Raising Children

Volume II

Vivian K. Friedman
Ph.D.

Raising Children

Volume II

Selected Columns from The Birmingham News

Vivian K. Friedman Ph.D.

Aardvark Global Publishing Company LLC
Printed in China

A selection of columns by Dr. Vivian K. Friedman that appeared in The Birmingham News, arranged by age and covering a wide variety of child-rearing topics. The columns are in question/answer format, and are intended to serve as a general guide. For specific guidance, consult your pediatrician or child psychologist.

Copyright © 2008 by Vivian K. Friedman

All rights reserved under International and Pan-American Copyright Conventions. Published in the United States by Aardvark Global Publishing Company LLC.

ISBN 978-1-4276-3212-8

Printed in China.

10 9 8 7 6 5 4 3 2 1

FIRST EDITION

Book design by Ari Friedman

Art by Jordan Anson, Zoe Benz, Savannah Freeman, Eva Gibson-Cook, Annie Nelson, Ashley, Madison and Savannah Oakman, Nicholas Osborn, Reid Owens, Chloe Sellars, Alex Villari.

Cover design by Ari and Michael Friedman.
Cover photography by Donald Moore

*This book is dedicated to my children
who taught me how to parent.*

Acknowledgments

Without the very tangible assistance and encouragement from my son Ari Benjamin Friedman, Volume I would not have come to be. From start to finish, the push for me to publish my newspaper columns in book form was his.

His experience as Layout Editor and then Editor-in-Chief of the Mountain Brook High School newspaper helped him to hone the skills he used in designing and laying out this book.

With Ari away doing a fellowship at the Harvard Initiative for Global Health, the torch was passed to my son, Michael. Michael, an honors engineering student at Auburn University, and photographer for the Mountain Brook High School newspaper and then the Auburn Plainsman, ably took over where his brother left off.

Thanks also to my good friend Steve Millburg, former senior editor for Coastal Living magazine, who carefully changed my hyphens to dashes and kept me attuned to detail.

Contents

Acknowledgments............xi

Introduction................xv

Birth to age 3 Infant and toddler

Only first children seem to have the terrible twos 4
Adoptive parents are indeed the real parents 6
Moms protect while fathers encourage independence ...8
Baby will speak without vocabulary lessons 10
The oral stage ends around the second birthday 12
Newborn babies don't tolerate overstimulation 14
Your child will be older next year than he is now 16
Mom and dad do things differently 18
Self-esteem begins with parent's love for the child 20
Potty training typically happens by age $3^1/_2$ 22
Enough attention for older boy lessens sibling rivalry ..24
Parental emotions affect child more than loss 26

Age 3 to 6 The preschool years

Parent must find cause of child's tears about school ...30
Barbie doll or baby doll — to please or to guide? 32
Child needs to learn to sleep in his own bed 34
Teachers have a right to discipline fairly 36
Don't define gender roles too narrowly 38
A bad experience is no excuse for bad behavior 40
Clear task, toy bins and company yield clean room 42

Life is easier for child without bearing a secret 44
It's hard to have a handicapped sibling 46
Some things are choices and some things are not 48
Children don't appreciate any gift if given too many . . .50
Calming the fears of a preschooler won't spoil him 52
Children shape their parent's behavior too 54
Schedules at home prepare child for school and life . . .56
Better to tell the children than to have family secrets . . .58
Five-year-old girl dreams of Prince Charming 60
Will vacation shortly after move confuse children? 62
Happy children get love, discipline and a role model . .64
Holding back a grade will aid maturity 66
You can't teach skills before the child is ready 68
Teach child to give — not only to get 70
Stage is scary for 3-year-old, ground level is better 72
Shallow water reduces swimming fears 74
TV to be watched passively must be chosen actively . . .76

Age 6 to 12 *The remembered childhood*

Balance structured activities with free time 80
Creative and introspective or Attention Deficit? 82
Teach children to read between the lines 84
Let child make complete transition to new grade 86
Family turmoil can overwhelm a high-strung child 88
Motivating a child works better than forcing her 90
Passive and less-favored children are often angry 92
Early trauma yields poor behavior at adolescence 94
Other diagnoses may mimic ADHD 96
Bilingual home is not the cause of speech delay 98
Behavior modification can quell problem behavior . . .100
Help child deal with dominating friend 102

Contents

Expect good behavior, don't beg for it 104
Parents need to intervene when child is bullied 106
Camp can be enriching for a child who is ready 108
Answer child's questions at his developmental level ..110
Buy to meet child's needs, not to match what sib gets .112
With one body you can't dance at two weddings 114
Troubled teens, not stable ones, turn to drugs 116
Give attention to child for independent work 118
Children need structure and predictability 120
Shelter child from conflicts of divorcing parents 122
Nurturance produces softer and kinder children 124
Adults are proud of parents who dared to parent 126
Positive self-esteem prevents drug abuse 128
Children are kinder one-on-one than in groups 130
Camps allow handicapped child to be the norm 132
Children spend carefully if the money is their own ...134
It is better to draw aggressive pictures than to hit 136
Your child is much more than just his illness 138
Parents relieve child's frustration too quickly 140
The less children get, the more they appreciate gifts ..142
Camp is good for some but not for all children 144
Habits save time by cutting down decision making ...146
School is for learning academic and social skills 148
Motivate, don't force, older to include young brother .150
A few good friends are enough 152
Parent must oversee child's remediation 154
ADHD not the only cause of poor performance 156
Motivation begins early in life 158
Child rejected by peers needs secure home base 160
Gift-giving rules vary with the social subgroup 162
Recreational reading can be below grade level 164
Failure to admit fault can be learned from parent 166

Mom's reading disability returns in her children 168
Recess serves to release tension in young students 170
Daily failure is worse than a grade repeat 172
Preteen wants to dress as a teenager 174
Preteen and mom disagree on style and fit of clothes .176
Separate poor spelling from other academic grades ...178
Should only gifted children go to school? 180
Help child to put loss into a framework 182
Worried child's self-talk is scary, negative and critical 184
Curbing unkindness is part of raising children 186
The meaning of money is learned from parents 188

Age 12 to 18 *The bridge to adulthood*

Teachers select students for advanced classes 192
Behavior and emotions are separate issues 194
Parent must set limits to create a likable child 196
Parents should be parents — not peers 198
Assess child's effort at schoolwork — not grades 200
Song choices reflect child's beliefs 202
Send a child away only from a secure home base 204
Parents don't need to solve problem, only to listen ...206
Teen won't stay in "time-out" chair 208
Maturity determines if 16-year-old may drive 210
Address the real issue, not just the wish to drop out ..212
Consequences must follow logically 214
"Do as I say and not as I do" does not work 216
Parents' influence typically is stronger than peers' ...218
Child doesn't need to know mom's mistakes 220
Teach child to make wise decisions on his own 222
Restrictions need to be fair and rational 224
The child who does not feel heard stops talking 226

First girlfriend is unlikely to be the final choice 228
Son struggles with move to new town 230
Competitive child shuns correction 232
Don't pressure child to get grades — motivate him ...234
"I don't care" may be cover for "I can't" 236
Disrespectful son treats parent as peer 238
Teach child to make lemonade out of lemons 240
Needs of individual and group are not always same ..242
Teens should have only the freedom they earn 244
Rudeness is not a developmental stage 246
Cooking and sewing are still important skills 248
Smiling child is easier to like than moody sister 250
13-year-old has the right to be told the truth 252
Recovered child simply needs to catch up 254
Artsy son feels he can't please athletic father 256
Parent's job is to help child evaluate risks 258
Crazy and angry are not the same 260
Many older siblings can be capable family babysitter .262
Child with plenty is still stealing 264
Strong will works better for adult than for child 266

Of general interest

Tenth year anniversary column 270
Healthy conflict resolution can be model for children .272
Nurture the young child, wean him as he grows 274
Nurturing sick grown child is probably OK 276
Too high self-esteem can lead to rage at reprimand ...278
Stability and happiness are not forged out of money ..280
Too high self-esteem is as bad as too low 282
The value of neatness must be parent-taught 284
Young children cannot be left alone 286

Some children are easier to love than others 288
Teach child to see the other person's point of view ...290
When behavior is out of line, the parent must act.....292
Arrival of child can change your life 294

Index *296*

How it all began

I moved to Birmingham in 1983 to join the psychiatry department faculty at the Medical School of the University of Alabama at Birmingham. From this position, I was often consulted by The Birmingham News on stories involving child psychology. After the first few months, I began to write out my answers for the reporters who called me. Then I began to call them and suggest topics. After I spent four years as a consultant, Betsy Butgereit, then a fledgling reporter, approached me and the senior editors at the paper with the idea of doing a parenting column. This was a novel idea at that time. There were few psychologists writing directly for newspapers then. And so the column was born. It debuted on March 14, 1988 and ran 17½ years twice per week. It ended with the demise of THe Birmingham Post Herald on September 22, 2005.

Raising Children

Selected columns
from
The Birmingham News

Birth to age 3
Infant and toddler

This is the stage in which there is the largest developmental change of any three year span of life. The helpless, sleeping newborn becomes the child who can express his feelings in words, can walk, draw a circle and play cooperatively with his peers.

He learns to sit at 6 months of age and to walk at a year. He puts short sentences together at 18 months and balances well by age 3.

Parents are the primary sources of pleasure and nurturance. Problems in this relationship lead to defects that will follow a child through life.

During the oral stage (birth to 2), the child's pleasure comes from sucking. Trust is learned from the regular arrival of the need-fulfilling caretaker.

The anal stage, beginning at age 2, is the start of autonomy. Now the child can refuse to do his parent's bidding. Only he can hold on or let go on the potty. Because language is still limited, this is the age of tantrums. Because concepts are primitively understood, this is the age of fears.

Only first children seem to have the terrible twos

Q. My 18-month-old daughter has changed overnight. She has gone from an easygoing, good-natured, perfect baby to one who definitely wants her own way. I used to be able to direct her activities. Now if she doesn't get her way she is mad and she cries.

Bedtime used to be pleasant. She would welcome sleep. Now she doesn't want me to stop reading the book or turn the light off. She screams when I put her in the crib drowsy so she can learn to put herself to sleep.

How can I make an 18-month-old understand that she can't always have what she wants? How do I get her to sleep at bedtime? Any hints would be appreciated.

A. Mothers with more than one child will often tell you that only their first child had the "terrible twos." This is not because the later-born children are better, but because first-time mothers are unprepared for the sudden change from docile infant to willful toddler that occurs around age 18 months to 2 years of age.

This phase will pass around age 3 as she enters the pre-school years where most children are again eager to please adults.

Your wish to make her understand your reasoning will have to be postponed until she develops more language and increasing understanding. A young child does not comprehend the world as you do. For now, you can tell her your reasons in simple words, but she will not grasp all that you say.

The frustration that parents have with the terrible twos is that the child is not rational. An explanation will not overcome the irrational resistance typical of this stage.

During the terrible twos, patience and diversion work better than explanation. Picking up a child without anger and putting her where she needs to be works well. You should not have trouble getting your child to move through the daily steps but you will probably find that it is not as seamless as it was when she was a docile infant.

Distraction is the best way to handle a willful toddler. Instead of saying, "Get into the bathtub. It's time for your bath," you might say, "Which bath toys do you want today?" This keeps her focused on the choice of toys rather than on whether or not to take a bath.

Preparation for transitions can help your child to avoid the balky resistance that comes at times of change. Give warnings of change shortly before the transition is expected.

Express this in time concepts your child can understand. "We have just enough time to finish the story before it will be time for sleep."

Routines go a long way. Habit reduces choice as behavior is done automatically without much thought. Less thought equals less resistance.

If bedtime is a struggle consider shortening your daughter's daytime nap. Alternatively, you might want to put her to bed somewhat later, so that she is tired when you put her down. Don't however, let her stay up so late that she is exhausted. Overly tired children are irrational.

Once you have established a calming bedtime routine and you have adjusted bedtime so that she is tired when you put her to bed, insist that she stay in her crib.

Allow her to cry for a few minutes before going back in to reassure her that you are still there, but do not take her out of the bed.

Increase the amount of time between your reassuring visits. You can talk to her at set intervals to calm her but do not take her out. While the first few nights will not be pleasant, if you are consistent, she will learn to settle down.

For most children the irrational stubbornness of the terrible twos will pass with the third birthday. If it does not, you may be seeing your child's temperament — most often inherited from one or both parents.

Adoptive parents are indeed the real parents

Q. We have recently adopted a baby. We plan to tell him that he is adopted. Obviously we can't tell him now, at age 2 weeks. What is the ideal age to do this?

A. Because you are not the whole social world for your adopted child, he will inevitably find out at some point in his life that he is adopted. If you wait until he is 10 before telling him, he is likely to find out from a relative, neighbor or acquaintance rather than from you.

You shouldn't wait until he is old enough to understand all the aspects of adoption before you say the first words. The process should be a gradual one, not a sudden shock.

If he hears it from other people, it may cause him to mistrust the adoptive parents who withheld information from him. It may leave him feeling that there is something shameful or secret about adoption.

Once the issue of adoption is out in the open, the adoptive parent need not discuss it at every opportunity. The desire to be honest can be taken too far. Repeatedly referring to the adoption can prevent the child from bonding to his family.

You do not need to feel pressured to explain adoption to your child before you are ready. Work through your own feelings of sadness or anger at infertility before explaining adoption to your child.

Young children accept the explanation of adoption without distress and may ask to hear the story of their adoption over and over again. They love to hear how excited you were when you found out he was born and how you fixed a room for him and shopped for a special outfit to carry him home in. He will learn from your attitude that adoption is a happy event.

The explanation does not have to be long or complex. You might simply say to your 1-year-old, "I'm so glad that I adopted you," just as a birth mother might say, "I'm so glad I had you."

The toddler doesn't understand what this means yet, but he hears the word *adoption* paired with his mother's pleasure and affection. A parent's open use of the word *adoption* gives the child permission to ask questions. It says that adoption is not a secret.

When your child asks how he was born, you can answer him with both, "Babies grow inside the mommy," and with a brief explanation that you were lucky enough to adopt him from a family who couldn't keep him.

By the school years, some children create fantasies about who their biological parents are. They may fantasize that their birth parents were rich and beautiful. Some may imagine they were kidnapped from parents who wanted to keep them. Many wonder if they were given away because they were bad.

As the adopted child gets older, he may ask why his biological mother gave him up.

Unless it contradicts the facts you know, you might want to say something like this: "Because your parents could not take care of you, they gave you up for adoption to a family who very much wanted you and could give you what you need."

This reframes giving the infant away from an act of abandonment to an act of caring. When discipline issues arise, as they inevitably will, some adopted children will hurl, "You can't tell me what to do. You're not my real parent."

If you calmly continue your discipline, your child will come to see that his place in the family is permanent and that you are indeed the real parents.

Moms protect while fathers encourage independence

Q. I have an 18-month-old baby. My husband accuses me of being an overprotective parent. While it is true that I love to be with my son and don't want any harm to come to him, I don't feel I am overprotective. I worry that my husband doesn't watch him closely enough and so I rarely leave the baby with him alone. How much protectiveness is too much?

A. Your child is lucky to have a mom who is so happy in her role as a mother. The early years of the life of a first child can be some of the most joyous years of life for the mom.

This is the basis of emotional stability for the child. There is little harm in bonding intensely as long as you don't prevent his progress from stage to stage. Your aim should be to mother and not to smother.

Moms and dads parent differently. Generally, mothers tend to protect and nurture, while fathers encourage independence and tolerance of a few small hurts.

Mothers teach caution while fathers encourage taking a few risks. Neither parent is wrong. This system works quite well for the child. With two parents playing different roles, the child gets both encouragement to venture out and protection from harm.

You cannot over-parent a newborn. The younger the child is, the more he needs his parents for survival. At this phase, the baby is completely helpless and dependent but around age 1 the baby learns to take steps away from his caretakers.

While most parents are delighted in their child's increasing skills of independence, a small number of mothers feel hurt when their child squiggles out of their arms to freedom.

Watch your own reactions to these first separations and consider it a warning

Raising Children

sign if you are sad or anxious.

Just as children can't grow up happily without love, they can't grow up emotionally stable without the freedom to be a person apart from the mother.

You need to give your child a clear message that he is competent and that he can be safe even when his mother is not with him. Without this, he cannot go on to school when the time comes without feeling excessively anxious.

Most new mothers are just delighted with the experience of being a mother and can't get enough of that wonderful closeness between mother and infant. If this is all that is going on for you, there is no harm in pulling back from other commitments in your life for now to enjoy this time. The baby phase passes by very quickly.

But if you sense that you have a tendency to smother your child, make an extra effort to allow him to form relationships with other people. Letting go can be difficult for a mother who needs her baby's exclusive love, but it is essential for the child's emotional health.

Children can attach to more than one person. His ties to others will not lessen his love for you. It is kinder to let him feel safe with others than to have him fearful of harm and abandonment when you are not with him. No mom can be with her child all of the time.

Let the grandparents have a turn, or if this is too difficult, allow someone less attached to spend time with the baby.

Get a babysitter now and then, and reconnect to your husband. His comments about your overprotectiveness may really be his way of saying that he misses you.

Baby will speak without vocabulary lessons

Q. I have a 4-month-old baby. I have heard that you can increase the baby's IQ by giving her the words for things so that she can understand the concept. Is there a special way to teach babies to talk?

A. You can't teach a baby to talk before he is developmentally ready, but a baby reared in silence will speak later and differently than a child who hears speech.

While language does help the development of understanding of concepts, it is not important for the baby to have words before the age when speech occurs naturally. You will not increase IQ through a strict schedule of language instruction for an infant.

A newborn baby's tongue is large in proportion to the size of the mouth. The baby can make the movements necessary for sucking food, but can't control the fine movements needed for true speech.

No matter how hard you try, you can't make a newborn, or even a six-month-old, say "carnivorous."

Gradually, as the mouth and tongue change proportions and as the brain and nervous system develop, the baby acquires increasing degrees of speech.

Language develops in a set pattern. Vowel sounds precede consonants. Baby's first coo is really "ooh." Repeated sounds (ma-ma, pa-pa, da-da, na-na) come before mixed sounds (mommy).

It doesn't matter what language the baby will eventually speak. The pattern of learning is the same. "Mama" and "papa" summon the parents in many countries simply because this is what baby is likely to say before anything else.

If you try to mimic your baby's first sounds, you will find them hard to imitate. This is because his language is still universal and yours is not.

He can make the vowel and consonant sounds of all languages, while you have long ago dropped all those sounds not used in the languages you speak.

The sequence of learning is a fixed one. It's unlikely that you will be able to alter the pattern with training, but that doesn't mean that it is not important for you to talk to your baby long before your baby can talk to you. Your baby will understand language before he can say the words to tell you what he wants.

Language is learned through hearing. Babies who are born with a hearing impairment will make some sounds at the expected age, but will gradually stop making those sounds. Without the feedback provided by hearing, the baby stops trying to talk.

Babies can hear speech sounds from the time of birth, so no child is too young to benefit from being spoken to.

Parents often intuitively use "baby talk." That is, they speak in a high-pitched, soft and melodic voice. This is just what the baby likes and responds to best.

Short sentences and repeated phrases combined with exaggerated facial expressions hold the young baby's interest and help him to learn to speak as soon as he is ready.

If you feel compelled to rush speech, you might want to examine your own motives. Learning to talk is fun for babies, and all but a few handicapped children will do it spontaneously.

Even if you could push your child to be the first baby on the block to talk, it won't matter in a few months anyway, when all the other children are talking too.

While you can delay speech development by not talking to an infant, you won't be able to rush development by establishing a rigorous lesson plan.

Enjoy your baby and do what comes naturally. Don't make your interaction with him a grueling lesson.

Your baby will enjoy your attention and your babble. The secure and happy baby is often an early talker.

The oral stage ends around the second birthday

Q. We have a little girl who will be 2½ next month. She was bottle-fed from birth and has never given up the bottle. At this time, her only bottles are at nap time and before she goes to bed at night. I let this continue for this long because she has never used a pacifier or sucked her thumb. The bottle used to put her to sleep, but does not really do so anymore.

I read that the sucking reflex diminishes at about age 2½. With this age fast approaching, I would like to try to take her off the bottle. What is the best way to do this? Will it harm her to just completely go "cold turkey," abruptly removing the bottle? Which method would cause the least trauma for her and for me?

A. I hear that you are feeling guilty and maybe a bit anxious as you imagine a scene of howling protest when you take her bottle away. While most mothers find it hard to deprive their children of something they want, particularly when the child is young, weaning is not stressful when the child is ready.

Different children are ready to wean at different ages. While many pediatricians urge parents to wean at one year, the oral stage, the stage where the child gets pleasure from sucking, is not over until after the second birthday.

I don't recommend going cold turkey from six bottles per day to none, but your situation is different. You have already tapered from many bottles per day down to just two, and you have weaned from milk to water. Your baby is no longer nutritionally dependent upon her bottle and won't take in fewer calories if weaned.

Since the bottle no longer soothes her to sleep, you will probably find that if you just take the bottle away she will adjust without too much fuss. She has all but given up the bottle already.

You will need to replace the bottle with other activities to help her make the transition from active to quiet, from awake to asleep. Children often have trouble with this change.

Substitute a storybook for the bottle at naptime. Give her a stuffed animal or a blanket to snuggle. Sing a lullaby if you and she enjoy this.

At nighttime, begin a bedtime routine. Age 2½ is a good time to start to form the evening habits that will carry you through the middle years of childhood. Bedtime routines take away the struggle of the evening hours and create a secure and loving nighttime separation from the parents.

Serve dinner at about the same time each day. Set a time for her bath. Be sure to include time for play in the tub. Then allow quiet play in her room, with dolls for example, or use this time for quiet play with her.

Board games are better for this time of day than rough-and-tumble play. Then read a story, give hugs and kisses, and put her to bed in her own bed for the night.

If she asks, you might return to her room for one extra hug or drink of water, but be firm that she is to stay in her bed after this.

If you have a predictable and soothing end to the day, your child will be able to separate from you without much fuss. Even though this is the age when fear of the dark is common, she will be secure and half asleep by the time you leave the room.

She will easily give up the bottle because she has outgrown it and will welcome the new comforters appropriate to her more grown-up stage of life.

Newborn babies don't tolerate overstimulation

Q. I took my 1-month-old baby to an adult party thinking that he would sleep through most of it, as it was after his bedtime.

When we got there, he wouldn't settle down. After he cried for an hour, I finally left with him. At home he went to sleep right away.

Aren't newborns supposed to be able to sleep through some noise? He is also colicky at home. How do you handle colic?

A. The troubles you mention are related to the immaturity of the newborn. Once they are frazzled, newborn babies have trouble soothing themselves.

They often need an outside source to calm them and to help them make the transition from awake to asleep.

You were hoping that he would fall asleep on his own, so that you might chat with some friends.

Although he is not old enough to be plotting consciously, he had other ideas for your time. He needed you to help calm him so that he could slip into sleep.

While babies can often sleep through noise, they do not tolerate overstimulation. The lights and noise of a party, coupled with your excitement and unfamiliar surroundings, led to a sleepless and crying baby.

Newborns don't do well with chaos. They are calmest with routine. While some babies can sleep through some noise, especially if they are already asleep, many need a soothing, if not quiet, environment to transition from awake to asleep.

You intuitively did what your baby needed. You left the noisy and light-filled party and removed your baby to greater calm.

By that point he had probably worn himself out. With both the change in environment and his own exhaustion, he fell asleep.

Some babies are more high-strung and sensitive to lights and noise than others. To help a particularly sensitive baby sleep, you can purchase special white noise machines which make a soothing, wind like noise to drown out more chaotic sounds.

Some mothers find that the gadgets that mimic mother's heart sounds are soothing to their baby. Some colicky babies like to sit in a baby seat near a clothes dryer that is running, because that repetitive noise seems to be calming.

Some babies are calmed in a swing, although many babies do not like the swing until after they are 2 to 3 months old.

Newborns like to be closely swaddled — that is, wrapped in baby blankets so that their limbs are securely against their bodies.

Of course, being held by a loving parent or caretaker is soothing for most infants.

However, mothers can't hold the baby all day and some colicky babies don't respond, leaving the mother even more frustrated.

Many babies respond to music, particularly to their mother's voice singing. Most babies like classical music. Babies, like adults, are different, and you may have to experiment to find what works for your child.

After you have made sure that your baby is fed, dry and comfortable, it is OK to put him in his crib for short periods of time, even if he is crying.

If your baby is crying for long periods of time, get help for yourself. Ask a grandparent to take the baby to give you some time off.

Colic usually only lasts about three months. As the baby matures, the seemingly irrational crying fades away. Some experts attribute this to the increasing maturity of the baby's nervous and digestive systems.

Not only does the baby cry less, but also, after age 6 weeks, he begins to smile. The baby's ability to relate to others makes it easier for the mom to get through the crying spells.

Once he smiles at you, you are hooked for life.

Your child will be older next year than he is now

Q. My fifth-grade son is talking about going to a high school other than our local public school. It is one in which the students have a lot of freedom, almost like a college campus. I'm not sure that he is organized enough to handle this much freedom. How do we talk him out of going there?

I also have a 12-month-old baby. The preschool that I want him to go to has a long waiting list for admission, and I really should register him now if I want him to go next year. When I observe the 2-year-old class, it just seems to demand so much of the children that I can't imagine him fitting in. Should I keep looking at other programs for him?

A. While planning ahead is generally a good thing to do, sometimes you can plan too far ahead. Children change rapidly, and even a few months can make a big difference in skills. It is not always possible to look at a 1-year-old and see how he will fit into a class of 2-year-olds or to look at a 10-year-old and see him in high school.

All 2-year-olds will be very much more mature than they were at 1 year of age. Most children will be more organized at 14 than they were at 10. A 40-year-old adult may not be very different in skills or style than that same person was at age 35, but five years in the life of a child can make a world of difference in maturation, organization and ability to function independently.

If you are concerned about your child's fitting into a particular program, of course you should keep looking at other ones. At this point you should keep all your options open, but do try to look at the programs from the eyes of a parent of a 2-year-old rather than as the parent of your child at his age now.

Your child is not static

and will not be a 1-year-old in a 2-year-old class. He will be the same age as the other children by the time he attends.

As you observe, look for the intrinsic merits of the program: how many adults there are per child, how discipline is handled and how calm and nurturing the environment seems.

Look for duplicates of toys so that children do not have to fight over them. Look for cleanliness and safety. Your child will need these at age 2 just as he does now.

Rather than assessing how aggressive the children are, look for how aggression is managed by the teachers. Your child will be the same size as the other children by the time he attends, but conflicts will happen now and then.

A teacher who is quick to respond, and an environment that provides enough structure, space and toys will keep conflict to a minimum.

Your 10-year-old should not be discouraged, at this point, from looking at all his options. He is too far away from high school to narrow his choices. It is admirable that he is thinking that far ahead and probably suggests that he is a good student with long-range goals.

The child who needs structure and close teacher and parental guidance at age 10, may very well be ready for independence in high school.

Many parents of 10- and 11-year-olds despair that their children will never remember the books they need for homework or will never come home from school with the sweater they left the house with in the morning, only to be surprised at how well the children do by age 12.

Rather than talking your son out of his choice, help him to broaden his options. Let him see several schools and talk openly about the similarities and differences between them.

Most schools with increased freedom also have high standards for admission. Encourage him to meet these high standards but be careful not to push a child who is already self-motivated. Don't take the control away from a child who is already on the right track.

Mom and dad do things differently

Q. We have a 2½-year-old son and we both work. I go into work before my husband does, so he feeds our son in the morning. The problem is that my husband likes to watch sports news on TV in the morning and so our baby gets breakfast in front of the TV five days per week.

Then in the afternoon when I have the baby, I have to fight him to keep him from the TV, which I think is not a suitable activity for a toddler.

I have a weight problem and don't want our child to get used to eating unconsciously in front of the TV. I feel strongly that meals should be at the dining table.

I like to keep our child on a schedule, especially since we have begun to potty train him, but my husband gets him up at different times each morning and then works potty trips and brushing teeth around his sports news show.

Are meals at the table and schedules important? Who's right?

A. Children do better with schedules and predictable routines. So do adults. If you had to decide each morning whether or not to brush your teeth or to put on your shoes, you would lose a lot of time making decisions that most of us do automatically without much thought.

Once your child is in grade school you will have to have a schedule, as he will have a set time to start, unlike day care where he can be dropped off at any time. Although even young children fare better with routine, you do not need to worry about an exact schedule quite as much right now. Very young children do have a sense of order but do not have a good sense of clock time.

TV is a passive activity which generally is good for children only in small doses, at carefully selected times of day, with actively and selectively chosen programming. While sports news shows

Raising Children

aren't likely to harm your son in content, watching every morning is setting up a habit that replaces other, more educational and social morning activities.

Most nutrition professionals would agree that people eat more when they eat in front of the TV. You are wise to take steps to break the unhealthful habit of eating without thinking about the meal. In addition, you will want to develop eating as a social, family event. Mealtime should be a time when the family gathers to reconnect and share experiences and feelings.

The easiest way to get things back on track is to do them yourself. Many dads complain that their wives want them to help but then want to tell them how to do it. If your schedule does not permit your taking over, you may have to allow your husband to do it his way.

You might also get your son on a schedule by getting him up at the same time each day and starting the routine as you prefer it. Dad might catch on, if you set it up.

While it does not sound as if you can convince your husband to give up his morning sports news, you can set limits on TV during other times of the day.

A 2-year-old can be taught that TV is only OK at a certain time — the morning in your situation. As long as your toddler is eating lunch and dinner without TV, he is learning an alternative way to eat.

As he grows older, you can set different rules for daddy and child. While dad can watch his show in the morning, your son may be required to eat at the table with you and any future siblings. While it is better to teach by example, adults do have certain privileges.

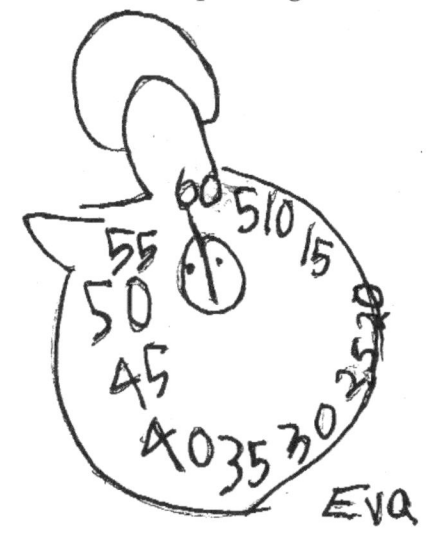

Self-esteem begins with parent's love for the child

Q. Our 1-year-old baby was born with a strawberry hemeangioma, a birthmark on her forehead. We are amazed at the amount of conversation and unsolicited comments that we get when we go out with her. People in stores and restaurants have stopped us to say, "No matter what the doctors tell you, it will become cancer and you should have it taken care of." The birthmark tends to go away on its own as the child grows, and if it doesn't, it can be removed surgically when she is older. We are not worried about her medically, but are concerned about the psychological effects on her from the rude and insensitive comments.

How can we protect her from unkindness? What should we tell others? How much should we tell her friends when she gets old enough to have play dates? At what age, to spare her self-image and self-esteem, should we give up on it's going away on its own and accept the scar surgical removal might leave? What about baby photos? Should we have them touched up or let the birthmark show?

A. While the rude and insensitive comments of others are very distressing to you, fortunately, at age 1, your baby is not yet harmed by them. You can immunize her from the potential harm by making her feel very loved and secure within her family. You can start this right now because self-esteem begins with the love that parents show to an infant.

Your explanation to other adults should be short and simple. "She has a birthmark and we have plans to take care of it." No further explanation is needed.

As she ventures out of home to preschool, she might encounter stares and questions, but at age 3, her peers are more likely to be curious than mean. At this age, you will need to give her the words to say to others, as her command of language will not yet be developed enough to explain in her own words.

While some parents explain a birthmark as having been "kissed by an angel," I favor a more factual approach. I tell children that their body is made up of millions of tiny cells and there are lots of different kinds. I marvel with them that so many hair cells, skin cells and fingernail cells knew just where to go, but only a few cells went to the wrong place. You can then explain that those cells in the wrong place may just go away, leaving new skin, or that the doctor can take them off when she is older if she wants.

In the meantime, keep in mind that the mark that seems so prominent now on a small face with little hair, will not seem so important as she gets older. Once she grows hair, you can style it with bangs to cover her mark, but do so only in a natural way. Don't go to excessive lengths to cover her face or you will give her the message that she is unattractive.

You can use a special covering makeup to lessen the color of the mark. Used along with hairstyle, this should take the focus off the birthmark. Be causal in your use of the cream and don't panic if one day she leaves the house without it. Your attitude will be more important in determining how she feels about herself than all of the strangers in stores.

Keep baby pictures of her both with and without the birthmark. You do not want to create a dark family secret that will loom larger than the problem by touching up all the photos. Yet you do want her to have some touched up pictures should she want to choose these when she needs baby pictures later in life.

If you are calm and supportive, your daughter should come through childhood with her self-esteem intact. As she grows, you can inform her of her options and give her the choice of how to deal with the mark.

Note: This column was written before laser surgery was commonplace.

Potty training typically happens by age 3½

Q. What are your tips for potty training the world's most resistant 2½-year-old?

A. Potty training is one of the first areas where the child is in charge. Only she can hold on or let go. In resisting potty training, your child is not pathologically willful or defiant. She is just passing through a stage in which she is establishing herself as a person separate from her mother.

The ideal time for potty training is between the ages of 2 and 3. Some children are ready earlier than others, and there is no reward for doing it first. Your child is right in the middle of this range, and she may just need a few more months before she is ready to take this step from baby to big girl.

Her seeming lack of interest in the potty process may actually be an expression of her fear of taking this new step. Young children do not know that their waste is not a part of their own body. In their eyes, you are asking them to flush away a part of their body as valuable as a finger or a toe.

No wonder a sticker or a piece of candy can't overcome the reluctance to produce in the potty until the child is just about ready to do so on her own.

While the conflict between your wish for her to use the potty and her determination not to seems as if it will never end, keep in mind that she might change her mind any day. Even as she resists, she is working on the problem in her mind and one day will surprise you.

She is approaching the age where most children give up their reluctance to comply in favor of the pride of being a big girl. I know of no healthy child who attended kindergarten in diapers.

Summer is a good time to train a child because she can wear little clothing. Training pants and a long T-shirt or dress make it easy for her to potty herself. Avoid clothes that are hard to remove, as toddlers will give you little warning when they need to go.

Don't keep her in diapers once you and she are ready to take the big step. She needs to feel the consequences of not going to the potty in order to learn.

Don't over-focus on potty training or you might increase her resistance. Take a casual approach. Get a storybook about potty training from your bookstore or library.

"Stop and Go Potty" by Judith Blau (Random House) or "KoKo Bear's New Potty" by Vicki Lansky (Bantam) are stories that your child might enjoy. The first has a Velcro doll to put on the potty on each page. The second book has comments for parents in addition to a story for the toddler.

Read the story together every night at bedtime just as you might read any other book. Because your child is at the right age for potty training and is nearly ready to take this step, she is likely to be interested in the story and to even to ask for it — unless potty training has become a battle of wills.

While extrinsic rewards such as candy can be used for some children when they are just about ready to go to the potty anyway, rewards related to the task are often more effective. Take her to the store and let her pick out her favorite big girl pants. Tell her she can wear these if she will use the potty.

If your child is in daycare or preschool, the group can be used effectively to help her want to potty. Modeling her peers can help her overcome her fear.

Potty training is not always straight-line progress. Expect accidents and regression especially when your child is sick, tired or anxious.

Be patient with her and remember that there is no particular advantage to being potty trained a month earlier or later.

As long as your provide instruction and gentle encouragement, she, like all other children, will do it when she is ready — most likely before she is $3^1/_2$.

Enough attention for older boy lessens sibling rivalry

Q. We are 34-year-old parents of a 9-month-old baby and a boy who is almost 3 years old. Our situation is somewhat unique.

We adopted our older son from Russia. Two weeks after we arrived home with him, I got pregnant. This instant parenting has been quite stressful. My husband and I are still trying to adjust to going from no children to two in a very short period of time.

Our toddler is driving us crazy. When we first adopted him, he was so sweet. He is in day care five days per week. He has made great strides since starting the preschool program. He is the only student in his class who can say his ABCs. We are very proud of him but our sweet child has suddenly turned.

He back talks us and will not obey us. He is jealous of his baby brother, which I am sure is normal. We have tried all of the discipline strategies we know to try, and nothing seems to work.

Don't get me wrong. He isn't bad every day, but most days he is a whiny and uncooperative kid. Do you have any suggestions? We sure could use some advice.

A. You seem to take for granted that parenting is hard and that the normal behavior of children is bad. This is not the case. It is not normal for a child to be jealous of a baby brother, although it does frequently happen.

Nor is it automatically stressful to suddenly become the parent of two children — busy for sure — but not necessarily stressful. Let's look at what you might do to put the joy back into parenting.

Providing enough attention to the older child can lessen sibling rivalry. Being in day care five days per week leaves him little time with his parents. When he has to share the precious few moments with a cute and biologically-yours sibling, he noisily, and maybe even obnoxiously, clamors for his share.

The more he demands, the less appealing he is to you. He senses this and increases his demands. He gets into a downward spiral of attention-seeking behavior.

In addition to increasing your hours at home with the children, it may help to include him in your time with his brother. Ask him to help you change the baby.

Maybe he could hand you the clean diaper or put some lotion on the baby's legs. While you give the baby a bottle or nurse him, you might softly chat with your older child. In this way he might not feel left out.

Being under the age of 3, he is likely to still be in "the terrible twos." This is a stage when the docile baby turns into an independent being and learns to say no.

First-time parents are often shocked at the resistance they encounter from a child so young, but some resistance is developmentally normal.

You do, however, have to set firm limits on unacceptable behavior. You are setting the pattern for many years to come. It is easier to get a 2-year-old under control than to try to fix an adolescent.

Instead of clashing head-on with him, use distraction. Give two choices (not more) when either would be acceptable to you.

Give warnings of transition time. Young children often don't transition from one activity to another without resistance.

Set consistent consequences for back talk and follow through. If you are inconsistent, discipline becomes a game.

Balance negative consequences with catching him when he is good, rewarding him with your time and attention. Don't use candy or toys to bribe for basic good behavior. He wants his parents, not sweets or trinkets.

Alter your schedule to reduce your stress. It may not be possible to do all that you did in the years before children, now that you are the parents of two.

Enjoy your little ones. The years go by fast.

Parental emotions affect child more than loss

Q. My sister had an infant who was born with a medical problem. She is not expected to live more than a few months. Their older child is 2 years old. How do you prepare a toddler for the loss of a sibling? Will it affect him later? How do you explain it to him?

A. The toddler's experience will be colored by the parents' feelings and behaviors more than by the loss of the sister. He is not likely to be bonded to the infant, who has probably spent most of her short life in the hospital.

She is a part of his life mostly through the parental attention she has taken from him, as her illness absorbs his parents' time and emotions.

While he is certainly affected by the illness and upcoming loss at the present time, he will not necessarily be affected for life. How it will affect him will be dependent upon the parents' reaction to the death.

If parents become depressed and unavailable to him, he will suffer for a long time. If they mourn and then go on with life, he will have little long-term trauma, although he may still have many questions.

It is probably best not to take a 2-year-old to the funeral, not so much because the child will be harmed by the service, but because the parents need their own time to grieve without having to hide their sadness from the older child. They will be more comfortable if they can attend to the service, rather than having to hush and chase an active 2-year-old.

Plan ahead of time for a babysitter who is familiar to the toddler so that he doesn't feel abandoned by his parents in their grief. Children have radar and they pick up on parental emotions. They know the difference between being left while mother goes happily to a birthday celebration and being left while parents go to bury their child.

Bring in the babysitter to spend time with the 2-year-old in the weeks before the infant's death so that when he is left with her for the funeral, it is part of his routine rather than an emergency event.

Even a 2-year-old should have some explanation of what is to come. Tell him about the imminent death in simple words that he can understand. Tell him only what is certain and don't burden him with possibilities. Don't tell him too far in advance. A young child will expect what you tell him to happen immediately.

Explain the death to him in terms that are consistent with the family's religious beliefs. Above all, do not lie to him.

Don't say that the baby went to live with another family. He will fear that you will send him away too. Even with a good explanation, you may hear him ask if you will leave him. He will need reassurance.

Children worry about being cared for, and this will be his concern for the deceased baby. Reassure him that the baby will be comfortable and safe and not alone. Tell him God will look after the baby, if that is your religious belief.

Reassure him that while his sister was born sick, he is a healthy boy who will live for a long time — until he is an old man. Reassure him that while he may see you cry, you are happy to have him.

Although you might not get many questions now, you may hear questions as he grows older. At age 4 or 5, the questions may not come from his memory of the event, but from hearing family members discuss the sister he once had.

Answer these questions honestly but in terms he can understand at his developmental stage. Young children don't think abstractly.

Be careful not to overprotect the living child. Parents who have lost one child often fear they will lose the other.

Take time to grieve and then try to go on with the care of your living child. It is the parents' reaction that will determine the impact of the loss on the living child.

Age 3 to 6
The preschool years

The child from age 3 to 6 is delightful. He still has the appeal of a toddler, but he has acquired language and can communicate. Because he can use words to express his needs, the temper tantrums of the terrible twos gradually disappear.

This is the Oedipal phase, where boys want to marry their mother and girls flirt safely with the father. It is from these safe and harmless flirtations that children set the groundwork for romantic relationships in adolescence and later life.

Play moves from parallel — where children play side by side but don't really interact — to cooperative where the children share a theme or take turns. This enables them to attend early childhood school programs and to gain from interaction with other children.

Parents still remain the focus of the child's security but preschoolers are able to leave home for a few hours each day and to accept the substitute nurturance and authority of a teacher.

Parent must find cause of child's tears about school

Q. My 4-year-old child was physically (without marks) and emotionally abused by his private day care teacher. He used to love school, but after a few days in this class he began to cry in the morning on school days.

We encouraged him to go to school. We told him pre-school was fun. We tried to be around the school to see what was wrong. We saw nothing for two months while he continued to cry and regress. How can a parent tell the difference between a child who cries because he just doesn't want to go to school and one who is in an inappropriate setting?

A. Most children like preschool and kindergarten. When they don't, the problem is usually one of anxiety over separation from the mother.

This crying typically begins at the time of separation — not the night before or during the weekend. The child with a separation anxiety may have stomach pains, but he does not usually regress to wetting his pants after being potty trained or to sucking his thumb once he has given it up.

He is happy when he comes home from school. In contrast, the abused child, while happy to return home, is upset at the end of the school day.

If you suspect abuse, ask your child about his experiences at school. Don't assume that all is well just because he shrugs his shoulders and does not confess. Abusers may threaten their young victims with consequences if they tell.

If you ask him about abuse and he doesn't answer, tell him that when adults are hurting children they often scare them and tell them not to tell. Let him know that it is always OK to tell parents and that parents can protect him from harm by the abuser.

When abuse seems to be happening in a classroom

setting, it is important that you talk to parents of other children in the classroom. Don't stop calling if the first parent says his child is not having a problem.

Some parents may need to deny what is going on out of their own need for day care. Additionally, an abusive teacher will not torment all of the children in the classroom. Abusers select their victims.

If abuse is happening, you are likely to find other parents whose children are suffering in the same way as your child.

Typically, time passes as you put together the clues to the problem and conduct your investigation before going to authorities and pulling your child out of the program. Communication with other parents can speed up the process as you share your suspicions.

Young children can generally be believed when they tell a parent about abuse. They do not have the life experience it takes to make it up, and there is no secondary gain in it for them. If your child seems upset, he probably is.

Notice when the change in your child's behavior occurs. Is he happy on vacation? Does he like weekends? Do his regressive behaviors stop during school breaks?

Look for symptoms of stress. Daytime wetting his pants, thumb sucking that increases or returns in a child who had given that up, stuttering that was not present before the stress may be clues to what is going on.

Don't blame yourself for taking two months to make a change for him. It takes this long to find out the facts. Parents should encourage their child to like and attend school, and most kindergarten problems are ones of adjustment — not abuse.

You took all the right steps. You encouraged him to like school. You listened to his complaints and took them seriously. You increased your surveillance at school, and you made a change for him when you found a problem.

With a good experience in his new school, you can expect that he will once again attend school happily.

Barbie doll or baby doll — to please or to guide?

Q. My granddaughter wants a Barbie doll for her birthday. As she is only 5 years old, I think a baby doll would be more suitable. I don't want her to grow up too fast, worrying about being thin, fashionably dressed and all the other female stereotypes Barbie represents.

Is it OK to give her a baby doll instead, or would I be better off getting my granddaughter exactly what she asked for?

A. If your goal is simply to please her, you could accomplish this easily by buying her what she asked for. If your goal is to guide her development and to expose her to your ideas, you might want to make your own choice of a gift.

Baby dolls and teen fashion dolls, such as Barbie, fill different needs and are suitable for different ages. The baby doll allows the young child to identify with the mother. The child can care for her baby just as her mother cares for her and her brothers and sisters. Through this kind of play, the child practices for her future role as a mother.

She can also identify with the baby doll she is caring for, feeling cuddled and loved. She can nurture or be nurtured in fantasy.

A baby doll is a particularly important gift for both boys and girls who have just had a new brother or sister born. It allows them to work out feelings of jealousy. They can feed the doll while mother feeds the baby. They can pinch the doll instead of the baby.

The wish to be a baby and the wish to grow up exist side by side in all healthy young children. While the baby doll allows the child to express his or her need to be a baby, the teen fashion doll allows the young girl to pretend to be grown up.

As she dresses Barbie, she can try on roles in play

Raising Children

and practice for the future with little risk. Having some of both types of dolls would allow her to play out both baby and growing up roles.

The play and play materials of childhood can influence adult ideas and skills, but a teen doll alone will not cause your granddaughter to grow up too fast.

The doll is a means through which the child expresses her concerns. If she is overly focused with romance in her play with Barbie and Ken, it is likely that she is overstimulated in her life. The dolls facilitate the expression of feelings. They don't create the issues.

While teen dolls don't make a child grow up too fast, they can influence the child's perception of beauty. Yet, the Barbie image is not all bad. Barbie can encourage the positive values of grooming and attention to attractiveness.

She can allow the young girl to fantasize and practice future roles, but she can also make a child whose body doesn't conform to this exaggerated caricature feel imperfect.

Whether Barbie is just a toy or a carrier of a standard of attractiveness depends to a large extent upon how the child is valued by her parents and what is taught in the home.

In the end, the choice of a gift is yours. If Barbie is not your style, feel free to give something that reflects your personality and values. You might want to give a different kind of gift altogether — one that creates a special relationship with your grandchild, such as a craft kit to assemble together or a book to read together.

Barbie is not the only toy she will enjoy. There are many ways to please a child.

Child needs to learn to sleep in his own bed

Q. I am a single parent with a 4-year-old daughter. My daughter likes to sleep in my bed at night. Is there any harm in letting her do this while she is young?

A. All children, regardless of age or of their parents' marital status, need to learn to sleep alone. Learning to be apart from others, without feeling anxious, is an important developmental step.

The way we fall asleep is largely habit. If a person who usually sleeps on his back is forced by circumstances — a broken bone, for example — to sleep on his side, he is likely to have difficulty falling asleep until a new sleep habit is formed.

If you sleep with your child, you become part of your child's sleep pattern. You will likely find that she will have difficulty sleeping without you.

A good part of your child's fussing when you try to remove her from your bed is not just her emotional need for you, but her resistance to changing a habit.

While many parents start out putting a child in their bed to help the child feel more secure, it can actually have the opposite affect. It can rob the child of an opportunity for independence.

When the child takes the place of a spouse in the bed, it can make the child feel confused and anxious rather than reassured.

If you want that cuddly closeness in bed, do it on a weekend morning rather than every night for sleep. Alternatively, you can spend a vacation afternoon in bed together reading books.

If your child wakes with nightmares, it is better to go to her bed with her than to allow her to sleep in yours. Comfort her but don't change her sleep place.

After a divorce, a parent can be tempted to sleep with his or her child, especially if he or she has only one.

It feels comfortable to replace the spouse with a child, but while the youngster can feel comforted by the parent's presence, he also feels burdened with the responsibility of meeting the parent's emotional needs — needs that previously were filled by an adult.

If you sleep with your daughter while you are single, and then put her in her own bed when you remarry, she will feel rejected.

She will literally be displaced by your marriage and will rightly blame your new husband for her displacement. She may act out in ways that will cause stress on the marriage.

A son in bed with his mother would carry an additional burden. He would likely compare himself to your adult partner in the competition for his mother and feel inadequate.

Problems can also arise in two-parent families. A child who sleeps between married parents is separating them.

One or both parents may use the child's presence to avoid emotional or physical intimacy. Having a child in bed allows the parents to avoid facing problems in the marriage.

If sleeping between the parents is followed by a separation or divorce, the child actually comes to replace one parent in the bed. Children are prone to blame themselves for parental divorce anyway, and may feel that they were the cause of the separation.

If a child never learns to sleep alone, she may be vulnerable when she reaches the age where she moves away from home. She may settle for an unsuitable relationship out of a need to have someone — anyone — with her just to avoid being alone.

The competent parent gives his child the gift of autonomy — the ability to fend for himself.

You do this by beginning in infancy to allow your child to separate from you at developmentally appropriate times.

Sleeping alone comes easily if you insist on this from the start. Cuddle your child during the day and let her sleep alone at night.

Teachers have a right to discipline fairly

Q. Two other women and I teach 5-year-old children at Sunday school. Last week, we were doing an art project, and one child kept demanding attention, interrupting the teacher who was giving instructions and then asking for more than his share of help.

I finally had all I could take of this behavior and went over to him and said, firmly but not rudely, "Hush!" The child and the other teachers looked shocked, but he did behave more acceptably for the rest of the class. Was I wrong in what I did?

A. Teachers and parents alike are caught in a current fashion of putting the child's self-esteem above the need for discipline.

Like all fads, this represents an extreme position of the pendulum, which swung away from the other extreme — overly harsh discipline. The current emphasis on developing self-esteem makes those teachers and parents who discipline and set limits feel like ogres.

It is never wrong to set limits for a misbehaving child if that child is your own or if you have responsibility for that child as a teacher, Scout leader or caretaker.

Your first responsibility is to the group as a whole. You need to do what makes the experience not only safe but also worthwhile for the majority of the children.

It is the parent's job to ready the child for a group experience. The parent who teaches his child appropriate behavior enables that child have a better time wherever he goes.

The badly behaved child is rejected and punished at every turn. Behavior that a parent will overlook will not be overlooked by others who are not bonded to the child in the way that a parent is. Teachers, Scout leaders and coaches will evaluate the child's behavior objectively without making allowance for the child's idiosyncracies.

Teaching acceptable behavior begins with saying no when it would be so much more fun to say yes. Parents love to see the child's pleasure at getting the latest trinket or treat.

However, the child who gets gifts and favors all the time soon turns into a monster who has to have things and attention all the time. He feels less and less pleasure from each gift and needs more and more to feel excited.

Saying no to trivial demands teaches a child to tolerate frustration. It enables him to do things he doesn't want to do — an essential task for school and learning. It is not easy to master new concepts, but in the long run, this mastery is what makes life interesting and fun.

The child who gets what he wants all the time is typically a poor student — not because he can't do the work, but because he isn't motivated to try. The child who gets, ends up feeling entitled. The child who feels entitled to anything he wants doesn't put out effort.

Be assured that you are doing the right thing for the children you teach when you help them to get back in control. Respond to the message the child is giving, "I need attention," without accepting bad behavior.

Set limits when he misbehaves but provide opportunities for him to be noticed in a positive way.

Tell him to finish his project quietly at his seat because you would like to have him show it to the class when he is done. Ask him to work extra carefully, because you would like to put it up on the display shelf.

If all attempts to meet his needs fail, you can ask his parent to attend class with him as a requirement for his participation. You can explain to the parent that he needs more attention than a teacher with responsibility for the whole class can give.

This will give the parent a chance to view her child's behavior first hand, and it will give her child attention from the person he wants it from the most.

Don't define gender roles too narrowly

Q. Are differences between boys and girls taught by parents, or do babies come into the world with gender differences? My son is very active in sports, while my daughter prefers to knit and play with dolls. Did I do this to them?

How do you raise boys to be boys and girls to be girls? What do you do if your child crosses the line?

A. Newborn babies are, for the most part, gender neutral, but by the time they are a year or two old, without any instruction, they begin to express preferences that are typical of their sex.

Psychologists used to think parents made their children into what they are. With increasing evidence, views have changed from the position that the baby is born as a blank slate for parents to draw upon to a view that the child is a combination of what he is born with and what he is taught.

For the most part, children will behave in a gender-typical way. Parents do not need to interfere with the way a child chooses to express his gender identity unless the child is having social problems at school.

The parent needs to be careful if he does try to steer his child. You cannot change a tomboy by putting her in lace dresses. If you try, you will convey that she is not acceptable to you. She may feel rejected for what she is, but she is unlikely to become her opposite.

Don't overinterpret what you see. Even if the boy chooses to play with dolls, the way he plays will be quite different from the way a girl plays. The girl will rock the baby and nurture while the typical boy will play out aggressive themes.

I observed a 7-year-old boy playing with a stuffed animal, pretending it was sick and doctoring it back to health. I thought this was a gender-neutral display of nurturance until I asked him how the animal got hurt. "Oh, he fell on his sword," said the boy. Few females would think of this!

With the exception of a small number of children who have true gender identity issues, most children find an acceptable balance between gender stereotypes and broader interests. Parents can make a mistake by focusing only on the atypical choices while failing to see all the preferences that are gender-typical.

There are many areas of overlap between the interests of boys and girls. Cooking and stuffed animals are interesting to both sexes during the early years. It is in these gender-neutral areas that parents sometimes make the mistake of defining a gender role too narrowly.

There is no harm in cooking with children of both sexes. Teddy bears, even as late as the sixth grade, bring comfort to children during times of separation from parents such as at bedtime.

We are generally more tolerant of alternative roles for girls than for boys. While it would not be in a son's best interest to encourage him to adopt a clearly feminine role, it is fine to develop his softer side. Boys who have some interest in aesthetics and cooking, or who are neat and orderly, often have a better marriage than those boys whose interests don't overlap the interests of girls at all.

For the best outcome for your child, don't define gender roles too narrowly. Focus on teaching skills but not roles and your child will find a balance between the feminine and the masculine traits that both sexes have.

A bad experience is no excuse for bad behavior

Q. My 4-year-old son was abused by an extended-family member. We are now seeing sassy and defiant behavior from him. We are afraid to punish him for these behaviors, as we don't know if this is part of his reaction to the abuse.

How can we tell the difference between ordinary bad behavior and behavior that is the result of what was done to him? Should we discipline him?

A. Generally speaking, it is not necessary, for purposes of discipline, to distinguish between behavior that is the result of abuse and that which is simply bad behavior.

Parents often make the mistake of excusing bad behavior for one reason or another, with the result that they simply have a badly behaved child.

Regardless of the reason for the undesirable behavior, your child will not be liked by others if you do not make him into a likable child. Instead of having one problem — the abuse, he will have two — abuse and rejection by others.

Some behavior is directly the result of abuse. Children who have been sexually abused often act out sexually.

In fact, knowledge of sexual issues before adolescence is often an indication that abuse has occurred. 4-year-olds simply do not have this kind of information unless they have been inappropriately exposed.

This kind of behavior, that is, sexual overtures, should not be directly punished but should be discussed with him. Professional help can be valuable in this case.

The child with sassy and defiant behavior, however, needs to know who is boss. The adult who cannot assert himself in the parenting role gives the message to the child that junior is in charge.

Divorced parents who compete for the child's love, parents of chronically ill children and parents of children who have been abused are especially vulnerable to shirking the role of the disciplinarian.

The child is the victim in this case, as he will be rejected by peers and teachers if he is not acceptably behaved. While his parent might excuse his sassiness, his teacher will simply choose someone else to be the line leader.

You most certainly do need to discipline him for sassy and defiant behavior or it will continue. If you do not like your child now, you will like him even less when he is older and less cute but still sassy and defiant.

Discipline needs to begin when the child is young. Age 4 is a good time to set the rules and expectations for behavior and values. 4-year-olds are natural parent pleasers. It is hard to change an adolescent.

If you tolerate rudeness, you are not only teaching him that he need not mind his parents, but you are also giving the message that he need not consider the feelings of others around him. You are creating a narcissist who thinks only of his own needs and who feels free to express every impulse.

Set limits on the defiance with consequences that catch your son's attention, but don't forget to notice him when he is well behaved.

You want him to strive for your positive regard, not only to avoid irritating you.

Don't pity him when he cries or when he resists the limits you set on his out-of-control behavior.

He is not the pitiful child who has been abused in the past. He is a child who has a long future ahead of him.

Clear task, toy bins and company yield clean room

Q. We tell our 4- and 7-year-old children to clean their rooms, but it doesn't get done. They aren't really defiant. They pick up one or two toys, and then they go on to other things. How do you get children to pick up their toys?

A. Children need a more specific instruction than the general "clean up your room" that most parents say. Even the child who wants to obey doesn't know where to begin when given an instruction that is too generic.

You will get better results if you say, "Put all your toys in the closet." You will get even more done if you say, "Put the Lego blocks in the purple bin." The more specific your instruction, the more specific the compliance will be.

Begin by organizing the room so that your child can clean up on his or her own. Provide bins to sort each type of toy — a bin for Lego blocks and a bin for toy cars for example. Create the organization for your child. He won't come by it on his own.

Keep the number of toys to a reasonable amount. Don't allow your child to have more toys than can be neatly put away.

Encourage him to give outgrown toys to charity to make room for the new ones or put them up in the attic to save for younger siblings or cousins.

Most children play with the same few toys over and over, while other toys just sit and clutter the room.

Stay with your child while he cleans up. He will be happier doing his chore with company, and you will be there to redirect him when he gets stuck or sidetracked.

Use this time not only to get the room clean but also to chat about his day. If he is talking while he works, it won't seem like a chore. He will remember cleanup as warm fuzzy time with his

Raising Children

parent, rather than chore time isolated and alone.

Most children don't retain multiple commands at once. Give the steps one or two at a time and repeat the instructions as necessary.

Have a set time for cleanup each day so that it becomes a routine. Most children brush their teeth without fuss or resistance. This is because it has become a habit. Cleanup time can become routine as well.

I hear from many parents that their children clean up at day care without a problem but they won't do it at home. At day care it is part of the routine and there is a place for every toy.

Start young but keep the expectations age appropriate. I am always startled at what parents expect from young children. (I am also startled at how little some other parents expect.)

A 3-year-old child cannot make up his bed without help, but young children can do a part of nearly any task if an adult works with them.

Not only does the adult provide the longer arms and the expertise, but he also provides the company that keeps the task from being a punishment. Being sent to do a chore alone is a powerful punishment for a young child.

Once in a while you can add extra incentives to make cleanup fun. Some moms hide pennies on shelves they want dusted or under beds where toys are hidden that must be picked up.

Of course the child could take the penny without doing the task. This provides an opportunity to teach honesty and rules of the game.

If you organize the toys, limit the number of toys in the room, keep your child company while he straightens up, give specific instructions and have a set time each day for pickup, you are likely to find that your child gradually takes on your value for neatness and organization — and makes it his own.

Life is easier for child without bearing a secret

Q. My child who is in kindergarten has a chronic illness. It is not something that others can see, but it does affect his energy level and cause him to miss some school. Should he share this with his classmates? How much should he tell them?

A. While few things in life are without some downside, it will make things generally easier for your child if he doesn't have to bear a secret.

By bringing out his illness into the open, you take the burden off the child. It gives him permission to go to his teachers for help when he needs it and to talk with peers about the experiences which make up his life but which are different from theirs.

Rather than letting him just blurt out his disclosure, take some time to plan the event. Use a moment in the curriculum to talk about the disease to his class where it won't come out of the clear blue.

You might adapt "show and tell" to this personal disclosure or use a science lesson about the body to inform his peers. The relevant disease foundation can often provide literature, pictures or even a live speaker.

Don't leave your young child to handle this issue on his own. Be sure to be there in the classroom to answer the questions his peers will have. A 5-year-old may have mastered a group of facts about his disease, but he cannot answer the questions of his peers.

Kindergarten-age children are typically accepting of others who are different as long as the teacher creates an accepting atmosphere. The most likely question the children will ask will be, "Can I catch it from you?" Young children are self-centered and will have concerns about the disease as it relates to them.

While the disclosure will make it easier for the young child, he may have moments of regret at disclosing his difference as he gets older. Fifth- and sixth-graders can be mean. Yet there is little choice for most chronically ill children because at one time or another, they will have visible needs or symptoms related to their disease. It will be better for their peers to understand that he is sick than to just think the ill child is odd.

Just as in every group there will be a child or two who is mean, there will also be some children who will become the allies of your child and will offer support to him. When he is teased by his less kind peers, remind him that they tease most children — sick or well. If they did not pick on him for his illness, they would tease him about his clothes, his sports skills or academics. The mean children go after anything they think will hurt.

Help your child to cope by arming him with facts. Explain in words he can understand and can use again when his friends ask questions. You are not protecting your child from his illness by keeping him in the dark. Don't overwhelm him with possibilities that are far into the future and may never happen but do prepare him for likely events. Increase the amount and depth of what he knows as he grows in maturity and ability to understand.

Be sure to emphasize the ways in which he is just like his friends. Don't become so focused on his abnormality that he and others begin to think of him only in terms of his disease. You don't want him to become "the diabetic boy" or "the boy with juvenile rheumatoid arthritis."

Avoid activities where his disease will be a significant handicap but do steer him toward clubs, teams and classes that showcase his strengths. Don't be concerned with what his peers are doing. If his physical stamina is limited, offer him music lessons or boost his computer skills. While physical skills are emphasized in the early grades, by the middle school years a broader range of activities will provide your child with a peer group that shares his interests.

It's hard to have a handicapped sibling

Q. I have a seriously handicapped 2-year-old child who is wheelchair bound and has many medical crises. My other child is three years older.

The older child has difficulty coping with all the time and parental energy her sister requires and is jealous of all the attention her sister gets outside the home.

No matter how much attention I give her it doesn't seem to be enough. It is true that when both children call, I run to the handicapped child. I don't see how I could do any differently.

The child I am writing about is older and is able to do for herself. The other child is both younger and cannot move unless I move her. How do I teach the older child to be more content?

A. It is easiest to prevent this problem before it starts. The solution applies not only to parents of handicapped children but to parents of two or more healthy children as well.

Each child needs time to be a baby and to have his needs met. Some children will gladly give up the dependency when they are as young as age 3 or 4. You will recognize this child by his tendency to say, "I can do it myself."

Other children seem to soak up nurturance like a sponge. They enjoy having their shoes tied for them long after the age when they can do it by themselves. This is the child you will have to plan for carefully.

Begin as soon as your second child is born. Set up a schedule so that your firstborn has daily time alone with you.

Consider sending your older child to preschool each morning on weekdays so you can get the nursing care done while she is away. Put the younger child down for a nap at 11:45 if your older one gets home at noon.

With the birth of a

handicapped child, there is typically a period of mourning.

Not only is the mother away due to actual care demands but she is also often too depressed to be emotionally available. This time can be especially intense if the survival of the child is not assured.

During the time when the new baby is in the hospital fighting for her life, parents can easily forget that they have another child at home.

Remind yourself how you would feel if you lost your healthy child. Just because she is not in danger physically does not mean that it is safe to push her aside. While her physical health is not at risk, her emotional health is.

This is the time when you are establishing her feelings about her sibling. While certain absences are unavoidable, do not fail to plan for time with the healthy older child.

Remember that she is just a baby too, and she needs you and cannot safely be ignored.

When the handicapped child comes home, include your other child in her care but do so in a way that the older child gets the attention.

Do not expect her to care for the baby while you do other things. Ask her to help you with the baby while you nurture and hold your first born, as if caring for the baby were doll-play that you were doing together.

Make the older child the center of your verbal attention. The baby won't care if you don't talk to her as long as you make eye contact, but the older child will appreciate your words.

Find other family members who will fuss over your well child. Bring in grandparents, unmarried aunts and uncles or childless friends who will see her as special.

Let them take her for outings and overnights before there is a medical crisis, so that she will not feel pushed aside when she spends the night with them because you are away at the hospital.

Able-bodied children need parents too.

Some things are choices and some things are not

Q. My 4-year-old child needs to be on medication four times per day for two weeks. Each dose is a battle of wills, with me insisting that she take it and her running away, crying and clamping her mouth shut. How do you get children to take medicine?

A. Although most children will resist the bitter taste of most medicines, the child who is obedient in other areas of life is more likely to comply in this one as well. Maintaining a general level of discipline closer to order than to chaos will make this, and all issues, go more smoothly.

Explain to your child that some things are choices and some are not. Give her examples. Let her choose the color of her new notebook for school. Let her choose which pants to wear, but make it clear that taking her medicine is not a choice.

Explain to her why she must take the medicine. Tell her about germs and read a book about the body that is at her level. Tell her that she is in charge of getting herself well and that she has the power to get rid of her discomfort by taking her medicine.

Use rewards but use them sparingly. The child who is bribed for all compliance is soon sated with trinkets and candy. This child not only cannot be motivated with gifts, but she also learns to think that she need not comply unless the reward is to her liking.

The child who is rarely bribed can be helped over the speed bump of the bitter medicine with the thought that something bad will be paired with something good.

Don't reward each dose but keep a chart of her whole day. Let her put a check on the chart each time she successfully takes a dose and reward her at the end of the day with a star. After two or three stars, you can give her a bigger reward. You will have to adjust the frequency of stars and rewards to ensure that she can achieve success.

Behavior modification programs such as this one only work when the child is successful at achieving the goal and when the reward is something the child will work for. The best rewards are parental attention and time. A reward that works for many children is 20 minutes of time with a parent to play a game.

Give sympathy and nurturance. When your daughter is upset about taking medicine, hold her and comfort her. Sympathize with how hard it is to swallow something that you don't like, without excusing her from taking it. Try to give the medicine when she is calm, rather than when she is in the middle of a crying spell.

Make taking medicine a game. Have a race to see if your child can swallow her medicine before you eat your whole bowl of soup. Young children like to have the spoon fly into their mouth like an airplane.

Use distraction. Tell your child a story while she gets the bitter liquid. Stories that you make up, with your child as the heroine, are most effective.

Dissolve medicine in food when the child will take it that way. Be sure to use very small quantities of the food so that the child will get the full dose. Don't use a bowl of applesauce. Use a spoonful.

Teach your child to swallow pills. Pills are much less traumatic for most children as the taste is not as strong or prolonged as with liquid medication.

When all else fails, you will have to hold your child down and give her medicine to her by force. Some things in the child's life are choices but taking prescribed medicine is not.

Children don't appreciate any gift if given too many

Q. Our child has every toy in the store on her Christmas wish list. How can we limit her gifts without disappointing her?

A. You don't disappoint a child by not getting everything she wants. On the contrary, a child won't appreciate any gift if she is given too many.

Many parents can remember a holiday or birthday where, after opening a dozen gifts, their child has turned to them and said, "What else did you get me?"

There is no magic number of gifts needed to satisfy a child. You can teach your child to be satisfied with little, or you can teach your child to want and want and want.

If you ask your child for a wish list, it's best to do so when she is not at the toy store or in front of the TV. Once you have heard her list, you needn't feel obligated to fill all the requests, nor do you need to limit your purchases to only what she has asked for. Parents know about more interesting and more educational gifts than the heavily advertised toys that children request.

Parental judgment should override the child's wish list. Children do not always make informed decisions. They don't have an overview of all the options available and can't evaluate whether a toy will be durable or will hold their interest over time. This requires adult experience. In the end, it is the adult who must choose.

While some greed for gifts is normal, if your child is overly worried about getting, you might want to look behind the wish for gifts at the underlying problem.

The 10-year-old who must have a pair of expensive, specific-brand jeans may be telling you that she feels insecure or that she has no friends. She may need help in learning how to make friends. A gift of status clothing alone won't solve the problem.

The child whose parents are divorced may play one parent against the other, using parents' guilt and feelings of competition to get expensive gifts.

The gifts never make up for the family the child has lost and so the child, still feeling empty, searches for more and more material things. Rather than buying more gifts, the parent might address the child's feelings.

To tame holiday greed, focus on activities rather than gifts. Baking holiday cookies creates a childhood memory that will remain long after a toy loses its luster.

Spread the excitement over time. Don't leave everything for one overwhelming day. If a gift arrives in the mail, consider allowing your child to open it right away, when it can be special, rather than lost among the many other new toys.

If a relative brings a gift before the holiday, allow the child to open it in his or her presence. This makes ithe occasion special for the giver, and lets your child associate the gift with the person who brought it..

For young children, put away some of the gifts after the holiday and bring them out one at a time. Save some for a rainy day or a cranky time when your child needs a distraction.

Teach your child realistic expectations. Inform her in advance that she can't have everything she sees advertised or in stores.

Brainstorm a list of everything she might like and then ask her to pick the three best choices. Ask her to think carefully about just a few things that would really be special to her.

Focus on others. Help her plan gifts for other family members. Provide ways for her to earn gift money or help her to cook, bake or craft homemade gifts. Teach giving, not only getting.

Calming the fears of a preschooler won't spoil him

Q. My not quite 4-year-old son is taking swimming lessons. He loves the water when his dad is in the pool with him, but when he goes to the class with his teacher and fellow students, he cries the whole time and won't participate.

My inclination is to let his dad be in the pool with him during the class, but my mother says if I give in to his crying, I am babying him. What do you think?

A. What is wrong with babying a baby? We are talking about a 3-year-old and not about a teen.

Nurturance never spoils a child. Calming the fears of a preschooler won't spoil him and will enable him to learn from the swim class experience.

If you don't do what it takes to make him feel secure in the pool, you will waste the money and effort you put into the lessons. He will not learn to swim until he feels safe.

For this reason many swim programs for young children require that a parent be in the water with the child. The feeling of safety is essential for progress.

If you put him in the water week after week feeling scared, he will pair the water experience with the feeling of fear. You will set him back in his learning to swim, and it might take months to undo the fears you will have taught him.

If the program does not allow a parent to be with him, it would be better to take him out of swimming lessons than to let him learn to be afraid.

If the teacher is not flexible, you may need to find another class. A teacher who doesn't adapt to make the students feel secure is not suited for teaching very young swimmers.

Choose a program that makes learning fun. Look for a teacher or program that uses toys to encourage progress. Swimming through a hoop or gathering pennies from the bottom of a shallow pool can be a nonthreatening way to get a child to put his face in the water.

Children should be encouraged or motivated to take the next step. They should never be shamed or forced.

Look for a program that adapts the pool so that the children have their feet on a solid surface. This can be either a shallow pool or a platform placed in deeper water. Young children typically don't like to swim where they can't stand.

The problem your child is having in the water is not one of obstinacy or poor upbringing. Many children are naturally afraid of the water.

This fear is protective, keeping them from getting into situations that could be dangerous. Your child's fear will subside as he gets older and as he masters the successive steps of swimming.

Grandparents' advice can sometimes be of great value. They have completed rearing their children and have the perspective of time.

On the other hand, they do not live with your child on a daily basis, and you are likely to know your child's needs better. Every child is different. What works for one, might not work for all children.

Listen to their advice, but trust your own judgment. Tell an insistent grandparent, "I have heard and carefully considered your suggestion, but we have decided to do it a different way."

If a 3-year-old continues to cry every lesson no matter what you do, it is best to simply stop the swimming lessons and try again when he is older.

Continue to take him to the pool in a less structured way. Let him play in shallow water if he enjoys that. Bring pool toys and let him pour water from one bucket to another or fill his dump truck with water.

If you do not force him, he will find his own level of comfort. He will reach a time when he is ready to learn to swim. For most children this readiness will come between the ages of 4 and 8.

Children shape their parent's behavior too

Q. My friend caters to her 4-year-old child. When they go to an amusement park, she even goes on the tame rides meant for preschoolers with her child because her child cries if she doesn't. The result is that her child is shy and clingy. I encourage my 4-year-old to be tough and independent and therefore she has turned out assertive and outgoing. Please tell moms that they don't do their children a favor when they pamper them into babyhood.

A. Your assumption is that the mom influenced the child, but you might want to consider that the child influenced the mom. While parenting style certainly makes a difference and parents do shape their child's behavior, children also come into the world with their own personality. If this were not true, children in a family would be alike except for influences such as birth order. In fact, as parents of more than one child know, each child is different.

It is not usually the mother who makes the child timid. More often, it is the mother who responds to her child's fearfulness with protection. It sounds as if your friend, rather than babying her child by riding with her, is encouraging her child to try the ride. She might otherwise not ride at all. By offering a little extra security, she is broadening her child's world by breaking down the barriers to autonomy. First she tries it with mommy, and then gradually she goes alone.

Most parents are in tune with their children. They do what works for their individual child. It is only when a parent tries to apply one way to all children that things go wrong. We see this when the mother of a learning-disabled child wants the whole school system to slow down to her child's level or when the mother of the gifted child wants more stimulating classes for everyone. Each parent is making the assumption that what works for her child will be good for all. This is not typically the case.

Growth and development are usually on the side of the child in overcoming problems. Shyness or reticence to try a new experience tends to go away with increasing age. This does not mean that you won't recognize your child when she gets older. She is not likely to change to be her opposite but the sharp edges of temperament tend to be sanded down by increasing maturity.

The mother of the reticent child who won't get on the ride has two choices. She can do as she is doing and give her child the experience of going on the ride without experiencing the fear or she can decide that this experience is not important and can steer her child to other experiences that capture her child's talents and interests.

As he gets older, the child with artistic talent can use his time to develop that skill and does not necessarily have to spend his time playing football or riding roller coasters if he hates it. We expect our children to be good at everything, but as adults we focus on only the few things that we do well.

It appears that you are matched to the temperament of your outgoing and venturesome child. It is also probably good that you are not the parent of the more timid child. Things have a way of working out like that. Most children tend to match their parents in temperament and skills.

It is when they don't that the parent must be careful not to make the child feel as if he has failed. The choice may not be between having an outgoing, brilliant, athletic child or not, but between having the child you've got with or without self-esteem.

Schedules at home prepare child for school and life

Q. My 4-year-old daughter has been asked to leave her preschool because she won't follow instructions. They want her evaluated for attention deficit disorder.

Not only won't she stay with a task such as story time or coloring, but she also won't go in from the playground when the class goes inside.

The school staff feels it is not safe to keep her because when they tell her to do something she won't do it. We feel that she is just stubborn.

She has never attended school before this year. At home we just let her play, and we have made few demands upon her. She did not have set mealtimes or bedtime until she started school.

They expect a lot of these children, both in terms of schedule and academics, while we feel she should just be a child. Shouldn't the school just give her more time to grow up?

A. Teachers and day care directors see large groups of children of the same age. They are not just looking at your child individually but comparing her to both her current class and to other large groups of 4-year-olds whom they have taught in the past. When school staff sees a problem, they are telling you that she stands out from other children of the same age.

While attention deficit disorder can be seen in preschool-age children, it is not the only explanation for a child who doesn't stay on task or mind adults. The lack of schedule and discipline at home is just as likely to be causing your child's disobedience as ADD.

Your child has not learned to respect and obey those who are in charge, and so she does not do at school what she has not been asked to do at home.

She is not used to a structured schedule and seems to feel that she can do what she wants to do, when she wants to do it. This will not work at school or later in life either. For her to succeed you will need to bring some structure into her day.

Children feel out of control when they can't predict what is coming next. Her seemingly stubborn behavior may be simply an attempt to be able to predict and control what will come next.

The inability to stay on task at school may not be due to lack of attention span. Many children who are disobedient at school have developmental delays. They don't persist at a task because it is too hard for them.

Ideally, the task assigned should challenge your child just a bit, to stretch her from her current knowledge and skills to a slightly higher level. If the leap is too great, the assignment won't hold her attention because she doesn't understand it.

Schools vary in their academic demands and their degree of structure. Parents tend to match the school to the home environment. The parent who has little structure at home tends to find a school low in structure as well. Often the child needs the opposite of what he has at home.

The child with little structure at home needs to learn that the day can be ordered. He does this by attending a school where the activities occur in a predictable pattern each day.

Academically, however, a match to the level of the child is desirable. The schools with the best reputation are often those which are academically most advanced. This is wonderful for the gifted child, but is not always the best match for a child who needs to catch up in skills.

While it is not wise to blame the school for the child's delays, occasionally and for some children a different school might offer a better match. Most of the time, however, the child takes her problems with her to the new school.

Have your child evaluated by a professional to sort out the cause of her behavior problem, and increase structure and discipline at home so that school is not totally different from her experience at home.

Better to tell the children than to have family secrets

Q. We lost a baby at the age of two months to a birth defect. I have since had two more healthy children who are now 2 and 6 years old. I feel that I ought to tell my older child about her brother, but I am afraid that if I tell the older child the younger one will learn about it before he is ready to understand. Should I tell her and if so, how?

A. It is better to tell a child about a family loss than to have a family secret. Withholding will lead the child to sense that some subjects are taboo.

If there is a secret that no one can talk about, she might fear telling you about the everyday events of her life as she tries to avoid treading on the forbidden topic. She may fear that the secret is about something worse than it is. She may think that the secret is about something she did that will cause you to leave her.

Children can be told about events that actually happened but should be spared worry about things that might be. A 6-year-old can be told that she had a brother who died shortly after birth but she should not be told at this age, for example, that she is at risk for having children with the same genetic defect.

She does not need to worry about something over which she has no control, which is years away and which might never happen. You can spare her the burden of worry that you carry.

The actual loss of the baby is a different matter. If you don't tell her, she is bound to find a photograph or a birth announcement or to hear about it from a relative or neighbor at some point. It is better that she hears it from you, where you can tell her the facts in a way that is not frightening to her.

Many children, upon hearing that a sibling died, will ask if they are likely to die too. Be sure to reassure her that while the baby did die, she is not likely to. Even if she could be at increased risk, do not burden her with what might be.

Limit your explanation to what has actually happened. Answer her questions honestly and in words that she can understand but do not share aspects that might scare her.

You need not worry about the 6-year-old giving information to her younger brother. The younger child will not understand it at a level that will be damaging to him. His world is the here and now, and he does not yet have the capacity to understand that others lived before he was born.

As long as his world is a happy and stable one, hearing about another baby won't be traumatic. The loss is a major one for the parents, but does not have the same intensity for later-born children. They will only be affected if you are depressed to the extent that it interferes with their care.

When your daughter asks where the baby is now, give her an answer within the framework of your religious beliefs. There is no one answer that is correct, but do avoid any explanation that could be frightening.

As children are most worried about being alone and uncared for, many children find it comforting to be told that the baby is in heaven with grandmother or another caretaker.

Some tenderhearted children will cry when they hear about the loss. Do not feel that tears indicate that she is damaged by knowing the family tragedy. It is OK for children to feel sad at times. Parents can't, and do not need to, take away all pain. Her tears will not last long, and her feelings about her sibling may lead her to closeness to you and to her brother.

On the other hand, don't be hurt if your child shows no response at all. Many children will not relate intensely to an event that happened before they were born. The mother's feelings about the loss will affect the living child more than the loss of the baby itself.

Five-year-old girl dreams of Prince Charming

Q. Our 5-year-old daughter is obsessed with marriage, love and weddings. She watches "The Little Mermaid" and other Disney happily-ever-afters over and over, and dreams of her own prince. Is there reason for concern or will she grow out of this?

A. Children's interests change as they grow through the various developmental stages. Your daughter's interest in love and marriage is tied to her developmental stage. She is in the so-called Oedipal period where it is quite common for little girls to be flirtatious and attentive to daddy.

You may notice little girls of this age get excited when daddy comes home from work. Between ages 3 and 6, little boys can often be heard to say they want to marry their mom.

While children of this age love the parent of the opposite sex, they often fear that their love will cause the parent of the same sex to be angry. Because young children need both parents, the anger of one parent is quite scary for them.

This is likely to be why your daughter has chosen to express her feelings of love for daddy through an interest in the films about love, rather than direct flirtation. Your daughter has transferred her interest from daddy to the more neutral movies.

You probably do not need to be worried about her. She is likely to move on from her romantic interests to academic and athletic ones as she goes on to the next stage. During the years of 7 to 11, the concern moves from love and romance to mastery of skills.

This is the age where children measure the competence of their peers by how well they can play hopscotch or hit a baseball. They admire the children who are good readers and may ridicule the child who "doesn't even know how much two plus two equals."

Not only do children move on from interest in romance to interest in mastery of skills, but they also move from a primary focus on home and parents out into the world of the peer group. The school-age child begins to spend as many hours away from the family as she spends with it. Peers become more important.

Her interest in love and marriage is likely to lessen during ages 7 to 11, but will reemerge during adolescence in a more mature form. You have many years to broaden her interests and develop her talents.

You can impart a balance between independence and attachment. I would be concerned about a child who was excessively angry or mean, but not about a child who is interested in love.

While her interests will change with her developmental stage, temperament can be seen early in life and is persistent. A romantic child is not likely to suddenly change into a tomboy. Her interest in relationships may continue, but this not a negative thing. Some children and adults are more independent than others. The ability to form a close attachment can lead to a very happy marriage. Independence is a useful trait to have under certain conditions, but it needs to be balanced with an ability to bond to others.

I would not belittle her interest in romance at this age but I would keep an eye out for opportunities to catch her attention to other things as well. Within the next few years, I would offer her experiences that will broaden her knowledge and give her skills.

If she loves romance, you might offer her ballet or music lessons. You might develop her artistic talent or have her tested for the school enrichment program if she seems eligible.

Parents tend to view each stage as if it will last forever. It doesn't. Just when you think you have figured it out, your child moves on to new interests and issues, and you as parent must change along with your child.

Will vacation shortly after move confuse children?

Q. We are about to move to a new city with four children ages 3, 5, 8 and 13. The older two are concerned about leaving friends behind. They have been invited to spend a week with grandparents in yet another city for a week, one week after we move. Should we let them do this or will it be confusing for them? How can we make this move go as smoothly as possible?

A. Young children are primarily wrapped in the family. As long as the family moves with them, they will make a good transition. The key will be to make it clear that when the parents move, the children go too.

Parents take this for granted. Young children do not. You may need to say explicitly, "Mommy, daddy, Michael, Marc, Ashley and Allie are moving to Birmingham."

Your 8-year-old's security is still based in her family as well, but she has begun to move out into the world of peers.

She may worry about making friends in the new community, but she is at an age where friendships are easily formed. The sooner you can connect her to a social group or school in the new town, the sooner she will have a smile on her face.

If you move during the summer, investigate summer day camp programs. A day camp that meets at the school she will attend would be especially helpful, as she would meet some classmates and learn her way around before school starts.

As children approach the teen years, they move away from family and into the world of friends. Thirteen-year-olds are selective in choosing friends and no longer will connect with just anyone their own age.

You can expect that your teenager's adjustment will take longer than your younger children's. Yet, within a year, a typical teen will find a niche in the new community.

You may have to be patient the first few months. Parents often feel guilty about the move when a teen is unhappy, since the move is typically the parent's choice and not the child's. As your teen is complaining and moping, keep in mind that his adjustment will likely come soon.

It won't really matter if your children visit their grandparents out of town or not. The visit will just be the equivalent of moving a week later, as it will postpone their getting to know new children in the new place. They will make new friends either way.

Help your children with their adjustment by doing the things that good parents do anyway. Choose a school and neighborhood carefully so that your child fits in.

Place him at an appropriate level of academics, so that he will not be overwhelmed and discouraged, or bored and understimulated.

Help him find activities that will lead to friends. Children often bond more easily in small interest groups such as Scouts, track or band than in the larger group at school. If your child is a gymnast or a chess player, help him to find these activities.

Unpack as soon as you can to give yourself a sense of order in your home, but do take breaks to meet your neighbors and accept invitations. You will be better able to help your children adjust when you are feeling grounded yourself.

Don't expect the new community to feel like home right away. It takes connections to friends and community groups and a familiarity with the roads and shops that make a place feel like home. These take time to build.

In place of the comfort of routine, try to enjoy the newness. Your younger children will enjoy "going on adventures" to discover the grocery store, the hardware store and the ice cream shop if your attitude is upbeat.

For the most part, they will adjust if you do. The child's adjustment relects that of the parents.

Happy children get love, discipline and a role model

Q. Although I have no children of my own, I am around many of my friend's children. One friend has a child who is always sunshiny and positive although she has gone through some difficult times. This child is always ready to help and contribute and loves to make others happy.

Another friend's child is a self-centered kid with a chip on his shoulder. He feels that he is entitled to all he gets. When you ask him to help out with something, his attitude is "Why should I? What's in it for me?" How do you raise a child with a positive attitude?

A. To a large extent, attitude is taught and modeled. You can shape even a child who is not innately prone to be positive with your attitude and your actions.

Innate temperament plays a role but is not the ultimate determining factor. Temperament will determine how much effort you need to put in to get the desired happy child, and it will also influence just how you do it. Some children can be given much of what they want without becoming spoiled, while others need to have their gifts limited so as not to create a child who feels entitled to excess.

The earlier you start, the more influence you will have over your child's attitude. From age 2 or 3 you can teach your child to see the glass as half full rather than half empty. Each time your toddler cries or fusses, you can help him to see the situation in a different and more positive light. Your child won't grasp this right away, but over time he will.

External events will shape how your child sees the world. Steer your child to success, and place him in programs where he will have good experiences. Don't leave your child in a day care where he is ignored or ridiculed. Lead him toward his talents. Don't place him so that he is the worst kid on the team unless it doesn't bother him. Find his strengths and give him those opportunities.

Give your children lots of love. The child who has been nurtured and attended to during the early years can typically enjoy the freedom of being a latchkey child at age 12. The child who has seen little of his parents during his formative years will feel abandoned and scared when left alone. Yet at age 16, he will shun adult advice if no adults have been there for him when he was younger and needed them.

Balance bad things with good ones. Give your child a sense that life will be good for him and that he is protected. If he has to go through a painful experience, consider giving him a treat to balance his bad day.

When he is upset, listen to his concerns. Don't be too quick to solve his problem for him. Hear him out.

Let your children share in each other's successes. Don't make life a competition. Let your children know there is enough love and attention to go around. Let them know that they won't always get the same thing, so they need not compare — but that each child will get what he needs.

Make them responsible for each other. Teach them that they are their brother's keeper — both within the family and within the community. Show them how you care for others. Let them see you reach beyond the immediate family.

Watch your own behavior. If you are a jealous and competitive person, your children will be too. If they do not hear you speaking badly of others, they might think twice before they do.

Be a strong parent however. Being sweet to others doesn't mean that you don't discipline your children. You cannot beg your children for good behavior; you need to expect it and set consequences for transgression. Some very sweet adults have children who are out of control. Happy children are raised with love, nurturance, discipline and positive role models.

Holding back a grade will aid maturity

Q. My child's kindergarten teacher has just recommended that he repeat the grade. We are reluctant to do this out of fear that he will think of himself as stupid. What do you recommend?

A. Under the right circumstances, getting a second chance at a grade can boost self-esteem rather than destroy it. It can place the child who is developmentally immature with children who function at the same level. It can bail him out of a situation where he is always at the bottom of the group struggling to keep up.

The benefits of retention decrease as the child gets older. While repetition in elementary school tends to give the developmentally slower child a chance to catch up, repetition in high school often leads the child to give up and drop out. At the high school level, it might be better to offer a lower-track class than to hold a child back.

Before you agree to another year in the same grade for your child, be sure you understand why and how your child has failed. You will want to obtain a careful evaluation, including testing by a psychologist or school system personnel, to determine the exact cause for the failure.

If the problem is due to bad behavior or lack of motivation, repetition is not the cure. If he failed to turn in homework one year, chances are he will do the same the next. You will need to resolve the underlying emotional problem. A psychologist or psychiatrist can help you uncover the issue.

If your child has a learning disability, simple repetition might not do the trick either. You will need to approach your child's school and request evaluation for special education services. If he has failed to learn by the traditional methods once, chances are he won't do much better the second time around. An ungraded class with a specially trained teacher may enable him to learn and prevent the loss of self-esteem that comes with failure.

The hyperactive child may benefit from medication to increase attention span and decrease hyperactivity. On medication, he may be able to absorb the material of his grade the second time around, improving upon his first unmedicated try. Just putting him back in the same grade without any change in his ability to pay attention may result in another lost year.

The child who is simply a slow learner should be grouped with other students at the same level of ability and proceed with his agemates. Younger bright children and older slow learners are not alike, even though they may be at the same level of math or reading achievement.

Should your child repeat? It depends upon why he is failing. Certainly a child who is not learning shouldn't just pass through the system, but no child should repeat more than once.

Hyperactive children might bring grades up to par when they are helped via medication to pay attention long enough to learn.

Emotionally disturbed children need psychological help. Children with specific learning disabilities need a different approach to the material.

Repeating the grade is useful for children who are chronologically young for their class (summer birthdays) and for children who are simply immature.

For these children the repetition is a gift of a year of childhood. Repetition, with the increased maturity of being a year older, will restore a balance and allow them to make satisfactory progress through the rest of school. Correct grade placement makes the whole thing work.

You can't teach skills before the child is ready

Q. My child attends an excellent school with an accelerated curriculum where reading is taught in kindergarten. Even though she has had an adequate exposure to reading, my daughter still can recognize only a few words. When we try to practice with her, she resists. She says that she can't read the words but we think she can. What can we do to help her to stop fighting us when we try to help her read better?

A. Skills have their "teachable moments." You cannot teach a newborn to walk or a 1-year-old to read. When you try to teach a skill too early, it takes an enormous amount of effort to teach a skill that can be absorbed easily if you wait for the optimal time.

Reading is based on neurological pathways in the brain. You can't rush neurological development. If you push your child to read before she is ready, she will get the idea that she is a poor reader. If you wait until she is ready — probably first grade for your child — she will think of herself as competent.

Schools with a large group of gifted children are correct in exposing children to reading in kindergarten. Many of the children will indeed read by the end of the school year. Most good schools do not overemphasize reading in kindergarten but they do provide exposure and opportunity.

It is typically the parents who feel that because reading has been introduced, every child should read at age 5. They become competitive with other families and feel that their child is behind if he or she is not precocious. Instead of an opportunity to learn to read, the child who is pushed before he is ready becomes burdened with an overwhelming chore.

Children who read very young are usually bright, but it does not follow that children who read on time are not bright. Many highly gifted children do not mature exceptionally early. Maturity, precocity and giftedness are not the same thing.

Your daughter's resistance to your "help" suggests that she is not ready to read at the level you are expecting of her. To help a child read in kindergarten you need to go with the child's skills and interests. Back off on the pressure to read or you will achieve the opposite of your goal.

If a child learns to read without undue effort or stress, reading is fun. Once she is reading you can provide materials at an appropriate level and let your child enjoy them. If you read with her, keep reading sessions short. Ten to fifteen minutes is enough for most 5-year-olds. Take turns reading a page, or let her read until she tires and then finish the story for her if she wants you to.

If a child is not ready to read yet, read to her. The love of reading comes from the enjoyment of stories from a printed page. If you read to her now, she will read when she is ready. No child has become dependent upon others reading to her simply because she has had too many stories read to her.

Stop occasionally and ask her to read a word you know she can read. Ask only what you know she can do. Ask only if the game is fun for her. Make sure she doesn't fail.

Be sure to let her be her age in other areas too. Parents who push academics often push children to maturity and independence in other areas they are not ready for.

Let her sleep with a teddy bear or with a night light on. Let her sit in your lap when she chooses to. Don't call her a baby when she seeks attention or cuddling. Five-year-olds are still young children.

Teach child to give — not only to get

Q. I always give holiday gifts to my children, but I think I have been lax about having them give gifts to me. I want to teach them to give and not just to get, even though I really don't need a gift from them. I don't just want to hand them cash to shop with.

How do you get children to give meaningful gifts to parents when they don't have their own money?

A. When children are young it is OK to just let them enjoy the holiday and be on the receiving end of gifts, but as they get older, they should be taught to think about others.

Homemade gifts are a good way to start with young children. Most preschools and kindergartens make holiday gifts for parents at this time of year.

Gift-making serves to develop fine motor skills at the same time that it offers social instruction.

In early childhood education programs, the students often make gifts that help the parent remember his child at that particular age. Plaster handprints or picture frames with a photo of the child at school are typical.

Children take pride in the gifts they have made and are happy to have something to give. Gift giving builds self-esteem and is empowering for the child.

If your child's Scout troop, school or Sunday school class does not make holiday gifts, you might want to suggest that it does.

Search through craft books for a project that is both personal and appropriate to your child's developmental skills.

The craft needs to be something that the child can make rather than one that requires lots of adult input.

As children get older, allowance should include some money that is intended for others. Small donations to charity, and holiday and birthday gifts for family might come out of this money.

Be sure to teach your child not only to give, but also to budget and use money wisely. You do not want to teach him to overspend.

Use gift shopping to teach your child to be a wise consumer. Ask him to evaluate the value and quality of his selection.

Use this time to teach him to think about the other person as he chooses something that person would like. Young children often give what they want, not what is suitable for the receiver.

Mom probably does not want a Hot Wheels racer. Encourage him to list several gifts that would be within his budget and then to select the one that best matches the person the gift is going to.

Pair up with other adults to help the child select a gift as a surprise. Have dad help with the gift for mom and mom help with the gift for dad. Single parents can pull in grandparents, aunts and uncles and friends to help.

Your child doesn't necessarily have to pay for the whole gift. Match his money with yours. A gift of a dollar or two toward a present is just as valuable a lesson as paying for the whole thing.

Gifts can be from a group. A child can shop with grandparents and select a gift to give from grandparents and child.

Siblings can pool their money for a gift for mom and dad. Gifts can be to more than one person. A gift for the kitchen can serve both mom and dad.

The effort of giving a gift is just as important as the money spent. Let your children wrap the gift whether they bought it or not.

Put several choices of paper out on the dining room table along with scissors, Scotch tape and an assortment of ribbons and bows.

You might even want to cut out pictures of pretty, wrapped gifts from magazines and let your children have a craft experience while they have the joy of giving.

Young children will enjoy coloring their own wrapping paper. The wrapper will seem like a gift too.

A stage is scary for 3-year-old, ground level is better

Q. My 3-year-old is going to be in a play at the end of the summer at the day care he attends. He doesn't want to participate. On the mornings that he has rehearsals, he wants to go in late. He likes the rest of his camp program and has friends and competent counselors. Is this just a case of stage fright? How do I handle it?

A. Stage fright in young children is primarily a fear of separation from the parent. Young children don't like the feeling of being high up on stage, apart from the audience. Being unable to find and make eye contact with the parent, who has come to see him, can unnerve a 3-year-old.

You might want to suggest to the camp staff that the children perform on the floor, at the same level as the audience, rather than up on stage. This makes it harder for the parents to see, but more comfortable for the children.

Darkening the house lights in an auditorium takes away the child's ability to find his or her own parent too. While for older children, this can cut down on the distraction, for younger children it increases their fear of separation. It is best to have young children perform with the lights on.

Instead of the whole camp performing at once, young children do better if each age group does its own skit in the child's own classroom.

With the smaller group, the parents will not have a problem seeing over the heads of those in front of them even without the use of a stage.

The smaller audience will allow each child find his own parent and will generally provide a less intimidating situation.

When your 3-year-old tells you that he doesn't want

to perform, ask him to tell you about his thoughts. Hear him out before telling him that he can make that choice as the date of the performance approaches.

Do encourage him to participate in the rehearsals. If he doesn't practice for the play with the group at all, he will miss a good part of the camp program, as rehearsals can become the main activity as the performance nears.

Let the counselors know about his fear right from the start, and ask them to put him in a role that is duplicated so that if at the last moment he still doesn't want to perform, he can be excused. Forcing a fearful child to do what he doesn't want to do may well increase his fear.

Get him involved with aspects of the play other than acting. Encourage the staff to include him in making the costumes and stage sets. Many children who are afraid of acting can become involved with the production in ways that are not threatening to them.

As children get older, stage fright is a different thing. In the place of a fear of separation is a fear of looking foolish. The older child worries about forgetting his lines or looking silly in a costume.

While older teens can enjoy the humor of a male in a female role, an elementary school age child may be humiliated by being asked to play the part of a girl if he is a boy.

Performing in a group rather than alone can lessen the fear of looking foolish. It is far harder to sing a solo than to sing in a choir.

The fearful child will be more comfortable with a small role than with the lead, and might prefer a nonspeaking part for his first or second acting experience. Not every child wants the lead role.

Having a role in a play can teach public speaking skills and build self-confidence, but it can only do this if the child is comfortable. The very young child may just not be ready for this kind of autonomy.

A relaxed approach will allow him to watch his peers and learn from watching so that he may be ready to join in as he gets older.

Shallow water reduces swimming fears

Q. My 3-year-old is afraid to swim. It has gotten so bad that she won't even get near the water unless she has a float toy with her.

She will happily bob about in the water with a floatation device but is terrified when you ask her to let go of her crutch. How can we overcome her fear?

A. Most children who fear the water are afraid of being in water over their head. By keeping your child in shallow water and by emphasizing that she can put her feet down and stand any time she wants to, you may lessen her fear.

In pools which lack a shallow end or for children who are too short to stand, it helps to put a platform in the water for them to stand on. Some community pools have these available for their preschool swim classes.

At age 3, you need to be careful not to expect too much of your child. When parents expect a child to do something he or she cannot do, the parent sets the child up to fail. Having failed once, the child may refuse to try again. Failure sets back learning.

The child is too young to know that the expectation is unrealistic and so he thinks that he should be able to do what the parent asks, but he can't.

From this he concludes that he is defective or inadequate. This is not the message that most parents mean to convey.

Teaching at the right time will allow developmental readiness to work with you rather than against you. At 3, you daughter might just be too young.

If you wait a year for formal swimming and spend another year doing pre-swimming skills, you might get results with less effort.

Her fear may stem from her own sense of not being ready for this skill yet.

Raising Children

If you try to teach her to swim in a year or two, you may find that her fear has disappeared without your exerting any special effort.

Feeling that she has no control over what happens to her when she lifts off to swim contributes to her fear. You can help her by giving her control.

Don't throw a fearful child into the pool. Let her get in at her own speed. Let her play on the steps for a while and gradually make her way into the water.

There are some children who are just temperamentally fearful. These children need a slow and understanding approach to swimming with much reassurance.

Use small incremental steps in what you ask of them. These children may swim later than daredevil personalities but they will achieve the same skills in the long run.

Floatation devices are useful to help preschool children to overcome their fears and to give them the experience of floating.

Older children, however, can become overly dependent upon floaties to the point where they are making no progress at swimming on their own.

Put the floating toys away during swim lessons by age 5, and work on steps toward real swimming.

You can use a kickboard, though, to teach. Ask a child 5 years or older to hold the kickboard so it keeps her head up while she makes her body float.

Teach her to kick — not only because it is a part of swimming, but also because it gives her something active to do. It gives her a sense that she can keep herself up.

Get some of her friends in the pool with her and play games. Throw pennies or plastic rings on the bottom of the pool and let the children dive for the pennies or toys to get used to putting their face in the water.

Build a general sense of confidence in your child. Praise her skills in other areas but do so only when your praise can be genuine.

A general "can do" attitude will go a long way toward motivating your child to try new physical skills.

TV to be watched passively must be chosen actively

Q. I have heard that watching TV causes children to become aggressive. Is this true? When my 4-year-old daughter has a friend over, she wants to watch TV with her. Should I allow this?

A. A psychologist named Albert Bandura explored the effect of observed aggression on children's behavior. He put children in a room with many toys including a punching bag. He found that the children only rarely punched the punching bag, choosing other toys to play with much more often.

He then took these same children and had them view other people punching the bag under various conditions. After viewing others acting violently, the children chose the punching bag over other toys with much greater frequency.

Because children do imitate what they see, what the child watches on TV certainly makes a difference. When your 4-year-old watches Masterpiece Theatre, she sees not only a good story with many levels of meaning, but she also sees politeness and a use of language that you might want your child to imitate.

Contrast this to a bit of a Power Rangers show I saw recently where a character said something like, "Do it or I'll blow your lights out. You got it?" If this type of show is on at your house, don't be surprised when your children talk to you like this. They repeat what they hear.

It is not only what they watch, but also how much they watch that affects their development. The child who spends hours in front of the TV is not active physically and is not interacting with other children. He is substituting a vicarious experience for a direct experience as an active participant. He is missing social exposure.

No matter how educational the show might be, it

Raising Children

cannot substitute for the give and take of two children playing together. With passive entertainment, the child does not learn to compromise or to assert herself, to share or to defend her turf, as she would in play with a friend. She doesn't write the script for the fantasy play that happens when children get together.

Should children not watch TV at all? Not having a TV doesn't harm children but it does make them different from their friends.

They may feel left out when the children talk about a particular show, but they will make up for this by having skills that they develop in the time they are not watching TV.

The child who can roller blade or figure skate will be admired, as will the child with advanced computer skills.

Quality shows on TV, in moderation, are not harmful. If your child wants to watch TV with her guest the minute she steps in the door, I would steer the children to other, more interactive activities.

If after several hours of play, when they are tired or tired of each other, there is no harm in using the passive entertainment of a quality TV show to wind down at the end of a day of play.

Two children who have been playing for hours can watch TV together as they wait for the guest's mother to pick her up. This may be a better alternative than two children being forced to interact after they are worn out.

Parents can use the TV to "babysit" for young children while the parent takes a shower or pays some bills. In moderation, TV is not harmful if the shows that are to be watched passively are selected actively.

Age 6 to 12
The remembered childhood

Your childhood memories come from ages 6 to 12. Prior to this, most people have only scattered memory fragments. In contrast, many people can remember complex series of events, and the emotions that accompanied them, from the elementary school years.

By age 6 the child's romantic feelings for the opposite sex parent are lessened, and the child's energy is freed up for learning. Mastery is the key task for this age, and popularity at school is typically based on competence. Children admire the best athlete, the best speller or the best piano player.

The child can now consider more than one dimension at a time — length and width for example. The younger child focuses on either length or width but not both at the same time.

He has a conscience after age 6 but thinking is concrete. Rules are rules, and motivation doesn't count. Tattling is common, as he is outraged when rules are broken. Fears diminish as understanding increases.

Balance structured activities with free time

Q. My son needs after-school tutoring to keep up with his school work. He also plays soccer, which requires two practice sessions and one game per week, spring and fall. Now he wants to do karate, which would be two or three classes per week year round. Should we let him or is this too much?

A. Children vary in their stamina, and what is too much for one child may be OK for another.

However, two activities, which are each three days per week, plus tutoring is probably too much structure for most children.

Even if your child could keep up with the physical demands of this schedule, it would not be wise to fill every moment with something to do.

Children need time to just play and think. With the exception of a small group of behavior-disordered children, most children do not need every moment to be structured.

It is when the child has nothing to do that he must discover his interests and create a meaningful way to fill his time. This won't work, however, if you allow him to turn on the TV whenever he has free time.

Yet not every child has the luxury of quiet time at home after school. For children who would otherwise be in day care, structured sports every day might not be very different from their time in day care.

Whether or not karate, soccer and tutoring are too much for your child will depend upon what your child would do with his time if he were not in these activities.

The fact that your child is asking for the activities makes it more likely to be successful than if it were the parent who wanted his or her child in every sport.

Consider your child's wishes but do not rely solely

on his opinion. Children don't have the adult perspective to see the whole schedule.

A child thinks only of each sport, without being able to think about how the activities will fit in with homework, meals, family time and relaxation.

Some children do better in adult-directed activities. The child who has difficulty getting along with others can gain a lot from interacting with peers within the stricture of a team or a Scout troop.

For these children, the group lends rules for interaction to the child who has not learned these on his own. If the experience of participating as a team or group member is successful, the learned social skills will carry over to one-on-one interactions.

Some parents worry that if their child is not in every activity he will lag behind his peers in skills. These parents need to remember that no child will excel — or even participate — in every activity as he gets older.

The younger years serve to allow the child to find his interests and talents from among many skills, not to make him excel in each one.

He can explore different skills sequentially, without having to do every one at the same time.

Some skills that seem so important in childhood are those which he will have little occasion to use as an adult. Try to save some time for life-long skills rather than only group activities. Individual skills such as swimming, piano or chess carry over into a time of life when it may be harder to get a team together.

For most children, two to three days per week of structured activities is enough. This gives the child time to be alone and time to invite friends over to play.

This unstructured one-on-one play time teaches valuable social skills. While teams do foster friendships, there is little opportunity for the children to work out their differences with their peers on their own.

Find a balance among group activities, time alone and unstructured time with one or two friends.

Creative and introspective or Attention Deficit?

Q. I hear so much about attention deficit disorder now. I don't remember hearing anything about it, even by a different name, 30 years ago. Are there actually more children with this problem today or is it just that we are noticing it more?

My grandson has been labeled ADD but I think he is just creative and introspective. He is not a behavior problem. He just marches to the beat of his own drum.

A. Several factors have changed over the past 30 years that have made children who can't sit still or can't pay attention stand out.

Increased academic demands have highlighted children who are developmentally immature. The child who could just play in kindergarten years ago now is expected to sit in a chair and work on academic skills.

While many children are ready for these increased academic demands, moving first grade curriculum into kindergarten causes those children who are not ready to stand out as learning and behavior problems.

Because of the increased academic expectations, we are less tolerant of the child who stares out the window when he should be paying attention in class.

Because we now have the term ADD, we call the child by the "disease" name instead of the kinder and more tolerant "absent minded professor" or "spacey kid."

Many spacey children do just fine in life and don't have problematic ADD. These children often are the more creative ones — the children who become writers or architects or cartoonists.

Some recent developments have increased the prevalence of ADD. Drug abuse and prematurity can cause the symptoms of attention deficit disorder. More children are born to parents who used drugs during pregnancy. More low birth weight babies are being saved.

We have limited the use of physical discipline but have not replaced it with other equally emphatic methods of parental control.

The mother who would have spanked her child for discipline now fears having her child taken away. Parental control is less than it used to be for many families.

Teachers have less control as well. Some parents are quick to defend the behavior of a wayward child.

While a generation ago the teacher could get the child back in line, now she fears the wrath of the parent who defends the out-of-control behavior of her child. The child falls into the cracks and gets medicine in place of discipline.

Parents and professionals may be too quick to label, yielding larger numbers of diagnosed children.

A percentage of the children who are referred for ADD evaluation, who stare out the window during class, who forget their homework and who never seem to have the right book with them for the assignment will become more focused and organized as they mature.

The spacey child does not need medication to control his wandering attention but he may need repeated reminders to stay on task.

Instead of sending him to his room so that he is less distracted by the goings-on in the family (any room has enough distraction for a child with wayward attention), keep him in the family areas of the home and lend him your focus.

Instead of giving your spacey child a diagnosis, return to the "absentminded professor" label and think of him as creative and introspective. Accept him as he is and redirect him when his attention wanders.

Organize his binder or notebooks for him while he is young, lending him your organizational skills until he develops his own. Note his weaknesses and work to correct them but don't pathologize them.

Separate out real attention deficit disorder from simple dreamy, creative traits or immaturity.

Teach children to read between the lines

Q. My 8-year-old son is a sucker for advertisements. He takes the TV ads as gospel and wants what he sees. How can we teach him that things are not always as they are advertised?

A. There are several issues here. The first is that your child seems to be watching too much TV. Enroll him in structured activities — sports, music lessons or specific interests such as art classes or chess tournaments.

Turn off the TV and insist that he play with his toys or play outside. Invite friends over for him and direct their play when they get stuck. Some children will need adult suggestions for activities until the TV habit is broken.

Another problem is his desire for everything he sees. Are you buying him the toys he asks for? Children who get gifts constantly always seem to want more. Children who get just what they need, but not everything they want, tend to be content with what they have. Limit gift giving to set occasions — birthday, holidays and rewards for achieving goals.

Next you will need to educate your child to be a wise consumer. Limiting children's exposure to TV and advertising is my first choice, but if they do watch, turn their exposure into an educational opportunity.

Give your child some hands-on experience. Choose a toy or a food product that your child has requested after seeing it on TV. Pick one which you suspect might prove to be disappointing. Ask questions to get your child to think about both the advertisement and the product.

Ask him to guess how long he thinks this toy would be fun to play with. Ask him to say what the TV advertisement claimed the toy could do and if he thinks the toy will really do what is claimed.

Be careful to listen to his answers and not to criticize. Open discussion. Don't close it.

After buying the toy or food product, ask your child what he thinks of it. Can it really do what the ad claimed it would? Ask him again a month later to help him see the difference between something that is fun at first and something that has long term value. If you have been nonjudgmental, your child should be able to see how his choice fell short.

Talk about how advertising is aimed at selling and how therefore it will likely exaggerate the strengths of a product and minimize its weaknesses. Discuss how it is important to think carefully before you buy. Remind him that you can spend each dollar only once.

By going through this process several times, your child will soon do it by himself. Learning this way of thinking will help him not only to make wise consumer decisions but to think critically in other situations as well.

The experience of negotiating for and discussing the merits of a new toy with his parents prepares him to do the same outside the family.

Your child learns not only to evaluate a situation rationally, but also to be prepared to defend his choices in a logical manner. Children who learn to do this tend to value their own opinions and are better able to resist social pressure.

Even after learning to make wise choices, your child might make some decisions that will seem irrational to you. Occasionally it may be in the child's best interest for the parent to allow the purchase of a fad toy — out of the child's own money — even if it is overpriced or poorly constructed.

The need to have the same toy as his classmates may outweigh the practical considerations. Having a fad toy may foster social skills.

If the toy turns out to disappoint him, it can serve as a powerful lesson. The advertised cereal that tastes awful or the toy that is not what is claimed to be may be worth its cost in educational experience.

Let child make complete transition to new grade

Q. My daughter repeated the first grade last year. Now she is going into second grade. We allowed her to make the transition by staying with her old friends from the class she left for Brownies and ballet. Now it is her second year with the new group. Do we continue to do after-school activities with her old class or move her to be with her new one?

A. Holding a child back a grade is as much an issue for the parent as for the child — sometimes more so. The ambivalence you felt in holding her back led you to make an incomplete shift.

While parents may try to appease the child's hurt at being held back by taking the step gradually, it is usually better for your child to make a clean break. Switching friends all at once both in school and after school is better than dragging out the transition over several years. Young children make new friends easily and after an initial adjustment, they blend right into their new class.

To keep her in both groups — one at school and one after school — is just to remind her of the repeat and to cause the transition to the new group to take much longer than it needs to. Despite some convincing tears and powerful emotions at the time of the change, your child's smile is likely to return as soon as she makes friends in her new group.

Better would have been to let her go to Brownies and ballet with her new friends. This would have allowed her to become a part of the group she will be with from now on.

Being with her new friends after school as well as at school will help her to become part of the new group quickly. Just seeing her old friends after school will not keep her in that group. She will just be "the one who used to be in our class."

Do switch her this year to be with her current classmates. She will have to make the transition at some point anyway. Since promotion from Brownies to Junior Scouts is based on school grade, the group will move on without her when she gets to the third grade. You can't keep her with this group forever.

Work through your own feelings about the grade repeat so that you too can become a complete member of the moms of her new grade. You can continue to see your old friends made through your daughter, but be clear to yourself that these friendships are now independent of your daughter's membership in that group.

Encouraging her to become a part of a new group doesn't mean that she cannot continue a friendship with a specific child from the old group. One-on-one friendships have little to do with group membership.

Grade repeats are usually done for developmental immaturity. Most teachers are quite accurate in choosing the children who need another year to grow. If your child was carefully chosen to repeat, her interests and developmental level should fit better with her new class than with her old one.

Most children who repeat are the younger ones in the class. Remember that your child is not a year older than her new class. She may only be a month or two older than the fall birthday children of her new group.

Ballet might offer an ungraded activity for her. After the early grades, ballet placement is based on skill rather than on age in most ballet schools. She may find that ballet is a good place to mingle with old friends and with children of different ages.

You may find, however, that she may prefer not to be with her old classmates. She might want to just enjoy her new friends, without having to face the children that went on without her.

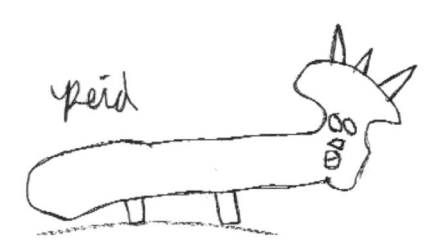

Family turmoil can overwhelm a high-strung child

Q. Our 8-year-old grandson gives his mother and his teacher at school fits. He can be aggressive, defiant and disruptive.

He behaves very well when he is with us alone, but when his two older brothers are around, he often stirs up trouble.

He can do his school work well, but often does not want to. So far, neither rewards nor restrictions seem to work. What can be done to improve his behavior?

A. There are many reasons why a child could be having the very general behavior problems you describe.

You mention only his mother but not his father. Is he responding to a divorce and the turmoil which leads up to the separation?

Some children are born very active and with a temperament that tends toward the aggressive. Yet, with a soothing environment, these temperamental tendencies can be kept in check.

When emotional turmoil occurs along with a high-strung temperament, the child's controls are overwhelmed and poor behavior results.

Many parents think they are offering discipline but are really ambivalent about setting limits.

Discipline is not the fun part of parenting, and few of us pictured ourselves punishing when we decided to have a child. However, without clear and firm limits, we create a child who is not likable — even to the parent.

Rewards and punishments do work if they are selected appropriately and applied consistently.

Most punishments fail because they go on for too long ("You are grounded for three months!"), because the parent backs down and does not really carry out the punishment (inconsistency) or because what is taken away was not really important to the child in the first place (e.g. taking away his bike when he is just as happy watching TV).

Do not give up on using punishments and rewards to get your grandson's behavior under control, but do seek help in finding what will work.

Sometimes it is the parent who needs support in carrying out discipline because the punishment evokes emotional issues in the parent.

It may be that the mother feels guilty about a divorce or that she was punished too harshly as a child, and so she doesn't want to punish at all.

The fact that your grandson behaves well when he is alone with you may suggest that he is jealous of and competitive with his siblings. These sibling rivalry issues can carry over into the classroom, where he competes with other children for the teacher's attention.

For many children, negative attention is better than no attention at all. The child who feels he cannot excel and be noticed for being the best may be disrespectful and aggressive to be noticed.

When both parents work full time, children may get little attention at home. The parents may have little time and energy left at the end of the day to do more than get supper on the table and do a load of laundry.

Some children get by with this, but many express their need for affection through angry, aggressive, hard-to-ignore behavior.

Too little time with too-tired parents is the most common cause of behavior problems today.

To remediate the situation for your grandson, define specific behaviors which need improvement.

Set clear expectations and consequences. Spend quality time with him.

Catch your grandson during those moments when he is behaving as you wish him to and reward him with praise and time with you.

Explore underlying emotional issues, which may be stirring up anger. Consider getting professional help for your grandson and his mother to look at the issues specific to your family.

Motivating a child works better than forcing her

Q. My 6-year-old daughter is strong-willed. Currently we are battling over what she will wear to school. She has four new outfits for this year and several that still fit her from last year. She refuses to wear the perfectly good clothes from last year. How can I make her wear the other clothes?

She also is supposed to put several pillows on her bed after I help her make it. Many mornings, she refuses to do this. I punish her by making her stay in her room after school, but this punishment doesn't seem to fix the problem.

A friend suggested that I use a star chart and reward her for making her bed but I don't want to give her a treat for doing the chores that are her responsibility as a member of the family. How can I make her do it?

A. Some children are more compliant than others. Your daughter seems to have come into the world with a strong-willed personality and a mind of her own. This might work in her favor in later life, but it is causing clashes between you and her right now.

Your aim should not be to "make" your child wear certain clothes or to "make" her put her pillows on her bed, but to motivate her to do it.

If you make her, she will resist and you will find yourself in a power struggle which neither of you can win.

I would recommend that you back off from the fight over clothes and let her wear anything that is in her closet that is appropriate for the weather and the occasion. She should not be allowed to wear pajamas to church or shorts in January.

If she is happy with her four new appropriate outfits, I see no harm in allowing her to avoid the other ones. Do not run out and buy her additional new clothes that you would not otherwise purchase.

If you back off from the conflict, you might find that she tires of the same four things and broadens her choices to include some of the clothes she hasn't worn for a while.

If you want to encourage her to wear other outfits, set up some natural consequences that leave you out of the equation.

You might try doing laundry less frequently, so that her favorites are not ready to wear when she wants them.

It is frustrating for a parent to see good clothing hanging in the closet unworn, but if you think about it, you will realize that it doesn't really cost you any more money for her to wear only her new outfits.

As to the pillows — all school-age children should have chores around the house but it is important to keep them age-appropriate in amount and difficulty.

The task of putting pillows on her bed is a reasonable one. Your friend's suggestion about using a reward chart is a good idea. This might sound like bribery to you, but let's look at it in another way.

You and your daughter are locked in a power struggle. Neither of you is happy with the current situation.

The techniques you are using will work with some children, but are not working with yours. You need to change tactics.

By using a chart to record and reward behavior, you are returning the control to your child. You are giving her a way to comply with your wishes without squashing her will.

It is not a terrible thing to use a reward to motivate a child over a hump, as long as the reward is appropriate.

If you think of it as an incentive, rather than a reward, you might be more comfortable with the idea. We all need incentives to get us to do tasks which are uninteresting or unpleasant to us.

While your expectations are realistic, your daughter is not complying. Back off and try another track.

Passive and less-favored children are often angry

Q. Our son is a fourth grader who is gregarious and athletically gifted. He detests reading and doesn't study for tests, but our real problem is with his temper and stubbornness.

To our knowledge, he has never hurt anyone because of his temper but it is still frightening in its intensity. Other than telling him to punch his pillow, how can we channel his anger?

A. Some children are born more intense than others, but there are certainly life experiences that can contribute to making a child angry. The first step in reducing anger is to get at its cause.

A common cause of anger in children is sibling rivalry, that is, competition between the children of a family. When a parent favors one child or protects one child at the expense of another, the wronged child feels angry.

Parents can foster this kind of anger by using competition to control behavior. When a parent uses "Let's see who can get the better grades," as a regular means of encouraging studying, one or both children wind up feeling hurt.

This is especially true if one child is naturally brighter than the other and always wins. The child who can't ever win the competition comes out angry and defeated.

The humiliation of repeated failure can lead to anger. A child who can't read cannot perform well in front of others. Sometimes he will become the class clown. Other times he will become an angry child.

Anger is also learned. The parent who feels wronged at every turn models this behavior for his children. The child learns to see good things as being given or withheld by others, rather than as being within his own control. If you feel that you can cause the things you want to happen, then you feel that you can work harder to achieve your goals.

If you feel that things are outside your control and you can only wait for them to happen or beg others for the goodies, then you feel angry when your needs are not met.

You can reduce your child's anger by making him feel that he is in charge of what happens to him. Some children have learned to feel helpless and must be actively led through situations to re-learn effective behavior.

You can reduce your son's anger by giving him experiences with success. A child who hates to read is probably a poor reader. This affects all other school learning. Thus he probably does not have many moments of success at school.

At the same time that you insist that he do his best at school, you can give him outside experiences to balance his academic struggle.

Athletics are particularly good for angry children because it allows them to express aggression in a controlled and organized way. Kicking a soccer ball or hitting a baseball is a good vent for anger and is probably more meaningful than punching a pillow.

Teach your son to express his anger in words. While he should not be allowed to call you names or be disrespectful, he should be allowed to express his opinion about issues.

A child who calls his parents "stupid" needs to be taught to say instead, "I did not think you were fair when you gave my brother ten dollars but gave me only five."

In the first case, he is rude without solving the problem. In the second he tells you what he is angry about and gives you a clue about how to resolve his feelings.

Remediating his learning problems at school can lessen his anger as well. A reading tutor to bring him up to grade level might reduce his frustration at school.

With more success and better self-esteem he might feel less angry. This is an excellent time to do this, before the low self-esteem and anger become an integral part of who he is.

Early trauma yields poor behavior at adolescence

Q. My son is 12 years old. In the past few months I have noticed a very distinct change in his personality. The once quiet child has become irritable, rude and rebellious.

His teacher from last year also noted this change in his behavior and called me more than once to discuss it. He has never had much self-esteem. He has no real friends. Whenever he makes a friend, it doesn't last long. He has just entered the seventh grade at a new school.

At first I attributed the changes to the beginnings of puberty. Now I am seeing more and more unhappiness and rebelliousness with a general attitude of defiance and anger. Half the time he is rude to me and the other half he acts like his old self.

Our household has never been stable. His father has been verbally and emotionally abusive on numerous occasions. I sometimes suspect that my son experienced abuse when I was not at home. My son does not want to be left alone with his father anymore but he won't tell me that anything happened.

My husband and I have been in marriage counseling twice in the past. Each time he found an excuse to quit. I plan to file for divorce.

How can I help and protect my son? Will divorce help him or make the problems that are already there get worse? Should I try to stick it out or have I waited too long to separate from a bad situation?

A. While puberty alone does not account for changes in behavior from sweet to rebellious, if the early years have not been stable, you will see the problems as hormones surge.

Young children are dependent upon their parents no matter how bad they are and will generally try to please. Adolescents can and will rebel against situations which are less than acceptable.

The absence of friends who could support him as his family falls apart places him at risk. The friendless, unhappy child is vulnerable to attention from gangs and drug-abusing teens, as any friend may be better than none at all.

If he lacks the social skills for acceptance by even these children, then he becomes at risk for suicide or destructive acts against others, now or in his adulthood.

Consider helping him to develop a skill and to join a group based on this interest. Children who have trouble making friends on the playground or in the lunch room often do better in structured groups.

Now that he is in the junior high school there should be several such activities available to him during school and after. Let the coach or faculty sponsor know of your concerns and ask his or her assistance in helping your child to fit in.

Your son needs the help of a mental health professional. If abuse has occurred, it is important that he talk about this and that there be some safeguards in the custody and visitation arrangements. It is unusual for an adolescent boy to not want to be alone with his father.

Divorce should never be taken lightly but it sounds as if you have made many attempts to work things out. Some situations just can't be fixed. Children should not be left in abusive situations, but divorce does not always remove the child from abuse, as the court will nearly always give both parents access to the child.

Some children become angry when their parents divorce but others, particularly when there has been abuse, find it to be a relief. Your child is already in emotional trouble, and maintaining the situation as it is, without change, is not likely to lead to improvement.

Take steps now to deal with each aspect of the family issues. It is easier to help a 12-year-old than a child in his late teens. Follow your instincts, and you will do what is right for your child.

Other diagnoses may mimic ADHD

Q. My husband and I have been told that our child has attention deficit hyperactivity disorder. He is in a special class at school for children with learning disabilities. Will individual attention at home help him catch up with learning? How do I deal with his need for attention when I have another, normal child as well?

A. While learning disabilities often accompany attention deficit hyperactivity disorder (ADHD), they are not the same thing. It is possible to have one without the other.

Although you sound certain about your child's diagnosis, you might want another opinion. ADHD is overdiagnosed. There is no blood test or chromosome analysis for ADHD. The diagnosis is based on observations of behavior and so it is somewhat subjective.

Not all distractible behavior is ADHD. Some behavior problems at school are simply the result of emotional turmoil. While depressed adults slow down, depressed or troubled children speed up into frenzied activity to push away their sad thoughts.

"Learning disability" is another diagnosis that can be made too frequently. In accelerated school systems, where the majority of the students are above average, children with average ability are sometimes seen as learning disabled. This happens because the child can't make A's when compared to his gifted classmates, and parents or teachers may become uncomfortable with the fact that the child makes C's. Parents seem to be more comfortable with the label "learning disabled" than with "average." Sometimes C's represent the child's best effort and ability, and do not indicate a disability requiring a label.

For children with true ADHD, rather than active

behavior due to other causes, medication is often helpful in improving concentration and behavior. While many parents are reluctant to use prescription drugs, when used correctly, they can make the child's behavior manageable so that he can learn at a school. Without this help, he gets farther and farther behind and thinks less and less of himself. Untreated children with ADHD often feel dumb.

In addition, the ADHD child's high activity level and inability to wait his turn make teachers and other students not like him. He receives more than his share of scolding and social rejection. Medication, by improving behavior, can help your child to be accepted. When there are learning problems, it can be helpful to give your child special academic help at home. In addition to tutoring in areas of difficulty, you can boost his self-esteem by creating a home in which he feels secure and loved. While the extra help with homework might evoke jealousy in your other child, you can get around this by including him in your sessions. The extra help your child with ADHD receives does not have to be at the expense of his brother.

Instead of working alone with your child with learning problems, plan a homework session where the three of you sit together at the kitchen table. You can be available to answer questions from both children while you work intensively with the child with the learning problem. This is quite a different experience for the competent student than being sent to his room to work while mother sits with his brother.

When your child with ADHD does need one-on-one help, help your other child to understand. Point out to him that he is fortunate to be able to grasp school skills with relatively little effort but don't expect this to sooth his ruffled feathers if his handicapped brother gets all of the attention, all of the time. Special attention doesn't have to be equal but each child needs to have some. Practice the piano with your other son or quiz him on his weekly spelling words. Normal children need attention too.

Bilingual home is not the cause of speech delay

Q. My 6-year-old daughter, who attends first grade, is slow to learn to read. She also was late in learning to talk. She didn't say words until age 2. We spoke two languages at home to her when she was a baby. Do you think that this caused the delay in speech and reading?

A. Bi- or multilingual children, children raised with two or more languages at home, do not show signs of language delay. If you measure their vocabulary at very young ages, you may find that they have fewer vocabulary words in one language than the average child of the same age, but if you add their vocabulary in both languages, the typical bilingual toddler knows more words.

The bilingual infant may start to speak a few weeks later than the child who learns one language, but when he does speak, he quickly catches up. There is no evidence that bilingual children have language problems, although they may occasionally use two languages interchangeably when speaking to family members who speak both languages.

Rather than suffering delays in learning language, after age 4, most children who speak more than one language acquire vocabulary more easily than children who speak only one tongue. They seem to have the concept that things can be said in more than one way, and they have a larger grammatical framework to fit their new words into, as they learn structures from both languages. This advantage in learning language is especially apparent when the bilingual child tries to learn a third language.

Your child's delay in learning to talk does suggest that there is some problem with learning language, but it does not appear to come from being bilingual. While learning two languages can cause the first words to come a bit later, her language problems have followed her beyond the first three years of life.

Bilingual children do not have any more difficulty reading than other children, and your daughter's delay in learning to read does not come from her hearing two languages at home. You can continue to speak to her in whatever language is comfortable for you, without fear that you are holding her back in reading.

Without other evidence of delay, not reading at age 6 may not be prognostic. Six-year-olds vary more than any other age group in their reading skills, and your child may be showing a reading immaturity rather than a reading problem that will follow her through life.

Before kindergarten or first grade, only a small percentage of gifted children are reading. By third grade, all children, except those who will have long-term reading problems, can read. It is in this 6- and 7-year age group that you find the greatest spread in reading level.

On the other hand, children who read before age 6 typically have more or less taught themselves to read. These children read effortlessly by the age of 7 or 8 and use reading for pleasurable recreation. Reading can be work for the reader who must struggle to decode. It is only when reading is automatic that reading becomes pure fun.

Given your daughter's history of delayed speech, you may be right to be concerned about her reading difficulties. You may want to have a careful evaluation of her skills, including testing of her overall cognitive ability, as well as an assessment of her reading and math achievement. While she might have a specific language and reading delay, she could also have overall learning deficits.

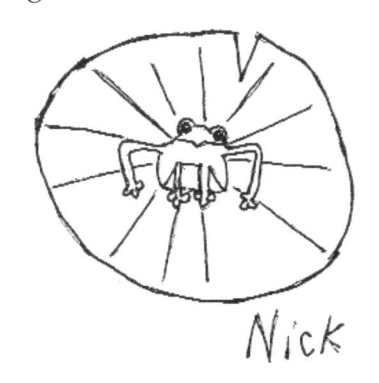

Behavior modification can quell problem behavior

Q. I teach second grade. One of my students talks out of turn many times each day. I've heard that behavior modification can be used to change behavior. Can you tell me how to apply it?

A. Behavior modification is a system of reward or punishment, targeted at a specific behavior and applied consistently, that motivates a person to change problem behavior.

In trying to change behavior, there are typically two goals: stopping the disruptive behavior and getting at the cause. Behavior modification is usually only helpful with the first goal.

The first step in any behavior modification program is called establishing baseline. Note how often the target behavior happens, what sets it off and when during the day it is likely to occur. Once you know the pattern, you can remove the child from situations that are likely to cause the problem. This should reduce the frequency. Then you can contract with the child, to involve him in the process of eliminating the problem. This contract will set the ground rules.

Work on only one behavior at a time and target something specific. "Being good at school" is too vague a goal for behavior modification. In this case, you will need to target "talking out during group discussion when you have not been called on." Tell him specifically what behavior you are working on with him.

Show him how the disruptive behavior is a problem, not only for the class, but for him too. Point out how he loses the respect of teachers and peers when he takes away another child's turn to speak.

While behavior modification can work as long as the child is motivated to earn the reward, even if he isn't interested in changing behavior, the results will last longer if the child understands the reason the behavior change is necessary.

Choose a reward that he is motivated to earn. For young children, stars or stickers on a chart are often effective. After earning a set number of stars for daily improvement, he should get a larger reward. The best reward is attention. Time with parents to play a board game is a reward for many children.

The child who seeks excessive attention at school is likely to have been deprived of attention at home. Special time spent alone with you might be quite motivating. Maybe he could help you clean the blackboard or sharpen pencils. Each child will respond to different rewards. You will need to find what is most motivating for each individual student.

In the classroom you will want to make sure the child isn't rewarded for his negative behavior. Don't credit his answer when he speaks out of turn. Don't notice him with a comment about his behavior. Ignore him until he raises his hand, and then do be sure to call on him to reinforce his appropriate behavior with the attention he is seeking. Call on him often enough when he does raise his hand to meet his needs.

Your attitude and feelings toward this child will affect the outcome of your behavior modification program. You can't hope to approach him with anger and dislike and expect him to improve. Try to find something likable about him and build his self-esteem as you help him solve his problem behavior.

To have a lasting effect, you will want to find a way to help correct the underlying problem. Work with the parents to increase his positive attention at home while you work on the problem at school.

Work with the parents and not against them. Blaming the parent for the child's problems will not help. Tell the mother, "I know that you are as concerned as I am. Let's work together and see if we can't make this better."

Help child deal with dominating friend

Q. Our daughter likes to play with the girl next door. However, this child, who is a year older than my child, intimidates her. She says thing like, "If you don't give me your gold crayon I won't play with you."

At my daughter's birthday party I overheard this child say, "If you don't let me sit next to you, I won't be your friend anymore." My daughter was afraid to let her guests choose their own seats.

We hate to see our child bossed around, and we don't want her to pick up this way of manipulating people. What can we do? How can we handle this without losing the friendship of the parents of the bossy child?

A. Children are born with different temperaments. It appears that your child is the less dominant one of this pair. Age gives the other girl an advantage, but personality probably plays a greater role.

Your daughter seems to be afraid that if she asserts herself, she will lose a friend. To combat this, you will need to give her words with which to assert herself in a polite way and to help her to see that some "friendships" are not worth having.

During the preschool and early grade-school years, parents have veto power over friendships. You don't have to allow your child to play with just anybody. If you feel that your child is picking up values, behaviors and language that are unacceptable to you, you can intervene.

Ending this particular friendship is complicated by the fact that this child lives next door and you value the friendship of her parents. If the situation is extreme, you will have to forgo the friendship and protect your child, but in most cases, it is not necessary to issue an ultimatum.

You can simply reduce your daughter's exposure to this child by getting her involved in other activities and other friends.

If you expect your daughter to stay away from the girl next door, you will need to invite other friends over to play. You can set a rule that she may have only one friend over at a time, to prevent the older, more dominant child from joining them.

You will need to be prepared to drive your daughter to other friend's homes when the return invitations come. Busy parents are often tempted to settle for the child next door out of convenience.

When they do play together, stick close by. Encourage them to play at your house rather than at hers for a while. Handle each situation as it comes up.

If you overhear a comment like the one you described, it is OK to say, "We can have more than one friend. I know you would like to sit next to Erin and it hurts your feelings when she sits with another friend, but we will all have to take turns with the birthday girl. Can I help you find someone else to sit with?"

If you anticipate the situation, you can prepare your child. You can explain that the reason the friend wants her all to herself is because she likes her. You can tell her that if the friend stops liking her because she won't do her bidding, then she was not a friend in the first place.

All of us encounter bossy and manipulative people at some point in our life. This situation is not unlike other social encounters she might have at school.

You won't always be there to speak for her, but if you give her the skills to deal with it effectively, she will be on her way to being able to resist manipulative friendships for the rest of her life.

Expect good behavior, don't beg for it

Q. I have watched some of my friends bribe their children into cooperation. This seems wrong to me, but I also sometimes reward my children for doing what I want them to do.

Is it OK to bribe for good behavior? What about paying children for good report cards?

A. There is a difference between a bribe and an incentive or reward. A bribe is usually given by the parent to buy peace and compliance.

It often benefits the parent more than the child. The parent usually has to give the bribe each time he wants cooperation from the child because the child never forms the habit of doing what he should do on his own.

An incentive, on the other hand, is given to help a child get over the hump of resistance. It is given during a learning phase and is for the benefit of the child. It helps the child form the habit of desirable behavior.

The difference between a bribe and a reward is that a bribe occurs before the behavior has occurred and a reward is given afterward.

You can reward your children for having a good report card by giving them a gift or money, but you can't bribe your children for a good report card because the behavior that is needed to get good grades requires effort over a long period of time.

The cash at the end of a semester won't motivate long hours of study over a period of months. The reward is too far removed from the immediate behavior. Bribing with money for grades can encourage cheating.

To bribe for a good report card, you would have to set up incentives for much smaller steps toward the goal. This can be done but it is time consuming and cumbersome.

More effective would be to teach your children the

importance of education. Many children don't really know why they go to school.

You can use incentives to help a child over an unpleasant situation. By pairing something pleasant with something traumatic you can lessen the memory of an unpleasant experience.

When a child has to go to the hospital for a medical procedure, it helps him or her to have something to look forward to. You can say, "This might hurt some, but after it is over we can go and choose a treat at the gift shop."

This is not a bribe for cooperation, but a pairing of something positive with something negative. If done correctly, it can move a child from resistance and tears to cooperation. It can allow you to avoid having to use force.

Parents began to bribe their children when spanking went out of style. As parents stopped coercing their children, they began to plead for cooperation.

The problem arises when the parent is begging the child for desirable behavior.

Instead of rewarding good behavior as the parent thinks he is doing, he is actually reinforcing bad behavior. Each time the child is badly behaved, the parent steps in with a treat.

Rewards for good behavior are best used during a learning phase and to help establish good habits. They should not be used for out of control behaviors unless you can catch your child being good and reward the good behavior rather than trying to bribe (i.e., reward) the bad.

The best reward is parental time and attention. Twenty minutes of board game time with a parent is a better reward than a shopping spree at the toy store.

You want your reward to be something that doesn't cost much and that can be repeated.

Rewards for good behavior are not necessarily evil, but they become a problem when you inadvertently reward bad behavior instead of desirable acts.

When you offer a bribe, think about what behavior you are reinforcing. Expect good behavior. Don't beg for it.

Parents need to intervene when child is bullied

Q. My fourth-grade son has only been back in school for three days but already he is being picked on. There is a bully in his class who has chosen him for his target. This would be bad enough, but he gets the other children to join him. My son can't possibly defend himself against the whole group. What can we do?

A. One of the most difficult things for a parent is to watch his or her child suffer daily, gradually losing the will to go to school.

Parents should not sit back and let the child work it out. He can handle a dispute with one child, but not the force of the whole group.

Once he is chosen as the target, even the kinder, gentler children are afraid to befriend him out of fear that they too will be outcast.

If the bully is just a large and aggressive child who uses his size to his advantage but comes from a decent family, you might get some help by contacting the parents of the bully. Tell them of your concerns without blaming them or their child. Ask them for help.

If, however, the bully is not only a big child but also a troubled one, the parents may be part of the problem and may to be unwilling or unable to help you and your son.

In this case, you might want to carefully select some parents of the boys who join the bully in his hurtful behavior and let them know what is going on. Some of these parents might be happy to help.

You might find that many of these parents have had concerns of their own about the bad influence of the bully. Your call may give them the reason they have been looking for to discourage their child from a relationship with the bully.

Do let your son's teacher know what is happening. Often children are only mean at those transition times during the school day when there is little adult supervision. His teacher may not actually see the bullying.

With notice, the staff can supervise your child more carefully and might even structure the day more tightly for the whole class so that peer abuse does not take place. In milder cases, they can separate the children who don't get along and maybe assign your son a buddy for certain activities.

Although parent involvement behind the scene is essential to the child who is constantly picked on, target children can be seen as even weaker when the parent is called in.

Keep your efforts between the adults and not obvious to the children. Work with your son to teach him ways to respond to the group. Teach him social skills in general, and teach specific responses to specific hurtful comments.

As he cannot take on the whole group of attackers, he will have to avoid situations where he is alone. Teach him to remain in the sight of the teachers, and pick him up after school rather than letting him walk home unaccompanied.

Encourage him to form friendships with other children like him. The more aggressive children label themselves "popular" or "cool" while the gentler children are isolated outsiders. If these outsiders band together, they are usually just as numerous as the popular, more aggressive group.

If all else fails, you might need to move your child to a new class or even a new school. This will help only if the problem lies outside your child. The child who provokes rejection will take his problem with him.

Don't just sit back for months or years hoping the situation will pass. Step in and help. The scars from peer abuse can have lifelong effects.

Camp can be enriching for a child who is ready

Q. We are considering sending our 8- and 10-year-old girls to summer sleep-away camp. Our 10-year-old has never been to overnight camp before because we thought the girls would be more secure attending camp together. Do you think an 8-year-old is too young for camp? How can we decide?

A. Children are ready to leave their parents at different ages. One 8-year-old might be ready, while another might want to stay at home. The age of your child is only one factor to consider in making your decision.

While camp can be a wonderful growth experience, it is an optional one. Summers can be used productively in many ways, and no child should be forced to leave home against his will. The best way to find out if your daughters are ready for camp is to ask them.

Although the presence of a sister at camp can be comforting for some children, it would be better to make the decision separately for each of your children. Your older child might be ready to go to camp even if her sister is not. You should not hold her back to wait for her sister. You can send her with a friend if she wants the company of someone she knows.

Don't send your child to camp for two months the first year, but don't make her stay so short that she doesn't have time to overcome the initial homesickness that most new campers experience before camp becomes familiar.

Most campers feel homesick until they get used to the routine, make friends and learn their way around the campgrounds. If she leaves before she has a chance to become comfortable at camp, she may leave with bad memories of an experience that would have improved had she stayed longer.

Evaluate your daughters' skills. Think about whether each child can make it on her own away from adult assistance. Can she tie her shoes and wash her own hair? Is she a picky eater who lives on mashed potatoes? The camp won't meet this need but she may widen her choices when forced to.

Remember that camp counselors are typically teenagers or young adults without children of their own. They aren't likely to nurture as you do.

On the other hand, this is why camp is a growth experience — because the child must do things for herself that parents typically do for her. She must blend into the ways of the whole group without special attention to her preferences.

Assess your children's skills at making friends. Children will generally respond to camp as they do to the social world at school.

The athletic child with lots of friends is likely to have a good time at a typical camp, as long as she is not overly dependent upon her parents. On the other hand, the child who has no friends at school might find herself in the same situation at camp, where she can't come home each afternoon to a loving family.

Match your children to the type of camp. Not all camps have the same focus or attract the same type of child. The one who might not do well at a sports camp, might really enjoy computer camp or foreign language camp, not only because the activities are fun, but also because she might find friends who share her interests and accept her.

Send your child to camp from a secure home base. It is only when the child is sure that his parents and home will be there upon his return that he can separate happily. If there are problems in the family, evaluate whether your child will feel as if she is being sent away or if camp will offer a reprieve from the stress.

The camp experience can be an enriching one for many children. It can give the child the exhilarating experience of independence. However, it is not a mandatory experience and no child should be forced to camp against his or her will.

Answer child's questions at his developmental level

Q. There is so much in the newspaper, radio and TV about the Clinton scandal that despite my most careful attempts to screen the information for my children I am afraid that they know much of the story.

My 9-year-old son has been asking many questions. I don't want to tell him too much, as I feel that he is too young to understand. I don't want him to think there are options to fidelity, although I do realize that he will learn this at some point.

How much should be discussed with a child? How can you shield your children from information you don't feel they are ready to have?

A. Children do their own screening to some extent. While you may think that they are hearing the whole story, for the most part they are hearing only the part that they can integrate with their own prior knowledge at their own developmental level of understanding.

Although children will miss what they don't understand, hearing a news story can prompt a child to expand upon what he already knows. You may hear questions about the parts that he does not fully understand.

You can answer these questions at his level. The key is to remember what that level is and not to give an answer that you would give to another adult. You do not have to reveal every detail. Just answer the direct question.

I am reminded of the story of the boy who asked his mother, "Where did I come from?" The mother gave her son a long answer about the facts of life. After listening politely the child said, "No mom. I meant, was I born in Chicago?"

This mother answered the question that an adult might have been thinking about. The child was reasoning with the much more concrete thinking of a child.

You do not have to discuss the details of the events catalogued in the Starr report with your children, but you can use this opportunity to discuss moral values.

You can tell your child that the president is in trouble for telling a lie and for bringing his private life into his office.

You can use this as an opportunity to discuss how to keep a job. You can use this as an example to show the consequences of lying.

You can focus on the fact that Mr. Clinton did something wrong and will be punished for his misdeed, rather than telling a 9-year-old the specifics of what he did.

As the story unfolds you can talk about the fact that there are consequences to bad behavior, not only for children, but for grown-ups too.

This will appeal to the elementary school-age child whose reasoning is concrete and whose rules are absolute.

You should not discuss the sexual deeds with a young child. Children need a childhood. Prior to preadolescence this information is developmentally inappropriate, not because the content is bad but because it is developmentally out of sync.

The issue of what to discuss with a teenager is more complex. If you don't prepare your child for what he will hear, he may hear it first from his peer group. Better would be to have the opportunity to hear his parent's view first.

Do this carefully, screening what you think is not suitable. Anticipate the issues and let your adolescent know that you are available for further discussion.

For the most part, both children and adults are less interested in the Clinton story than the amount of media coverage the scandal has received indicates.

Most children will hear a bit of it, but will then move on to more developmentally appropriate subjects.

Clinton's behavior is not one of the tasks or issues of childhood and won't hold the interest of a 9-year-old child for very long.

Buy to meet child's needs, not to match what sib gets

Q. My friend's children are very close, while my children compete with each other. If I give them a piece of cake for dessert, they compare who has the bigger piece. Even if I buy them the same shirt in different colors, they both seem to want the blue/green/red one. I have always tried to be fair, buying one child a gift if I buy something for the other one. Where did I go wrong?

A. When you tell your children that you will be meticulously fair, buying one child a gift when you buy something for the other, you teach them to compare. By saying that what one child gets will always be matched with a gift for the other, you teach them to look not at their own needs but at what someone else has.

Better would be to give the message that you will not always give them the same amount or the same thing, but that you will meet the needs of each child. When you buy one child shoes, you don't need to buy shoes for the other child unless his are worn out or outgrown as well. If you buy shoes for the child who doesn't need them just because his sibling got some, you are teaching entitlement. You are teaching your child that it is not his need that counts, but comparison to what others have.

Some children come into the world more jealous than others, but even these children can be weaned off their jealousy. By repeatedly focusing on what they really need, you teach your child to look at himself, and not at his neighbor. When he says, "No fair, Tommy got a new jacket," your reply might be, "Is yours too small? I thought it still fit you." This causes him to think about his need and refocuses his thinking away from: "If he gets one, I'm entitled to one too."

In addition to material things, examine how you distribute attention. Often the focus on material gifts and purchases takes the place of the deeper concern over who gets more attention and love — that is, who is the favorite child. The child whose emotional needs are met is less likely to worry about who gets more toys or clothes than the child who never feels he has his parent's attention or approval.

Your children's need for attention will not be equal. Once again, you do not have to give each child the same thing, but you do have to meet each child's needs. The oldest child who lost undivided attention will need more one-on-one time than later children who never had it. The sensitive, cuddly child may need to be held more than the child who lives by the creed, "I can do it myself." Differences in temperament will determine what each child must have to feel satisfied. Meet the real need for attention without encouraging a jealous nature.

Start when your children are small. If your 3-year-old comes home from preschool at noon, put the baby down for his nap at 11:45 so that your older child comes home to undivided attention. This is more important for the firstborn child who has lost your exclusive attention than it will be for later children who never had it and don't expect it. You cannot do this for his entire life, but that won't be necessary. Once a child is secure in his place in your heart, he won't need to be reassured forever.

When your children compare, carry it to an extreme to make your point. Tell you son that each time you buy his sister a dress you will buy one for him too. They will soon get the point that it is not what the other one gets that matters, but what their own needs are.

With one body you can't dance at two weddings

Q. Our 10-year-old is in his second year of playing ice hockey. Once, last year when he wanted to quit, we told him that he was committed to a team and had to finish the season and then he could quit. Things got better and he's now enjoying hockey and his team. Then we got the schedule of remaining games and seven of the next eight games were at the same time as Sunday school and church.

We feel that attending Sunday school and church are very important. However, so is being part of the team, and making him miss most of the remaining games didn't seem fair — especially since some of the games were all-star games and he had worked very hard to achieve this honor. We have occasionally been able to take him to church on Saturday night, but he still misses Sunday school and we cannot attend church as a family. How would you handle this problem?

A. My mother used to say, "With one body you can't dance at two weddings." You and your child will have to make a choice. For this season you are stuck with missing one or the other activity. Next year, you might be able to plan his sports schedule so that he can do both.

Church attendance has different meanings for different families, and each family will have to make its own decision and set its own priorities.

The best decision would be one which allows your child to have both experiences. Finding an alternative service, as you have suggested, might not be a perfect solution but it will give him some of each experience. No solution will lead to perfect attendance in two activities scheduled at the same time. You will have to bend on some aspect of one or the other.

You are looking at your schedule conflict as one

of religion verses sports. You might want to see the activities as more similar than different. The lessons taught in church are not only learned in the church building.

Participating as a member of a team, learning to be kind to team members who have not performed well, sharing the applause and the ball or hockey puck, controlling aggression, and tolerating failure are all very important lessons. Your son is learning values, even if he is not at a formal church service.

Learning takes place in a series of stages. Usually it is not possible to do or master everything at the same time. Development is a series of incremental events. Children do not master crawling at the same time as they learn algebra.

Maybe you could allow your son to finish the seven weeks, with the understanding that the whole family will return to the normal Sunday schedule when this is over.

For next season, you might want to find a league that doesn't play on Sunday morning. This should not be too hard, as most of the leagues don't. You might also be able to gather other parents to support you in your request to this league that games not start before the afternoon on Sundays. Before committing to sports teams in the future, you might want to find out the schedule for the whole season.

Include your son in the decision of which commitment will come first. A love of religion does not come from taking away something that is important to him without his having a say in it.

Even if you feel that you will ultimately choose church over hockey, it would be better to discuss your thinking with your son than to impose the decision upon him.

There are times when a parent should be firm and make an absolute decision ("No, you may not drive drunk."), but for most issues where there are equally valid arguments on both sides, involving the child in the discussion and choice, even if his ideas don't prevail, will give him a sense of fairness and of being heard.

Troubled teens, not stable ones, turn to drugs

Q. My children are still young — ages 6 and 8 — but I have seen children of friends of mine whose kids were nice when they were little turn to drugs in their teens. It seems that which kids wind up on drugs is just random.

What can a parent do to prevent this from happening?

A. The teens who turn to drugs are not a random group. Children who have few friends, who have trouble learning, who are undisciplined or who are attracted to excitement are those who get in trouble later.

Substance-abusing teens are typically children who have failed to master some developmental steps.

As early as age 2 the child learns right from wrong. At this age, he feels shame for wrongdoing but is largely dependent upon others to keep him on the right path. The "no" comes from outside himself, typically from mom or dad.

Gradually he takes their rules and lessons to be a part of himself. We say he "incorporates" the parent's values. At this point he feels guilt, not only shame, when he does wrong.

Parents foster the development of a sense of right or wrong by starting early with firm discipline and clear rules and expectations.

The parent who cannot say no or who shirks his job as a parent is setting his child out on the path to many adolescent problems, including drug abuse.

Nurturance must accompany rules so that the child feels valued and loved. Discipline without a relationship leads to rebellion. The child naturally wants to please a loving and giving parent. He models this parent, taking the parent's values as his own.

As the child enters school, the developmental task becomes mastery of facts and skills. If he fails at learning, he develops a sense of inferiority.

If he lacks academic or athletic skills, the nicer children will tend to reject him, leaving him vulnerable to seek attention from the group of children who abuse drugs and get into other sorts of trouble.

Parents can intervene at this point by valuing achievement and by making sure the child's class placement matches his abilities.

It is far better to hold a child back a grade than to let him dangle off the bottom of the class year after year.

Tutoring specific deficits not only teaches him that subject, but it also builds self-esteem, which buffers him from vulnerability to being lured into an undesirable peer group.

Treating attention deficit with medication can give the child the chance to succeed.

Parents need to set a good example. Not only should parents not use drugs or alcohol, but they must also actively participate in positive activities.

If your child sees you eating bonbons in front of the TV most of your day, he will not strive to contribute to the world.

If he sees you active in his school and the community, he will take on your values as his own.

Children see the world in black and white. If you experimented with drugs in your teens don't tell your children until they are older.

Young children are concrete in their thinking. Right and wrong are absolute. If you did it, they can too.

Teens can think abstractly but are likely to tell you that if it was OK for you, then it is OK for them.

The parenting strategies that keep children off drugs are not unique to drug abuse prevention. They are simply principles of good parenting.

Encourage and value your child. Love him and spend time with him. Set limits and rules.

Enforce your rules consistently. Start discipline young. Instill values and set a good example.

Give attention to child for independent work

Q. My 10-year-old daughter is not doing well in school. She has been tested and found to have adequate ability to succeed. There is no evidence of a learning disability.

She is somewhat active and has been given medication to control her excess movement, but even when the fidgets are controlled, she continues to do poorly in her work. When I sit with her she is able to do the homework with little trouble, but if I leave her on her own she doesn't get it done. The teacher finds the same at school. What is the problem and how do I fix it?

A. When a child is struggling at school, the first step is to do a careful evaluation of the problem. Testing should include an IQ measure to gain an understanding of the child's ability. Achievement testing should be done to measure what has been learned.

The scores from these two tests should be compared. If aptitude (IQ) is higher than achievement (reading, spelling and math) then the child should be able to do better.

If achievement is higher than aptitude, the child has done well for himself, even if he is trailing his grade placement.

But looking at aptitude and achievement alone won't tell the whole story. Ability is only part of what determines success. The other factor is motivation.

Some children, despite adequate ability, just don't do well at school. When other causes have been ruled out, you might want to look at the child's motivation to grow up. School success implies that one can be independent. Not every child sets this as his or her goal.

Some children are temperamentally passive. They just seem to live by the motto: "Never do for yourself what others will do for you." These children do fine when parent or teacher works one-on-one with them, but left to work on their own, they accomplish little.

You can tutor these children for hours, yet little will change. Tutoring doesn't help, because neither exposure to the material nor the ability to master the material is the problem.

The problem is that this child doesn't want to do for herself. Mastery, the typical goal of the child of school age, is not her goal. She wants to stay incompetent and dependent.

Parents of children with this problem often are ambivalent about independence themselves. They may give the message that finding someone to take care of them should be their goal in life. This takes the place of mastering skills with which to earn independence.

Sometimes the parent is ambivalent about letting go of the child and may foster dependency in order to keep the child close to home.

Other passive-dependent children have not had enough nurturing. Often children whose parents spend little time at home with them fail at school because only failure evokes attention.

The child whose parent has to sit with him for homework corners the parent's attention for at least the time it takes to get the homework done.

To turn this situation around, attention needs to be offered at times other than around school failure. Reward independent work but give attention at another time. Let your child work on her own but don't abandon her.

Encourage her to work independently but let her be in the same room as you are. Let her do her homework at the kitchen table while you cook dinner.

Then reward her success at independence with special attention. Play a board game with her when her homework is done or go out walking together for exercise.

Make sure the reward involves your time and attention and is something you can do repeatedly — not just an expensive gift she gets once.

Children need structure and predictability

Q. I am a divorced mother of three children. I have a court-ordered visitation agreement, but my ex-husband repeatedly wants the days changed. He asserts that it is good for the children to see their grandparents or that they benefit from a camping trip with their dad. I find all the changes very disruptive. What do you think?

A. Children need structure and predictability. While a variety of different schedules are workable, a constantly changing one is not. Children need to be able to count on what is coming next.

Children need to move from the routine of the marriage into a new routine in the divorce. They can make this change once, or even twice, without major harm, but they cannot tolerate multiple and continuing changes without the chaos undermining their sense of security.

While parents' needs may be best served by dividing the children half and half, the children fare best when they have a home, spending the bulk of their time in one place, and visiting the other. When they live in two places, they seem always to be missing what is happening, emotionally or socially, in the other one. Few adults choose to live in two places, but we sometimes expect this of children in a divorce.

Most requests for visitation changes are not for the benefit of the child but are instead a form of ongoing battle between the parents. If the visits were just for the purpose stated, they could easily be carried out during regular, scheduled visitation.

Typically, requests for changes in a court order are made by the parent who has the greater amount of money with the goal of hurting the parent who is less able to afford the court costs. Often, they are just filed for harassment. This is an issue between the parents. The child is the victim.

If we are to serve the best interest of the children, then we need to establish a routine that they can count on. Even a 5-year-old can look at a calendar and follow the first and third weekend or count the days until spring break. Routine and predictability are the guidewords. Changes are confusing.

All other things being equal, children benefit from having roots. Visits to grandparents can be positive, but unfortunately they are not always so. If the grandparents can provide a haven for the children where they are nurtured but not involved in ongoing disagreements between the two families, then the visits are in the child's best interest.

If the grandparents just extend the divorce battle, then the children are cut into yet another piece to be shared among an even larger group of people. Children don't divide as easily as crystal or silver. It is important for children to be able to know what is coming before the event occurs. Standard visitation, which typically asks the non-custodial parent to give only thirty days notice before a summer visit, may not be enough notice for summer planning.

Most summer camp programs fill by March. Classmates discuss where they will be going to camp starting in February. The child caught in divorce may be uncomfortable when his friends ask what he is doing for the summer and he does not know until the last moment. The child who has been attending the same camp year after year may be closed out of his summer routine by the parent who won't make his or her plans more than a month in advance.

Visitation schedules which are consistent and predictable for the child can serve to give the child access to both parents. Children are not served by constant changes, even when the specific trip or visit sounds like a good idea. Visits to grandparents, trips to the beach and special time with the noncustodial parent can all be arranged within a fixed schedule.

Shelter child from conflicts of divorcing parents

Q. My husband and I are getting a divorce. There is a good deal of bickering going on. How can I keep things calm for my 8- and 12-year-old children?

A. It takes both parents to keep things calm for the children. Unfortunately, one parent cannot easily do it alone. If you cannot control the fighting, it may be best to get the children out of the house at least some of the time during the initial negotiations.

While it is generally not a good idea to send children off to summer camp during a period of uncertainty and change, it just might work to time the divorce so that they are told about the situation and then given a respite from the ugliness by being out of the home.

This will not be the right solution for every child and will only work for a child who likes camp and separates easily from the family. It will work best for a child who has been to the camp before. A child prone to homesickness should not be sent away from an unstable home base.

Think of your children's needs first. Time your divorce with other pressures and demands upon your child. It might be best to separate during the summer, when there are no exams or homework.

Some children, however, might feel more secure in their normal routine. A summer day camp might be able to provide some structure without the demands of school.

Parents need to continue to parent together even though they are ending the marriage. Try to maintain a consistent role with your child during the divorce. Children need their parents to be adults. Often the parent less likely to get custody tries to become the playmate of the child. This is usually not in the child's best interest. He needs to continue to develop social skills with his peers. He needs his parent to be the parent — not the buddy.

Discipline often slides during and after a divorce. As each parent competes for the child's love, the parent/child role reverses. The child suffers when limits and rules go lax. Without discipline, he loses both parents — not just the one who moves out. Trips to Disney World do not make up for lost structure.

Don't hide all conflict from your child, but do keep the arguments civil. Ironically, children are often very confused when they see no conflict and the marriage suddenly ends without a clue that there were problems. Some open but controlled conflict can help the child prepare for the separation.

Discuss the reasons for the divorce with your child but don't burden him with adult issues. Explanation is necessary but should be at the level of the child's development. Children will not be able to understand the sexual nuances of an extramarital affair, but they can understand that daddy or mommy wants to be with someone else.

Maintain routines and activities for children during a divorce as much as possible. Both parents should make an effort to get children to sports practice or Brownies, regardless of the visitation rights of each parent. The court looks out for the interest of the divorcing adults. The parents must still parent their own children.

In the end, the children will fare only as well as both parents allow them to. Unfortunately, an angry and vengeful parent can destroy a child. In a few years the parent will move on to a new life, but the child will be scarred forever unless the parents put the child's needs and feelings above their own anger and need for revenge.

Nurturance produces softer and kinder children

Q. My 8-year-old daughter still wants me to brush her teeth and dress her. She can and does do it herself sometimes. Should I do this for her when she asks or insist that she do for herself because she can?

I am still dressing my 9-year-old son on school mornings. This happens because he has trouble getting up in the morning. If I want him to get to school on time, I need to dress him to speed things up. He dresses himself on weekends and vacations. Am I making a baby out of him by helping him in this way? What can I do to change this?

A. Nurturance doesn't ruin or spoil children, although it will keep a child developmentally younger and more dependent for a short time. Nurturance produces softer and kinder children — children who grow up able to nurture others.

Paradoxically, the child who is expected to take over all of his care too early in life may be the child who is least independent later. The nurtured child can easily be left alone for short periods of time by age 11, while the child who has always been alone will resist being alone at an age when he should be ready for this.

Nurtured children tend to have a more benign view of the world. They expect the world to be caring and may choose friends who are kinder to them. Children who have not been nurtured are often angry children who can be mean to others.

Mean children are often rejected by the nicer children, who choose their friends from among the children who are more like they are. Not only are these children not nurtured at home, but they also get little from the peers they are left with. Often they have behavior problems at school, and their behavior causes rejection by teachers as well.

Providing the warm fuzzies for your child probably will reduce his aggression and anger. The lack of aggression may make him less assertive on the sports field, but it is more likely that the child who seeks help from mom with tasks he could do for himself is not aggressive temperamentally to begin with.

As long as the parent is offering help out of the child's need, and not out of the parent's need to keep the child dependent, there is not likely to be any harm. Eight- and 9-year-old children are still dependent.

This dependency will pass with maturation and development as the child approaches adolescence. A healthy 12-year-old will not seek a parent's assistance with dressing — even if mom helped at age 9.

The danger comes when the parent has the need to keep the child dependent. By doing everything for his child, he gives the message that the child is incapable. The child who has absorbed this message feels that he cannot do for himself and generalizes his feeling of incompetence from simple skills such as dressing himself to complex ones such as choosing and holding a job later in life.

Children need more time to do tasks than adults do. While it is not harmful for you to help your 9-year-old dress, in order for him to have a chance at fending for himself, you will need to set up a schedule that allows for the extra time it takes him to do it. If mornings are difficult, set bedtime back a half hour earlier so that he will get up with enough time to get dressed on his own.

Help your child when he is tired or in a rush, but do provide opportunities for him to master basic skills on his own. Tying his shoes for him some of the time won't halt his development, but if he really can't do it by himself, he will be embarrassed in front of his peers when his teacher tells him to tie his shoes at school.

Find a balance between doing for him and giving him the chance to develop his own competence. Everything in moderation.

Adults are proud of parents who dared to parent

Q. My 8-year-old daughter wants to wear miniskirts and halter tops. We feel she is too young for this sexy attire. We want her to dress like a girl her age. Her friends do dress as we don't want her to. Their parents seem to allow this adult attire, making it hard for us to set limits. Can we say no without ruining her friendships with the other girls?

A. Just because other parents allow a particular behavior doesn't mean that you need to. Parents always have the right and the responsibility to say no. Adults looking back at their childhood are typically proud of parents who dared to parent.

Although it is possible to be different and to parent well, it is usually easier to parent as the peer group does. You might want to approach the parents of your daughter's friends and see if you can come to an agreement about dress code. These other parents may feel just as you do and may be quite pleased to set rules for all the girls as a group.

Just as young children play house or fireman to try on roles of adulthood, your daughter is trying on clothes that model the teens and adults she admires. As long as she is free to go back and forth between her own stage and the one she is trying on, there is no major harm in being ahead of herself some of the time.

If, on the other hand, she can't play ball because she refuses to take off her clogs or won't swim because she does not want to mess up her hair, then something is amiss.

Just because your 8-year-old is wearing skimpy attire doesn't mean she is sexually precocious. She may be unaware of the seductive message these clothes can send.

The message to others may not be the same either.

The halter top that may be seductive on an adult may be simply cute on a young child. Without adult development, the skimpy top doesn't necessarily have the same meaning.

Uncover the meaning of the clothes for your daughter. She may not wish for them for the reasons you think she does. Skimpy skirts may simply be the style for her while you see it as a conscious effort to attract a certain kind of attention.

If she is truly trying to be seductive at the age of 8, there is a problem and you will want to work to restore balance to her life. If she simply thinks the clothes are pretty and has little understanding of the seductive aspect of skimpy clothes, she may simply need some guidance.

While the skimpy clothes may not carry the same message for your child as they do for you, others may read the message as you do. Your young daughter may need to be made aware of the message she is sending.

In moderation, an interest in clothes and attractiveness, although a bit precocious at age 8, is not a terrible thing. Appearance is the first thing others notice about us, and we do want our children to take pride in dressing neatly and attractively. It is the definition of *appropriate* that seems to need fine-tuning.

If her clothes turn on your alarm system and are outside your values, then you must set limits.

If you feel she is skipping childhood and propelling herself into adolescence before she can handle the challenges of that stage, then you will want to step in to slow her down.

If she is just playing dress-up, you may simply need to add age-appropriate activities to the time she spends trying on clothes.

Jordan

Positive self-esteem prevents drug abuse

Q. I have 7- and 10-year-old children. I want to start talking to them about drug abuse and how to refuse offers. Is this a good age to start or should I wait until adolescence? What should I say?

A. Parents talk to their children about drug abuse even without a specific conversation about the topic. Parents are talking to their children about drug abuse when they say, "I need a cigarette" or "Johnny, get me a drink" or "Let's go fill my prescription for tranquillizers" or even, "I'm falling asleep. I need a Coke." Children learn from their daily environment. These comments teach that everyday tensions can be managed with drugs.

When you use drugs correctly, your children learn that too. When they see you refrain from drinking at a party because you will be driving, they learn that lesson. When they see you eat healthful foods, they learn to respect their body.

Drug awareness education is taught at most schools. You might want to find out what your child already knows and to time your conversations to reinforce what is being taught at school.

You do want to be careful not to overdo drug education. The stable, emotionally healthy child does not need endless talks about drug abuse.

The age at which you need to talk with your children will depend upon where you live. In some neighborhoods, kindergarten is not too early to teach your child to say no and to walk away.

In other parts of town, it would be wasteful to expose children that young to drug education, because it would be outside their experience and it would have little impact.

Time the talk about drugs to the time you think

your child might need that knowledge. Work from your child's need to know rather than from your own anxiety.

Begin your instruction with family rules. Let your children know what you expect of them. Express your expectations positively in terms of your pride in your child. "We are Smiths, and Smiths don't drink." "We eat healthy foods and respect our body."

Watch advertisements with your children and teach them to be critical thinkers. When they see an ad for a cigarette that suggests that smokers have more fun, ask your child if it is likely that a cigarette could improve someone's social life or accomplishments.

When you see an ad for stomach remedies, ask your child, "If eating spicy foods makes the man need a certain pill, how else could he avoid the pain?" Teaching your child to think of alternative solutions to a problem gives him options to drug use when stressed.

Lectures about illegal drugs are a small part of drug abuse prevention. Drug abuse prevention begins with a broader set of morals. When you tell your child, "Even if your friends use that word, we don't use it in our house," you are setting the stage for resisting group pressure and doing what is right. When you give your child appropriate love and attention, you are buffering him from needing the approval of an inappropriate peer group.

Ongoing comments about good and bad help a child to establish his own value system. "We will take dinner to Mrs. Jones because she is ill," or, "You can't take that toy because we didn't pay for it," goes a long way to establishing a framework for behavior.

The children who abuse drugs are not a random group. They are children who are vulnerable and searching for acceptance or an escape from depression and anxiety. By giving your children values, self-esteem building experiences and a sense of feeling loved, you are buffering them from vulnerability to drug abuse. Talks about drugs won't work without this larger framework.

Children are kinder one-on-one than in groups

Q. I have a child who is in a wheelchair due to a progressive disease. How do I teach him to handle other children's ridicule? How and when do I tell his 8-year-old sister that she is a carrier of her brother's genetic disease and could pass it on to her sons?

A. Parents and professionals who deal with handicapped children sometimes forget that their children have the normal problems of growing up just as do their more typical peers. If your child is experiencing ridicule, I would guess that he is in approximately the fifth or sixth grade.

Younger children may express curiosity and may ask questions without censoring them. Their questions may be blunt but are not typically meant to be cruel. Young children are usually fairly accepting of differences and can easily be helped to do so by a teacher or other adult who takes the time to explain the situation to them. Assigning an offending child the role of special helper to the handicapped child can turn this child from abuser to advocate.

By the fifth and sixth grades, children are pulling away from parents and moving on toward reliance upon the peer group. In their insecurity, they try to be exactly like every other child around them. Differences are threatening as they could lead to peer rejection. Peer rejection is devastating.

To be accepted by the group, some children will take the role of aggressor in teasing others in order to make sure that they are not on the receiving end. The handicapped child poses both an easy target and a threat because he is a reminder that we are not all the same.

By the high school years, children are more accepting of differences, and your child will have an easier time. Cliques form around interests, and your child might find an interest niche. He may even find himself to be a celebrity known to everyone in the school due to his wheelchair.

In the meantime, as you wait for his peers to mature, give him loving support at home. Send him to summer camps with other handicapped children so that he can have his own peer group outside of school. Take an active role in educating his class about his disease. Some cruelty comes out of fear that the disease could be catching. Ask his teacher to assign selected children to be his helpers. Children are kinder one-on-one than they are in groups.

Remind your son that most children are being teased at this age — that this is a sign of his normalcy, not his handicap. Help him to see that it will not go on forever, but simply until his peers mature. Teach him to respond to teasing by including his peers in his world, maybe showing them how to drive his motorized chair.

At age 8, your daughter does not yet need to know that she is a carrier of this disease. She is not thinking about having children, and the issue is yours but not hers yet. While it might make you feel better to not have to bear the secret, it would put undue burden upon a child who needs to form her own identity with a sense that she is normal. Telling her too soon might make her feel handicapped or different.

As she approaches the late teens and begins to think about marriage and family, you can share your knowledge with her. Be sure to state it in a positive way, emphasizing the advances in medicine that make it possible to detect genetic diseases before the birth of the child. Emphasize that she will have choices in family planning and that being a carrier does not mean that she can't have a healthy child.

All this requires a level of thinking and understanding that is not possible for an 8-year-old. Facts should be given to her when the issue becomes her issue and when she is capable of making informed decisions.

Camps allow handicapped child to be the norm

Q. My 6-year-old son has muscular dystrophy. He is unaware of all the implications of having this disease. We have not even told him the name of his problem yet, just that he has weak legs.

We have been given the opportunity to send him to a camp for a week with other children with the same diagnosis. Should we send him, or will he worry when he sees the older children with more advanced disease who are in wheelchairs and who are much more disabled than he is now?

A. Camps for children with illnesses or disabilities provide a powerful emotional and learning experience. It gives the handicapped child, who is a minority in most settings, a chance to be in a group where he is the norm.

It offers a child, who typically has less autonomy than his age would merit, a chance to fend for himself. Even if he requires the help of camp counselors and nurses, it is different from being at home with his parents.

Being in a different environment will pose new obstacles and challenges. In overcoming these, he will gain a sense of mastery. He will do this without mom or dad smoothing the way for him and so the achievement will be unquestionably his own.

Having said this, we must remember that your child is only 6 years old. While he certainly can benefit from a camp experience, few parents of typical children send them away at that age.

A handicapped child is not just his handicap. He is a normal child as well — and normal 6-year-olds don't necessarily attend sleep-away camp.

If he does go, you can expect him to be with the other children of his own age. Just as typical 6-year-olds don't pay much attention to what the teens at camp do, your son is not likely to either. He is likely to play with other boys his age, who are at the same stage of his progressive neuromuscular disease.

It will be a self-esteem building experience to play ball with other boys who share his leg muscle weakness. At camp, he will not have a handicap relative to the children he plays with. His skills will be the norm.

While exposure to peers who share a disease and its problems is an important function of camp for handicapped children, camp is not just that. It is also an opportunity to learn new skills, to experience the out-of-doors, and to have fun.

Your child is more likely to tell you about the fish he caught or the zip line on the ropes course than he is to jump off the bus and tell you about an older child with more advanced disease.

Yet you are not incorrect in protecting him from the whole truth at this age. Although he will probably relate to children his own age, he will see the older children with more advanced stages of his disease.

If he asks questions, this will open a door for you to begin to discuss some of the aspects of his disease.

You will likely be surprised that he takes in only what he is ready to know. He is unlikely to seek more information than he can handle.

Follow his lead, and answer only what he asks. Do so in simple language, and stick to the here and now. Don't burden him with what might happen. Tell him only what is certain and what is coming up soon. Be honest but positive.

Base your decision about camp on whether he is ready to be away from home for a week and on such factors as the adequacy of supervision at camp, rather than your fear of his seeing too much of his disease.

If you decide not to send him this year, be sure to give him this opportunity as he gets older. Diagnosis-based camps are a positive experience for nearly all the children who attend. They let the handicapped child know that he is not alone.

Children spend carefully if the money is their own

Q. My 9-year-old wants everything he sees in the store. I'm afraid that I have set him up this way. We recently went through a divorce, and to make up for the stress he went through I bought him extra things. Now that money is tight, I can't get him to understand that he can't have everything he sees. How can I teach him the value of money?

A. Material things never make up for the absence of stability in the home or take the place of appropriate and loving parental attention. Money is just money, but buying can become a habit.

To turn your child around, you will have to teach him about money. The best way to do this is to give him his own money to budget. When he has his own money to spend, you won't have to say yes or no to his requests. When he asks for something, you can simply say, "Do you have enough money to buy it?"

In order for allowance to work as a lesson, he will need to have enough money to meet some of his wants but not all of them. Making decisions about what to buy while not being able to get everything he wants is the core of the lesson. He should not have enough money to be able to buy expensive items every month or small items nearly daily.

An allowance is a commitment. Parents should not withhold allowance as a punishment. If the child is to be able to budget and save, he should be able to count on the money coming in.

Allowance and pay for chores are not the same thing. Most chores should be done just because the child lives in the family. Children should not be paid to set the table or take out the trash. If you pay your child for chores, you are in effect saying, "If you don't want the money you don't have to do the work." If you expect him to do the chore whether or not he wants to, don't offer money for it.

There are times when pay is appropriate. Money overcomes resistance and motivates. Often parents look for a way for a child to earn money to pay for something that parents might not buy but don't mind the child's having. Before the teen years, it is hard for a child to find employment outside his home. Often the only way to earn money is to work for his parents. Paying a child for extra work does no harm and can help teach a work ethic. The best paid chores are those that don't have to be done daily. Be sure to make the task one that a child can handle, and then don't pay for a job that is not completed.

Don't undermine intrinsic satisfaction and pride with pay. The teenager who can change a light switch gains far more from the satisfaction of accomplishment than from the few dollars you give him. Take him out for pizza to express your thanks, but don't take away his pride by reducing his accomplishment to paid labor.

If your child has his own money, he will likely become a more selective shopper instantly. Most children are more careful with their own money than with yours. The child who has put in hours to earn money will think twice about spending it on something that he will tire of in a few days. If he doesn't learn this lesson spontaneously, you can probably explain it to him easily.

Set a good example and include your child in some of your thinking. Share with him how you save for new furniture or a family vacation. Don't burden him with details of adult financial worries but do include him in understanding the changes in the family situation.

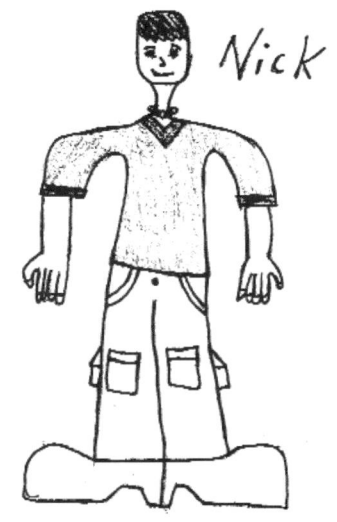

It is better to draw aggressive pictures than to hit

Q. My child draws quite a bit, but his pictures are always scenes of violence — guns, tanks, rockets and so on. He is not violent in his interactions with other children although he will play army and war with his friends. His life is stable and happy. Where is all this aggression coming from?

A. Based on the themes of his drawings, I would guess that your child is a boy. This type of play and art is typical of boys between the ages of 4 and 12 and usually does not indicate deep emotional problems.

A certain degree of aggression seems to be innate. The fact that your child is discharging his aggression in art and fantasy play, rather than against his peers or family, shows good mental health. When an event makes one angry, it is more mature to imagine revenge than to seek it.

The drawings of girls and boys can be very different. Girls typically draw houses and flowers, while boys often draw guns, cars and airplanes. If a boy draws a house occasionally, there is nothing to worry about. Even if he draws houses regularly, he may simply be a budding architect. Yet his work will stand out from that of the majority of his male peers, who are more likely to draw machines than dwellings.

While drawing war scenes is not abnormal, drawing mutilated bodies or squashed animals should arouse your concern. If your son is drawing not only tanks and guns but also people with their body parts severed, it may be time for a closer evaluation.

In considering anger

and aggression in children's drawings, you might want to look at how the drawing was made. A detailed and carefully done line drawing of a gun is less disturbing than an impulsive splat on the paper. Any subject matter done with fine detail suggests an interest in the subject but not a loss of control.

Line quality can give you insight into your child's mood. The angry child often draws heavy black lines, retracing his lines for emphasis, while the anxious child sometimes draws with sketchy lines of interrupted flow. The confident child will draw fluently.

Drawings should be interpreted within the context of the child's experience. The child who has witnessed a shooting is likely to repeat this experience in drawing, in play and in conversation to work through the traumatic experience. The child who has been in a car accident where someone was injured is more likely to draw a picture of blood the day after the accident than he was the day before.

Drawings can be used to get an idea of the maturity of a child. The more detailed the drawing, the more likely the child is to be older and intelligent. The 3-year-old will draw a circle to represent the head of a person, while the teen is more likely to draw the face as an elongated oval. If a teen puts in his best effort and can do no better than the stereotypic "smiley face" — a circle with two dots for eyes and a curve for the mouth — you may have evidence of delayed mental ability.

Your son's drawings sound like they are typical of his age and gender. If his behavior is pleasant and he gets along well with friends and teachers, there is probably nothing to be concerned about. To keep him on track, steer him away from violent videos and TV and balance his interest in aggression with instruction on kindness and service to others. Emphasize the needs of the larger group as a whole rather than just his own.

Your child is much more than just his illness

Q. My 8-year-old son has Duchenne muscular dystrophy, a fatal disease in which there is slow but progressive deterioration until death occurs, typically in early adulthood or late teens.

My child has asked me if he is going to die. He has suddenly developed a fear of going to sleep. When I ask him about why he can't sleep, he says that he is afraid that he won't wake up again. How do I answer his question about dying? How do I deal with his fear of going to sleep? He is up for hours every night.

A. When children with fatal illnesses ask if they are going to die, an honest but kind response is to say, "We are all going to die. Nobody knows exactly when that will be."

You can follow this with a realistic disclosure of the prognosis for his disease with emphasis that he has many years to live before he has to worry about dying. Point out to him that many healthy people can be suddenly killed in auto accidents or through diseases diagnosed unexpectedly. Each day of life is a precious gift, and no one is guaranteed a specific number.

His fear of going to sleep indicates that he does not understand the slow and progressive nature of his disease. Because he does not understand that he will deteriorate in function from his current high level, he thinks that at any moment his life could end. Since this is not likely, you can reassure him by helping him to learn more facts.

Expose him to children of various ages with muscular dystrophy, especially older children. Help him to see that he is a long way from death. He is expecting that his death will be sudden — that he will go from relative health to not waking up one morning. Help him to understand that death will not be sudden but that he will have plenty of warning before the time comes.

In the meantime, sit with him at night to reassure him, but don't allow him to form bad habits such as sleeping in your bed. Maintain normal discipline despite his handicap. Offer him a nightlight if this comforts him, and allow him to sleep with a teddy bear or other comforting object without ridiculing him or pushing him to be a "big boy."

He may need extra support and comforts to overcome his fear and to cope with not only the normal stresses of growing up but also the additional burden of his illness.

Search out children's support groups through the association for his illness — the Muscular Dystrophy Association in this case. Encourage him to attend a summer camp for children with his disease. In seeing other children with his illness, he will be better able to put his stage of illness in perspective. In his mind he is much sicker than he is in reality. He has gotten ahead of where he actually is, causing him to worry about dying.

Give him a religious context in which to place death. A child's fear of dying is often a fear of being separated from those he loves, especially his parents. Assure him that he will be cared for in heaven. Some children are comforted by the thought of being reunited with a deceased grandparent or other loved one. Do tell him that he will have to wait many years for this reunion however, as he has many years of living to do first.

Be sure that he attends school and other activities appropriate to his age and skills. Fill his present with goals. Set short-term goals that he can achieve. Don't allow him to sit in front of the TV but help him to find interests that are stimulating. He might enjoy chess or collecting Matchbox cars or comic books. Every child can be helped to find a hobby or talent.

Focus on the normal part of your child, without overemphasizing the fact that he is sick. Your child is much more than just his illness.

Parents relieve child's frustration too quickly

Q. As a teacher, I see some degree of frustration as being part of good learning, but some parents jump in to relieve their child of all frustration. As soon as the work becomes challenging, the parents ask for less demanding expectations. I feel parents jump in too soon. How can teachers help children and parents live through those periods when children struggle to master new material?

A. Parents today tend to be more directly involved with their children's schoolwork than were parents of previous generations. Like most things, this has its pluses and minuses. The advantage is that parents can quickly see what the child doesn't understand and can step in to help. The disadvantage is that they come to bear the child's frustration with him and sometimes bail out too soon.

Learning takes place when the level of new material is ahead of the child's current knowledge but not so far ahead that the child is lost. If the material is too easy, the student will be bored and unchallenged. If the material is so far ahead of the student's current knowledge that he doesn't have the background to assimilate the new information, the material will go past him and he will tune out.

Good teachers aim for lessons which make the child stretch. If this stretching becomes so painful for the parent that he steps in to take the work away, he takes with it an opportunity for mastery. Self-esteem is built on struggling with an obstacle and overcoming it.

If the parent takes away the challenge, he gives the child the message that he thinks the child is incapable. The child loses self-esteem not from having to work at something that is hard for him, but from hearing the parent in effect say, "This work is too hard for you. I'll ask the teacher to assign something easier."

All children need to succeed some of the time. The time for academic modification is when the child can't ever achieve success. The child who studies for hours but still fails the spelling test may need to learn five words per week instead of twenty. Constant failure takes away the desire to learn.

Even functioning at the absolute upper limit of one's ability all of the time can be very tiring. If a child must stand on his toes to reach every day, he might be better off in a class a year behind where success might come with a reasonable effort but not a Herculean one. The child who is so close to the edge of his ability that he cannot afford to be sick for one day is going to feel quite stressed by school.

Teachers can help a child through a period of challenge by offering encouraging words as the child struggles to master a new concept. Children don't understand that what is hard for them might be hard for everyone. Teachers can help both children and parents learn that acquiring new information takes work. Sometimes the child benefits from having a larger task broken down into smaller steps. The younger the child, the shorter the goals should be.

Parents may need help in remembering that the goal of education is learning. Often parents intervene out of the mistaken belief that every child should make the honor roll. They seek to make the work easy enough for their child to get a high grade.

Teachers need to let parents know that errors are OK. Sometimes the most powerful learning comes from the mistakes we make. I will never forget how to spell "chocolate" because I misspelled that word when I represented my third-grade class in the schoolwide spelling bee almost forty years ago.

The less children get, the more they appreciate gifts

Q. My 10-year-old son has seen a pile of gifts that I have wrapped for him. He knows what a few of them are but not all of them. Despite knowing that I have bought many gifts for him, he continues to point out other things that he wants. I am finding myself insulted and ready to return all that I have bought. How do you teach children to appreciate what they have and get, rather than always wanting more?

A. The less children get, the more they appreciate what they have. Giving in to your impulse to return all of his gifts would certainly turn his attention to how much you had purchased for him. Yet most parents, feeling more upset than the child at this very strong lesson, would not be able to carry this out.

Instead, take an active approach to limiting his demands. Ask your child to make a list of what gifts he would like to get this year. Tell him that all his communications about his desires must be through this list. Leave the list where he can add to it as ideas come to him, but make it clear that he will not get everything on his list. Do not allow further conversation about his wants, other than additions to his list. This is as much for the parent's benefit as it is for the child's.

Teach him to give as well as to get. For each gift that he wants, ask him to donate one of his current toys to charity. Alternatively, you can ask him to put some change in a piggy bank that you will donate to a good cause when it accumulates a significant amount. Change the focus from getting to giving each time he brings up the topic of gifts.

Bake and cook gifts for others. These are wonderful ways for the child, who has little money of his own, to give a gift that is not simply bought by the parent.

Often, in our desire to

express our love through gifts, we forget to teach that gifts are given as well as received.

Greed and endless wants are not created on December 1. Nor are they created suddenly at age 10. they represent an attitude that is developed slowly throughout childhood and is modeled on the parents' attitude and behavior. The parent who lives to shop and who competes with his or her peers by having the most expensive car, jewelry or athletic shoes should not be surprised to have a child with many holiday demands.

However, even good kids with altruistic values can get caught up in the season of buying. Teach your child alternatives to shopping and build self-esteem by reminding him that not all the things he wants must be purchased. Remind the child who wants a specific army base for his toy figures that he can build one out of construction toys. Teach him that when he builds it himself he can customize to his needs. Spend time with him guiding his project if he needs help. Children who have been taught to buy rather than create have temporarily lost the ability to think creatively. This can be reignited.

Teach skills related to his wants. The child who wants to buy a super-hero costume can be taught to sew the costume. If the parent can't sew, use materials that can be glued or stapled. Creating together leads to quality parent/child time.

Teach the value of money by giving your son an allowance year-round. When he asks for things beyond what you choose to get for him, simply say, "Do you have enough money for that?" You will be surprised at how much wiser consumers children become when they are spending their own money. Parents' money seems endless to a child. When they handle money of their own, children get a more realistic sense of limits.

Don't be afraid to say no. It is more fun to say yes to a child's demands, but it is the parent's job to prepare his child for life. In real life you can't have everything you want.

Camp is good for some but not for all children

Q. My 10-year-old daughter is at sleep-away camp for a week. On day three she called us and asked us to come pick her up because she hates camp. Should we go and get her? What should we do about camp next summer? Should we try another camp or simply assume that she is not the camp type?

A. There are many reasons why a child might not be happy at camp, and the parent's first job is to do some detective work to get a better understanding of the problem.

Talk to your child, to the camp director and to other parents to get a sense if the problem lies within your child (homesickness, lack of friends) or within the camp (not enough or the wrong kind of adult supervision, not enough to do).

Homesickness often sets in about day three. The first few days of camp are new and exciting, and most children do fairly well. Once the newness wears off, some children begin to think about home and to feel sad. Because your daughter's camp stay is so short, you needn't pick her up for homesickness. By the time you get there, either she will be feeling better or it will be time to go home anyway. Even if she continues to feel sad, she might feel better about herself if she sticks it out to completion than if she aborts the mission and comes home early.

A one-week stay is not too long away from home for a 10-year-old. Unless you uncover a real problem in the safety of the camp, you should probably let her stick it out. Let the camp director know about the problem. It might just be that with some additional support and attention your child can enjoy her last few days.

For longer camp stays, talk to parents of other campers and see if the problem is a general one or if it is just your child. Ask your child what specifically she is unhappy about. Your response should be different if she is just missing home than if she is being taunted by other campers with no staff intervention.

Sometimes discontent is simply a function of weather. When rain precludes horseback riding, baseball games and swimming and campers are confined to their cabins, children have more time to think about home. Many smiles are restored by sunshine and a return to activities that serve to distract a child who is prone to missing home.

Although temperament does not change, children's fears and concerns are not the same from year to year. Your child will be a year older next summer and may be more ready to cope with time away from home. Don't discourage her from going if she wants to. Express confidence in her ability to be happy on her own. Tell her how proud you are of her independence.

Let her practice changing her own sheets or washing her clothes if she will have to do these at camp. The children who have the most trouble away from home are those who have parents who love to do for them. The change to being on her own at camp will be more successful if there is preparation and encouragement before camp.

The child who isn't happy at camp for one week paradoxically might do better with a longer camp stay. Homesickness is usually worst at the beginning of camp and improves as the child makes camp friends and gains confidence in her independence.

If a child is away for a month and calls home on day three, it is best to investigate and to encourage her to stay. If she is still unhappy after another week, then you might want to consider the reasons for her unhappiness and bring her home if you don't expect her feelings to improve. While camp is a wonderful experience that promotes independence and growth for most children, there are some children who just prefer to be at home.

Habits save time by cutting down decision making

Q. I have a second-grade son. I would like to know how to get him to do his homework on his own without parental reminders?

A. Young children do not have the same goals as adults. They look at the world as an interesting place with many things to catch their attention. Unfortunately, homework is usually not the first thing they choose to do. It is often up to the adult to remind the child and to set up a structure and routine conducive to homework.

Habits save time by eliminating the decision process. If an adult had to decide each day whether or not to get dressed or whether or not to brush his teeth, it would take an eternity to get out the door. By having habits — things we do without much thought — we can speed up our morning routine.

Children are not born with these habits. Parents must teach them. Parents can help the child to develop homework habits so that certain cues in the child's day lead to starting homework.

Set a time for homework to be done. Within reason, when the child does homework doesn't matter. What does matter is that you establish a routine. Some parents like to set a rule that homework must be done before going out to play. Other parents find that letting the child play after school gives him a break.

Homework can be done after an early dinner. Different times work for different children and different family routines, but homework should be done early enough so that the child is not tired.

Not only will the tired child not absorb the lesson, but when the parent allows homework to be the last thing of the day, the child also gets the message that it is a low priority.

Your child is less likely to resist starting homework if you don't arbitrarily interrupt another activity. Transitions from one activity to another can be difficult for many young children. Set homework time for a natural break between activities.

Stopping play for dinner and then moving to homework is easier than allowing him to return to play after dinner and then expecting him to interrupt his play fifteen minutes later.

Doing homework right after school will be easier for many children than playing for twenty minutes and then stopping play to do homework.

Children enjoy homework more when they are not abandoned to do it alone. While some educators suggest doing homework in a quiet place such as the child's room, I find that children are happier doing homework in the center of the home, as long as there are few distractions and low noise. Turn off the TV and radio but do let your child be near you.

Before a child can do homework on his own, he must be able to handle the level of difficulty of his assignments. Most children will do work that they can do. A child who resists doing homework is sometimes one who doesn't have the skills to do it.

Some children who are resistant to doing their work can become cooperative with some parental involvement. Even adults enjoy doing laundry or dishes more when they have company.

If your child is having trouble with assignments, don't do the work for him. Show him how to do a similar problem and then watch him do it on his own. Notice where he makes his mistakes and retrain him. Participate by calling out spelling words to him or by asking him questions about a science chapter he has read.

As children get older, most will spontaneously shed their dependence upon parents. Wanting company or help in the second grade is not outside the norm. If he still seeks help past sixth grade, you will need a careful evaluation of his academic skills and emotional needs.

School is for learning academic and social skills

Q. My 9-year-old child does not want to go to school. He says that the children laugh at him. I can't seem to convince him that school is for learning, not for playing with the other children. Why is what the other children think of him so important?

A. School is for learning but it is for developing social skills as well. The child learns far more than the curriculum when he spends seven hours per day with his peer group. Much of the fun of school comes from the interaction with others, just as the adult at work enjoys not only the task at hand but also those he does it with.

While the young child's most intense fear is of separation from caregivers, the fear of being humiliated is the fear of the school-age child. Mastery of skills and facts is the developmental task of this age group. Humiliation is the price of failure to learn what is expected. For young children, parents are salient. During the elementary school years, the peer group becomes increasingly important.

When children are asked to report the things they fear most, right after losing a parent they ranked experiences that caused them to lose face. Wetting their pants in class, being thought of as stupid or incorrectly dressed, and repeating a grade were high on the list of feared experiences.

While adults said they worried about how a child would react to a trip to the dentist, the school-age children worried more about a trip to the front of the classroom to do a math problem that was too hard.

Adults chose having a new sibling, getting lost or going to the hospital as stressful events for children. The children themselves ranked those situations as less distressing than the ones in which they suffered humiliation.

When your child comes home upset about comments or taunts hurled by peers, be prepared to listen. Solutions tend to close conversation and are rarely helpful. Hold back on the comments "Just ignore him" or "He's not good enough for you anyway." Instead, ask questions which open up conversation.

Ask, "What exactly did he say?" or "Is he teasing other children in your class too?" These let your child know you are listening. They cause him to think about the problem in an analytic way. They lead him to continue talking, leaving you a way to help him.

After hearing him out, help your child understand human nature. Help him to see that some children are teasing him because they fear being left out.

Unless the peer group is undesirable, help your child to fit in with his peers. If the peers are too rough for your child, a transfer to a new school or a new neighborhood might be wise. In some cases, however, the problem lies within the child and he will take the social problems with him.

Teach your child to notice how others dress, talk or behave. Teach him to mirror acceptable behaviors. It is not until the teen years that children can really define their own style and be accepted by the group even when they are different.

You do not need to compromise your values, nor do you need to spend beyond your means to make your child fit in. An inexpensive pair of blue jeans is OK. Velvet knickers are not. If you dress your child totally differently from his peers, you will set him up to be a target.

Help your child to feel secure at home. A child who can retreat to home at the end of the day can withstand some teasing. Send him to school feeling loved. Give him social, academic and athletic skills so that he can hold his own in at least one area.

Going to school is not an option, but it does not have to be painful. Take your child seriously when he tells you he is upset. Take steps to correct the problem.

Motivate, don't force, older to include younger brother

Q. My 10-year-old son always wants to go with his 12-year-old brother wherever he goes. He doesn't seem to understand that it was his older brother who was invited and he wasn't.

When his brother does spend time with him, my 10-year-old is in heaven and just grins from ear to ear. Should we make the older child take his younger brother with him? If so, how much of the time?

A. Forcing a child take a younger sibling along is a sure way to breed resentment. Your 12-year-old is a child too, even though he is two years older. He is entitled to his own friends and activities.

Far better than making the choice for him and telling him he must include his brother would be to tell him of his younger brother's admiration for him.

Point out to him how his brother looks up to him and how he cherishes the time he spends with him. Let your older son invite his brother because he knows that it makes him happy.

If you need his help as a babysitter while you are out, be direct about your needs. Instead of telling him that he must take his brother along, tell him that you need to be away and you need his help.

Let him decide if it would be better to take his brother along to the ball field with his friends or to cancel his plans and stay home to watch his brother.

As long as you do not ask for his babysitting services excessively, he should take on the family responsibility without too much fuss.

How often he includes his brother can usually be left up to the older child. Except for the times he is actually helping you out with child care, the choice should be primarily his.

If he never includes his brother, you need to work on

the relationship between them. You may also want to address issues of self-centeredness on the part of the older child and teach him to reach out to others.

If he always includes his brother, then you might want to give him permission to have his own friends.

Talk to your younger son too. A case of big brother hero worship may be a healthy closeness, but it also might be a feeling that he is not as good as his big brother.

Point out the strengths that the younger child has and share with him that his skills will improve as his gets to be his brother's age.

Share with him the secret that when his older brother was the younger child's age he could not do some of the things he can do now.

Even if it would make your younger child happy to tag along, when only one child is invited, it is not appropriate to send two. Your younger child will need to learn this. Just as you would teach him other aspects of manners and social appropriateness, you will want to teach him the etiquette of invitations.

If a family invites one child for lunch or to spend the night, it does not expect two to show up. If he was not invited, he cannot go.

Plan some family events for the boys to have time together. Family camping, picnics or trips to a water park will create memories of a childhood spent together. Although generally there is no harm in having children invite friends along, in this instance you will want to avoid this and make this time for the brothers to be alone together.

Encourage your younger son to make his own friends too. When his older brother is spending the night with a friend, it might be a good time for the other child to invite a friend to your house.

Enroll the younger boy in activities which fall within the talents he can develop with practice. Activities not only lead to skills, but they provide a social group as well.

A few good friends are enough

Q. My sixth-grade son is a nice and good child. The students in his class tend to make fun of him because he is so straight. I am worried that he doesn't have many friends, although he does have one close one with whom he spends time both at school and outside. Should I worry about him? What can I do?

A. It sounds as if you are already worried but you probably need not be. Nice children tend to attract nice friends. He may be better off with one supportive friend than spending time with lots of the meaner children.

The bully who seems popular now belittles his classmates. He may intimidate his peers to silence at age 12, but he won't be in the same power position in a few years. In the fifth and sixth grades the popular children are the ones who are more aggressive and have athletic skills. This changes during middle and high school where are broader range of skills are admired.

As the children get older, they are not in class with the same group all day. They break up into social groups that are made up of children with similar interests and ways of interacting. The bully may find himself alone, or he may find himself in a group of children who relate by putting each other down.

Your son, on the other hand, is more likely to attract kinder, gentler children. You will probably find that his circle of friends widens as he grows and that you like the children he has chosen or who have chosen him. They are most likely to be children who are gentle, kind and straight — like your son.

The child to be concerned about is the child who is insecure. This child may tend to become like those around him just to be accepted. Often these children can be identified in the early elementary grades when they give away their lunch money to buy friends.

Watch also the child with no friends at all. One close friend is all it takes to make a child feel OK about himself at school. The friendless child, especially the child with little support and security at home, is a vulnerable child.

The child with poor social skills is not likely to do better in junior high because he will take his problem with him. The problem is not external, as it is for the child with a mean and aggressive peer group.

A problem that is outside the child goes away when the peers mature, but the child with poor social skills will not do better with the more diverse group in middle school because the problem is carried with him to each class period.

This child will need adult intervention. He will need help in understanding what it is he does to alienate his peers. Being unclean, talking too much, dressing out of style or missing social cues can be corrected — although not always as easily as it might sound.

Most children are born reading social cues, but a few are not. They can't seem to understand when a peer needs quiet or how to join in a conversation that is in progress.

The problem is perpetuated because these children often blame the others for not including them, rather than looking at what about their own behavior is turning others off.

The kind, gentle, straight child will outgrow his problem as his peers mature. He needs only a few friends now and support from a loving family. The child who has few friends because he lacks social skills will need adult or maybe professional help to learn to read social cues.

Parent must oversee child's remediation

Q. My 10-year-old child has trouble learning some of the math concepts taught at school. The school says that she is not learning disabled and doesn't qualify for any extra help. What is the teacher's responsibility and what is the parent's responsibility for making sure each child learns the grade level work? Are parents expected to put in extra time at home working with a student who has missed learning a lesson taught at school?

A. The school's job is to look out for the best interests of the group as a whole. The parent's job is watch out for the interests of his own child. The school's job is to make the child fit into the group. The parent's job is to make sure the special needs of the child are taken care of. The child fares best when these two forces are in balance.

A teacher is quite successful if all but one of her students masters the work. This is of little consolation to the parent of the child who fails. No teacher is going to be as concerned about your child as you are.

If you are worried about your child's learning, you will want to take the time to teach her or to hire someone else to do so.

All remediation requires some effort on the parent's part, but not all efforts are equal. You need to match the intervention with your own temperament and with that of your child. Some children are resistant to working with their own parent, and some parents simply do not have the patience to teach.

The computer can be a valuable tutoring tool, especially for basics such as spelling and math facts. The computer is infinitely patient and never criticizes. Even higher level math can be taught through the many step-by-step math programs available.

The parent's role in

computer tutoring will be to motivate the child to use the computer program. It doesn't work if the program sits on the shelf.

Help your child over his resistance by setting up a schedule for computer remediation time and by not allowing him to go on to other activities that he prefers until he has completed his assigned work.

Parents can typically learn material faster than the child can. A teacher who doesn't have hours to spend with a student might be willing to quickly show the skill to the parent so that the parent can then go home and work with the child.

Reading your child's textbook may bring back the skills for you. Even if you haven't done factoring or fractions in a number of years, you may find that you can easily relearn material you once knew.

Some parents find that they do not work well with their own children. Often parents are too invested in the outcome of the lesson to be patient. Some children resist doing work for their own parents that they will do for a stranger.

If hiring a tutor is not feasible, consider trading tutoring with a friend. You tutor her child and she tutors yours.

Or invite a group of students to work with your child. She might be more cooperative in the presence of others, and you may be more patient with children who are not your own.

Ask her teacher if there are other children having the same or similar difficulties. Invite one or two other children to join your tutoring session. It is often more fun to learn in a group.

As the deficits of the other children are not likely to be exactly the same as your child's, she might get a chance to shine in skill before her friends as you work on something they need to learn but she has already mastered.

It is the job of the school to teach, but no lesson will reach every child. If you don't want your child to fall between the cracks, you will want to help her learn. In the end, she is not the teacher's child. She is yours.

ADHD not the only cause of poor performance

Q. My child tests poorly on the Stanford Achievement and other standardized tests. He has attention deficit hyperactivity disorder. Could his ADHD be the cause of his low scores?

A. The effect of attention deficit on testing will be to produce widely varying scores. If a child is cognitively capable but lacking attention, his scores will be high when he is on task and poor when he is not. If his scores are consistently low, year after year, attention deficit is not likely to be the problem.

If you see wide swings in scores in a single subject from year to year, attention may be a factor. The child who gets a 90th percentile in math one year and a 47th percentile the next year may be off-task during the test where he got the lower score.

Attention is also a possible factor in the child who tests low in one or two subjects each year but it is a different subject each time. It is the inconsistency — and not the low score — that reflects attention deficit.

Test scores measure your child under test conditions. When we think of measuring accurately, we usually mean that the test is measuring the optimal ability of the child.

Actually, test scores give us a more realistic measure. They measure what a child can produce under test conditions — performance within a given time limit, under some stress, on a certain day. The test conditions, for most children, give us results similar to what the child does in his daily class work.

This may mean that you are not getting a measure of your child's absolute best performance, but you are getting a measure of his real performance. Tests do not lie unless there is a random type of error, such as moving all of his answers down one space on the answer sheet.

The child whose distractibility lowers test performance is performing as he will under most conditions — ones where he will have other things to look at and listen to. While his absolute potential may be greater, the test is measuring him as he is.

Some things, such as anxiety, can lower test performance. If you have a child who becomes anxious on tests, you may not be able to measure his potential by sampling his knowledge under pressure. His test scores may not be a measure of his potential, but are a measure of how he performs under stress.

Testing is not the only situation where an anxiety prone child will underperform. Even for the child whose anxiety lowers his test performance, the test is measuring how he will perform in some other situations.

Attention deficit disorder is often accompanied by learning disabilities. Low test scores, especially if they are limited to one or two subject areas, may reflect a specific learning deficit rather than a global problem in maintaining attention.

However, poor school performance has almost become an accepted characteristic of ADD. Children with attention problems who do exceptionally well in school are not usually labeled ADD but are simply seen as "spacey" or "the absent minded professor."

If your child is scoring poorly on standardized tests, the label is less important than the remediation of the problem. First you need to assess your child's potential for achievement by testing him one-on-one rather than in a group. Then you will want to measure his performance against what he is capable of doing.

Too often, parents expect high achievement without regard for what the child can realistically do. Once you have established that your child is capable of doing better than he is doing, you can work with him at two levels.

You can teach test taking skills and you can work on the content areas. Medication for distractibility can make a difference.

Motivation begins early in life

Q. My fifth-grade son is capable of doing good schoolwork but he doesn't try. He does the minimum to get by and is happy just to pass. The school won't fail him or hold him back because he has passing grades, but his achievement does not reflect his ability. How do you motivate a child to want to study?

A. Motivation begins with correct placement in a classroom. The child who cannot keep up with the work often drops out and tunes out and complains he is bored. Although you say that your son can do better, you might want to have him tested by a psychologist. You may be surprised to find that while his overall ability is adequate, he may have specific deficits in aptitude or specific gaps in mastery of skills he should have learned in earlier grades.

Motivation begins early in life. The child who is not allowed to watch much TV and is instead encouraged to read, play creatively or do arts and crafts projects is more likely to do schoolwork later on. Habits are formed early.

Attitude is more easily shaped when the child is young. Teaching your child that school is important when he is 3 will make him a willing student when he is 10 or 14.

Don't pull him out of school for vacations. Don't allow him to miss school without reason. Teach him why school is important. Make the connection between school achievement and career and life success.

Provide emotional stability at home. Your child's emotions will determine how he feels about school. Depressed and angry children are not typically the best students. The child who rebels against authority because he has not had any parental attention won't complete his assignments.

Gifted children are typically eager students. The work seems interesting to them because they make many peripheral connections, but the child of more limited ability can also be led to enjoy school.

Choose a school system carefully, looking for one that offers multisensory learning experiences. If a student has to master math facts in order to be the cashier at the school store, he just might be motivated.

But school can't be all fun and games. Parents have to teach children that they must work hard even if the task is not to their liking. Parents who bail their child out at the first discipline from the teacher are telling their child that he need not work too hard.

He learns quickly that if there is a consequence for failure, mom or dad will rescue him. The child who knows that missing assignments is not acceptable to his parents is more likely to do his work and turn it in than the child of the parent who will blame the teacher for the child's poor grade.

Yet pressuring your child to get all A's will not work either. Reward the effort rather than the report card. If your child doesn't do his homework, he needs to be more closely supervised. He loses his independence if he can't work on his own.

Incentives can be used to get a child over a hump, but these will only work for parents who don't use them excessively or give their children too much already. Many children today can't be motivated because they already have everything. Small repeatable rewards work better than one large gift. A dime per day paid at the end of the week for achieving a specific and small goal will work better than a trip to Disney World at the end of the school year for generic "good grades."

Child rejected by peers needs secure home base

Q. A friend is having trouble with her 8-year-old adopted daughter. She has severe learning problems and doesn't seem to grasp what she is expected to learn at school.

She has attention deficit disorder, and she is on medication for that. She does not seem to understand the social rules either, and so she has no friends.

She is never invited to birthday parties or to spend the night. She has delays in language and motor skills. What can my friend do to help her child? It is tearing her apart.

A. It sounds as if your friend's child has what psychologists call pervasive developmental disorder. Children with this diagnosis have problems in many areas of development, including cognitive (thinking), fine motor (writing), gross motor (clumsiness) and social.

Because the areas of deficit cover more than one skill, the treatment must be multifaceted too. Just treating ADHD with Ritalin will not lead to improvement in all areas.

Medication will be necessary to get this child to the point where she can benefit from any of the other interventions. If a child cannot sit reasonably still and concentrate, the tutoring efforts will frustrate both child and tutor.

A medication consultation with an experienced child psychiatrist may lead to a combination of medications to target several symptoms. The mood, behavior and attention problems that are often seen with pervasive developmental disorder may not respond to one medication alone.

The social problem can be approached both at home and at school. With parental permission, teachers can intervene as they see the problem come up. This child may not notice responses from peers. The teacher is there to observe and can make quiet corrections on the spot.

When the child talks too loudly or invades a classmate's personal space, the teacher can cue her clueless student.

When the awkward child gets lunch on her clothes the teacher can send her to the restroom to clean up. If her shirts are too short so her underwear shows when she bends over, the teacher can bring it to the attention of the parent and child to correct the problem.

Teachers can identify a potential friend in the classroom who might be a good match and can pair these children occasionally for group projects. The teacher can encourage friendships within the classroom while the parent extends this to the home.

Invite selected children over after school, but do be prepared that there might not be return invitations right away. Even if your child is not invited in return, she gains the experience of being with other children outside the structure of school.

Identify her learning disability and adapt the curriculum so that she can have a reasonable school experience. Don't "dumb down," because this gives the student the message that she is incapable, but do factor out learning problems from other subjects.

If a child can't spell, don't subtract points for spelling errors on her science test, but do keep on working on the spelling skills during spelling lesson time.

Lead the child to after-school activities that will develop fine and gross motor skills in a noncompetitive environment. Swimming lessons might be less humiliating than softball, where all eyes are on the batter.

Love each child as she is, without overemphasizing the need for change. The child who is rejected by peers needs a secure and accepting home base.

Madison

Gift-giving rules vary with the social subgroup

Q. I gave a birthday party for my 10-year-old daughter. Several guests arrived without presents. My child was disappointed. What do you think about people who accept an invitation, attend the party, but don't bring gifts?

A. We live in social groups that have rules about gifts and gift giving. These rules and customs serve to assure that things will come out fairly — that when one gives away something, one will get something in return. While this may sound crass and may not be necessary in an affluent society, it is essential for survival in social groups where resources are scarce.

Whether or not it is appropriate to attend without a gift depends upon the customs in your particular social group. Most social groups develop a level of gift giving that is adhered to by the majority of the group.

Most groups will quickly accept that a person with lesser means might give less or that a person who is wealthier may give more, but the group generally will set an amount to be spent on gifts that is comfortable for the majority of the group's members.

Generally, if you have given a gift, the other family is obligated to return one — not right at that moment, but at the appropriate occasion. There are exceptions to this, however.

Gifts are connected to social status. They are given by higher status to lower status. The parent gives a gift to his young child. The child is not under the same obligation to give a gift to the parent. The boss gives a present to his workers. The workers are not obligated to return one.

In fact, to do so would be to make a statement about equal status that might be read as a challenge to the boss's authority. The gesture may not be taken kindly.

If it is the custom to give gifts among your daughter's friends, then it is rude to attend without one. The gift need not be expensive, as long as it is chosen with the birthday child's interests and preferences in mind. It can be homemade, as long as it is age and gender appropriate.

Attendance without a gift can be a direct message. It may be that the child or parent who did not send a gift wanted to discourage a repeat invitation. They attended this time but said, in effect, "I don't want to make this a regular thing."

Gift selection is a social skill that involves sensitivity to others. People who select the most appreciated gifts, do so by putting themselves in the other person's shoes. They select not what the giver likes, but what the recipient would enjoy.

Self-centered people not only tend to give fewer gifts, but they also give gifts that meet their own needs and interests rather than those of the receiver.

If your child was disappointed or hurt at not receiving gifts, then it appears that she had reason to expect them and that the guests violated the social norms in coming empty-handed. Perhaps they see you as being of a higher status. Perhaps they just didn't consider your child's feelings.

Unless you think the guest lost a gift that a mother sent, it would be rude to mention the lack of a gift. Instead help your daughter focus on the fun she had at her party.

Use the experience to help her learn how to choose friends. The lack of a gift is unimportant, but the child who disregards her feelings will not make a good friend.

Recreational reading can be below grade level

Q. Our son is a fourth grader who is intelligent, gregarious and athletically gifted, but he detests reading. He won't study for tests. His grades are high even without studying. We have taken him to an eye doctor for glasses. We have set up a structured time for study. We read to him. We still have the same problem. Do you have any suggestions?

A. Children who don't like to read are usually those children who don't read fluently. When decoding is difficult for the child, reading shifts from recreation to work.

To help your son enjoy reading, you may want to have his reading level tested. If there is a problem in his reading skills, you can work with him to remediate this.

Knowing his skill level, you can then challenge him with books just a tad above his level that will stretch his achievement without frustrating him with a hopeless task. For his spare time, you can provide books below his level that are easy enough to be recreational.

For pleasure reading at home, go back one to two grade levels and choose books of interest to him. If he likes sports, get sports stories.

Serial books are a wonderful way for the middle elementary school reader to be propelled from one book to the next because the story continues.

Angel Park Hoop Stars and Angel Park Soccer Stars by Dean Hughes (Knopf) are two series that may catch your athletic son's interest.

Keeping the reading matter short may be a way to keep a reluctant reader from feeling overwhelmed. The Encyclopedia Brown series by Donald Sobol (Bantam) is easy reading of high interest that offers a complete mystery in each chapter. The child doesn't have to read a hundred pages to finish the book. He can read a chapter and get the story from beginning to end. Encyclopedia Brown is a boy whose father is a detective. The boy solves mysteries by using clever deductive reasoning.

Your son's reluctance to study may not be a problem right now, as you say his grades are solid. Bright children can often get through the early grades with little effort. Yet it will soon catch up with him as the work becomes more demanding.

In the early grades, children are taught basic skills which enable them to absorb more material later. While they do need to memorize math facts and spelling, bright children can get these with very little repetition outside the classroom.

By the fifth grade, they no longer learn to read but read to learn. At this point, no matter how bright the child is, if he doesn't read and study (studying is re-reading), his grades will drop. No matter how bright you are, the state capitals won't just jump into your head.

When the work overwhelms his laid-back study style, it may take a few low test grades or a bad report card for him to catch on to the change, but as long as success is important to him, he will make the transition from coasting to effort.

If he does not, you can deal with his motivation at that time. Right now he does not study because he doesn't need to in order to do well.

To motivate him, you might want to consider giving him a greater challenge through an enrichment program, or you might just let him have a last year of play before the work of school catches up to him.

When it does, you can increase his study time by being with him for company while he works. Many children don't like being alone in a room to work, but will put in time if they have someone with them.

Continue to set structured study time, and check homework assignments on the schedule his teacher suggests.

Avoid becoming overinvolved in a child who does not have poor grades. Remember it is he who is in the fourth grade — not you.

Failure to admit fault can be learned from parent

Q. My 9-year-old son won't admit blame for anything. It always is someone else's fault. If he can't find a book for school, he accuses someone else of taking it. If his shoes are not in the closet where he thinks he left them, someone else must have moved them. When there is an incident at school where one child pushes another, the other child is always at fault. How do you teach a child to own his own behavior?

A. One of the most difficult behaviors to change is the child's failure to take responsibility for what he has done. The reason it is difficult to change is because the child can see no need to change it. In his eyes, he doesn't own the problem behavior in the first place.

People who don't take responsibility for their own behavior are doomed to repeat their mistakes. A person who can't look at his own behavior is not open to change or improvement. While it may feel good for a while not to have to say, "It's my fault," over time, it causes the loss of relationships as friends move on to more equal and open ones.

Not taking responsibility for one's own actions can be learned through modeling the behavior of others. The parent who goes to school to defend his child when the school reports a problem does his child no service.

The child learns that he is always right, and that nothing he does is his fault. He learns that there is no consequence for bad behavior. He learns that he doesn't even have to admit that the behavior in question was his.

The parent who breaks a fragile object in a store and then denies it is teaching his child to do the same. The parent who can't say he is sorry or make amends teaches his child that apologizing is a shameful thing to do and that denial is better. Children watch the daily interactions within their family and tend to imitate.

The absence of punishment is a missed opportunity to shape good behavior, but excessive punishment can lead a child to deny that he has done wrong as well. When the punishment is harsh, the child's need to avoid punishment can be stronger than his need to admit the truth.

Parents can set goals that are too high for a child. The child who must always get "A" grades cannot admit that he made a mistake. The stakes are too high. He cannot risk the loss of the parent's love. If he gets a lower grade, it must be the teacher's fault.

Although the failure to own one's behavior can certainly be learned from bad example, there are a few excellent parents who have children who won't admit to what they have done. Some part of this may be related to temperament.

Often these children are competitive. They compete with siblings to be the favorite child and may feel that if they admit to a flaw, they will lose the competition.

Of course, their behavior leads them to be less desirable than the better-behaved sibling, but they cannot see this. They think if they don't admit to wrongdoing, they have done no wrong.

Getting a child to accept fault when he is guilty is dependent upon good examples and many repetitions. The parent must catch each time the child blames others and ask him to look at it in a different way.

The parent or teacher can ask the child to think of the worst possible outcome that would happen if he owned the misdeed. Helping him to see that owning his behavior will not lead to loss of love may give him the strength to admit to behavior so that he can change it.

Mom's reading disability returns in her children

Q. I am a single mother of three children. My twin girls, who are in the sixth grade, have struggled since grade one to make B's and C's.

One twin's fourth-grade teacher declared that she had ADD and said I was depriving her of treatment if I did not put her on Ritalin. My better judgment led me to believe that ADD was not her problem. She was tested and placed in special education for reading only.

Unfortunately, a job change led to a move with a change to a private school, and special ed ended. Now the private school says that both twins have a reading problem. They read at fourth grade level, two years behind grade.

I was never tested as a child, but I always had to struggle with reading and with understanding what I read. I was always the last to finish a test. I got OK grades, but getting to those grades took much work.

They are feeling bad about being the poorest readers in their grade. To compensate, one is acting the class clown. The other has frustration tantrums. Where can I get the girls tested?

A. While further testing may be helpful to sort out specific aspects of your children's reading problem, it appears that the diagnosis has already been made and you need a program of intervention.

A good reading tutor, especially one with a background in remedial reading, is what you should look for.

Reading problems are often inherited. Chances are that your children have the same disability that you had. The hurt is that having struggled with your reading disability for years, you now have to face the pain and the struggle all over again with your children.

The positive side is that you have the key to your

children's reading problem. Having learned what worked for you, you are in a good position to know what will work to help your children learn to read.

Think back to how you overcame your dyslexia. The strategies and methods that worked for you are likely to work for your children, as they are likely to have a similar deficit.

Reading is a combination of phonetic (letter sounds) and whole word recognition. Most children can learn to read with either method and alternate both methods when they read.

A few children process only one way. If you learned to recognize whole words at a glance, try this with your children. If you still sound out each word, strengthen their phonetic skills.

Because attention deficit disorder is not a disease that can be identified by a blood test or a chromosome analysis, diagnosis is largely a matter of opinion.

There are many other problems, including depression, learning disabilities, being upset over a specific situation such as abuse or a parental divorce, or simply "spoiled brat" behavior that can mimic the symptoms of attention deficit disorder.

It takes a careful evaluation to sort these out. Stimulant medication can be a miracle drug for some children, but it is not a cure for all.

Do not tolerate bad behavior at school but do let your girls know that things will get better for them. As children, they are expected to be good at everything. As adults, they will only have to do what they are good at.

Meanwhile, help them to find pleasure in their areas of strength while they work at improving their weaknesses. Most children can find a niche.

Recess serves to release tension in young students

Q. We have a new principal at my son's school who doesn't believe in recess. I think she is going to have problems with fidgety children. I feel that my child really needs a break during the day. What do you think about recess? Is it just a waste of time?

A. Sitting still, thinking, concentrating and making small, controlled movements (such as those required for writing or coloring) build tension in the naturally active child.

Fidgety or talkative behavior in the classroom indicates that the children need a break. Taking away that physical release is likely to prolong the misbehavior in the classroom as the students release tension in their own ways.

Recess should be a regular part of each school day for the lower grades. It works best when it comes as a break during a span of academic activity, but can also be used in the earliest grades at the end of the day to shorten the academic day.

By the fifth and sixth grades, however, recess can become a time when the powerful children pick on the socially weaker ones.

At this age, recess can be omitted to prevent aggressive or mean children from intimidating others during this less structured time. By now the academic load has increased, and recess may come at the expense of learning.

For the lower grades, recess is not just a waste of time but a part of the curriculum. It serves to provide an opportunity for socialization. Children learn how to talk to each other and to persuade and influence.

Through play, boys and girls learn both to conform and blend into the group, and to make themselves stand out as special.

Recess is a time when the child works out a place for

himself in the social pack. Without adult guidance, the children are free to make friends, change friends and leave others out.

While some of this seems cruel to observers, the children are learning lessons about getting along with others. They are learning social skills.

Recess gives the children a chance to play out angry feelings in a safe way. Hitting a ball with a baseball bat on the playground is preferable to hitting a classmate in the school room.

Recess allows time for fantasy, which vents the child's feeling of powerlessness. The child who was scolded by the teacher can play Superman or G.I. Joe to restore his self-esteem.

Through fantasy play the child can rehearse the teacher's rules and incorporate them as his own.

During this unstructured time the child might play school, imitating his teacher, or he might ride a tricycle, obeying the teacher's safety rules and noticing when other children fail to do so.

Recess provides time for children from different classes to play together, allowing friendships from previous years to continue. It provides the child with a larger group from which to find children with like interests.

Boys and girls handle recess differently. Boys are more likely to blow off steam in physical activity.

Girls often choose to relax in social games. In the middle elementary school years, the genders don't mix very much, and so recess serves to reinforce gender identity.

Recess provides training for large muscles. When sports are played, the time is used to train eye-hand coordination. These motor skills carry over into the classroom as handwriting and perceptual skills.

Recess gives the child who is not successful at academics a chance to show his skills at physical activities.

Recess makes school fun. The child's anticipation of seeing his friends and having time to play together makes him eager to go to school each day.

Daily failure is worse than a grade repeat

Q. My child's second-grade teacher has recommended that he be held back a year in school. We are not sure how he will take the news. We are worried that it will damage his self-esteem to not go on with his class. How do you decide if repeating a grade is a good idea?

A. Repeating a grade is best done for a child who is immature so that he can have another year to grow and develop before having to face the increased demands of the next school grade.

Holding a child back does not make him any smarter but it does give him a year to grow up. He may feel smarter when compared to children at his developmental level, rather than at his chronological age.

The ideal candidate for a school grade repeat is the child who is young for his class, small in height, immature in coordination and social skills, but with adequate intelligence. It should not be the academically slow child who repeats the grade, but the immature one.

Repeating a grade will not help the mentally retarded child. A gifted or even an average child a year younger has little in common with him.

The mentally retarded child will need an ungraded classroom where his curriculum is individualized to help him master specific skills of daily living.

Holding a child back will not change personality. A repeat will not make a leader out of a timid child, unless being older in the group overcomes his shyness.

Nor will it increase his motivation to write a story or read a book. Carefully chosen encouraging words and selected reward systems can do this.

Motivation can be improved without repeating the grade, unless his apathy is caused by failure to understand the lesson.

The child who should not repeat is the child who is aggressive and big for his age and who is precocious in physical development. The academically slow child who is big for his class often becomes the class bully, causing problems for the teacher and for the other students.

Most children will protest being held back because they focus on the immediate embarrassment of facing their friends. Parents will need to take a longer-term view.

Not holding an immature child back is not benign or self-esteem sparing either. The child faces humiliation every day as he doesn't know the answers to classroom questions and tests, and as he is the smallest, youngest or weakest player at sports.

To not hold back the child who is struggling means that he will have an even more difficult time in the next and subsequent grades, as he will not have mastered the background facts.

Instead of daily humiliation, it is better to face the problem all at once with a repeat, so that the child has the chance to succeed and build real self-esteem.

When you have the opportunity to hold a child back for immaturity early in his school career, it may be wise to do so. In my practice, I have never heard a parent regret having held a child back, but I have heard many who decided not to hold a struggling child back wish later that he had.

When a grade repeat is being considered, I would recommend that you have him individually tested by a psychologist to evaluate intellectual strengths and weaknesses and to see how his achievement measures up to his aptitude.

Ideally, if you are going to hold a child back you might want to consider changing schools. It is easier for a child to start the same grade over when the other children have not already identified him with a certain class or grade.

Yet, some children may prefer to remain in their familiar school. Talk to your child and individualize your plans.

Preteen wants to dress as a teenager

Q. My 9-year-old daughter wants to wear things that she says look "cool." We think that the clothes that she covets are too sexy for a little girl. We would like her to wear things that are cute and pretty. She wants slinky and bare. Can we rule over the dress code, and if we do will we make her an outcast with her friends?

A. The pressure to dress little children as miniature adults is an extension of the erosion of the boundaries between children and adults. Many parents compete through their children and equate having an advanced child with their own enhanced status.

These parents have little idea about the child's developmental stage. The result is a child who looks older and may say the words of a more mature stage but who is out of step with her own development.

When the child in a skimpy top and miniskirt cries like a younger child at a slight frustration, the parents can be surprised. They have forgotten just how young their child is.

Ironically, as children are pushed to dress in more mature clothes, parents are dressing like teens. It seems that we have idealized the adolescent years of dating and flirtation. Young children want to look like teens, and so do some adults. Yet adolescence is a time of uncertainty and upheaval. It has neither the stability of adulthood nor the carefree time of childhood.

Clothes symbolize the changes between stages of development. Some styles arise out of functional needs of each stage, such as snaps on the bottom of infant clothes to allow for diaper changes. Other styles come from body changes, such as the creation of a waistline in the clothes of girls past puberty. When you dress your child too maturely, others can misread her age and stage.

Pseudo-mature clothes attract attention the child may not be ready for. When a child dresses in a sexually attractive manner, she may just get what her clothing style asks for, much to the surprise of the child, who has no idea about the message she is giving.

Children are not emotionally prepared to handle sexual overtures and parents need to protect them from this by not allowing them to send out a misleading message.

Clothing manufacturers participate in the push for pseudo-mature clothes. As soon as children leave the little boys or little girls clothing department, it is hard to find styles that are suited for a 7-, 8-, or 9-year-old. The child in a size 8 must wear the same styles as a child in size 16.

Parents always have the right to set a dress code, just as they have the right to guide other behavior. At this age you control what she buys. Yet you might be able to find a compromise that pleases both of you. Maybe she can buy a top with thin straps and agree to wear it with a shirt over or under it.

My grandmother, a wise and nonconfrontational woman, upon seeing me in a bikini I bought at age 16 commented, "That's lovely and what else do you wear with it?"

Dressing your daughter in clothes that are different from her peer group's may elicit some teasing from her classmates and may even cause certain children not to include her in their social group.

This may be to your and her advantage, however. It may cause her to be with the children who are given the gift of childhood by their parents — parents who insist that their children look and act their age and stage.

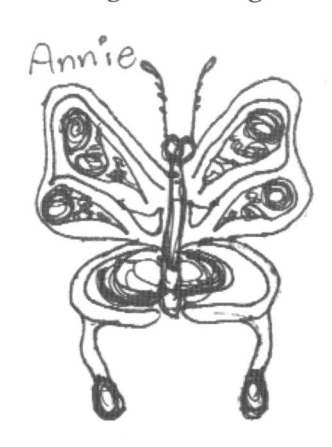

Preteen and mom disagree on style and fit of clothes

Q. I recently tried to shop with my 11-year-old daughter. She wanted a pair of pants that didn't fit her. They were too expensive for me to let her buy a pair of pants that she would hate in a month when the fashion changed from baggy and falling off her waist to correct fit.

She insisted that her friends wore their pants baggy and that she would "look like a dork" if she wore pants that fit.

How do I convince her that the pants she desires are unflattering?

How do you shop with a preadolescent girl and resolve the differences between what mother wants to buy and what the child thinks is cool?

A. Pre- to early adolescence is a time when both boys and girls are sensitive and insecure about appearance. They want to look exactly like the social group they desire to be with or they feel left out and awkward.

The peer group as a whole establishes fashion trends that are different from what adults wear.

They are trying to separate from the parents they have been dependent upon during their early years and make the transition to independence. Wearing different clothes is symbolic of the break.

Acknowledge to your daughter that you understand the fad of baggy pants but tell her that she can wear the style without wearing the wrong size.

Tell her that she may have the pants in the right size or not at all. It is her choice. Say this matter-of-factly, not with anger.

Do, however, let your child blend in with her peers. Don't make her wear frilly dresses when her friends wear blue jeans.

It generally doesn't pay to buy an outfit that

mother likes but daughter doesn't. It will hang in the closet unworn.

If your daughter does not feel comfortable in it, it is not wise to make her wear it. She will have more difficulty facing her peer group if she doesn't feel pretty.

Try to find a point of compromise. Usually there is something in the store that you both like. If not, the problem goes deeper than just choosing clothes.

If your child chooses a style that is totally unacceptable to you, you have a right not to pay for it. Parents always have the right to say no.

Your child won't like it for the moment, but she will appreciate your protection in the long run, and she will have the courage to do the same for her children.

Most preadolescents do not choose outrageous styles. That comes later in adolescence.

If cost is the factor — if she wants brand name and you want generic — give her the cost of the clothes you would buy and let her match the difference for the more expensive brand out of her own money.

To avoid making her hear that she is unattractive, make a neutral comment rather than a personal one. "The pants are too big," rather than, "You look ridiculous in those pants."

Appeal to her desire to be older. "The high school kids aren't allowed to wear pants that hang low." Educate her. "Each manufacturer makes a slightly different size and fit. In brand X, I think you need a size Y."

Don't expect a resolution. If you wait for her to agree with you and say, "You're right mom," you will probably wait until she is 25.

Just make your point in a matter-of-fact tone and accept that she cannot agree with you right now. It is OK to agree to disagree.

If shopping for clothes becomes a battleground, you might want to send someone else to shop with her. Sometimes a grandmother or an aunt can make the same guiding comments without arousing the defensiveness that a mother's comments evoke.

Separate poor spelling from other academic grades

Q. My 10-year-old child cannot seem to learn to spell. I have accepted his low grades in spelling, but both he and I find it frustrating that he cannot get a good grade in science or history because the teachers deduct points for spelling errors. Do you think they should make allowances for his spelling problem?

A. There are both pluses and minuses in adapting academic expectations for a given child. When you expect less of a child, you send a message that you don't think he is capable of doing what other children can do. This is a powerful message to a child whose self-esteem may already be shaky.

On the other hand, if he never has any experience with success at academics, he begins to see himself as incapable anyway.

For the child who can do well at science and history, not taking off points for spelling in his academic subject can limit his low self-esteem to one content area, while he achieves in other areas. It is better for the child to say, "I can't spell," than to think of himself as "dumb."

Sometimes though, it is not the child who is distressed but the parent. Most parents are intensely bonded to their children, and the child's failure can make the parent feel bad. Before you adapt a curriculum, try to sort out whose feelings you are sparing.

If your worry is just about his grades, you may need to relax and put your worries aside. Elementary school grades don't follow the child to college or later life.

If low grades motivate a child to try harder, then parents and teachers should not bail the child out. The child will benefit more from the lower grade that pushes him to learn than from an adapted grade that allows the problem to remain.

Some children, however, just give up when they don't do well. It is this child who needs a break in points off for spelling for academic subjects, so that he doesn't give up on all school and learning.

Some parents feel that their child must make an A in every subject. They will prefer to limit the child's exposure to material to only that which he can master easily enough to get that perfect report card.

Some children in challenging curricula may never make an A but are still mastering a good deal of content. The child who can hang on with a low B or a high C may gain more from the material he is exposed to than if he were placed in a less demanding class and never saw or heard the harder concepts.

In many schools the honor roll is based on grades alone, without noting if the grade was for an advanced class or a remedial one. Some parents find it so important to see their child's name on the honor list that they will lower expectations to the point where their child can get an A. Schools may need to weight grades for honor roll purposes so that parents and students don't choose less learning in order to get more recognition.

Be careful about the attitude you convey about grades and achievement. You don't want your child to limit himself in life to only what he can do easily. Growth comes from stretching to master new skills, but those skills must be within the child's ability to reach for them.

If a child is suffering from constant failure, parents and teachers should step in to help. No child can happily attend school if he fails most tests and assignments each day.

Homogeneous classrooms, where children are grouped by ability, can provide the child a chance to shine at his level.

Minor adaptations, such as not counting off for spelling during science and history tests, can go a long way toward giving the child the experience of academic success while he isolates and works on his problem in spelling.

Should only gifted children go to school?

Q. My fifth-grade son plays baseball. He and most of the other boys on the team play well, but there is one boy who just can't seem to hit the ball or catch at all.

Why don't these parents take their child off the team? He holds everyone else back, and he can't be having any fun.

A. Sports have moved from informal games arranged by children to organized teams and leagues. In the process of keeping score not only for the game but also for the season, there has been increased pressure to include only the best players.

Few would argue that classroom education should be limited only to gifted children, yet some parents ask that only athletically gifted children get to play team sports.

Childhood is a time to try out many activities and gain many skills. It is a sampling time, when the child tastes a broad range of things so that he can find his talents and his interests. Most children should have the opportunity to play, especially if they want to.

Children are developing beings, not finished products. They can't improve their skills without the opportunity to practice. Many children who begin sports as weak players go on to develop some degree of proficiency with time.

In the early grades, many children have the opportunity to play team sports. During this time, both the child and his teammates learn who is athletic and who is not.

If being a weaker player doesn't bother the individual child, the adult organizers of the team should not exclude him.

A league can easily absorb less-coordinated players as long as it distributes these players evenly over the many teams in the league so that one team doesn't consistently lose.

Most children, however, quickly learn where their talents lie, and they self-select activities that showcase their strengths.

The parent of the less-athletic child should not encourage his child to abandon sports, but he should provide opportunities for him in areas where he has a chance to do well. Many children who are not team sports athletes are good swimmers or tennis players or excel at chess or computers.

If a child comes home saying that he is the worst member of the team or if he is experiencing taunts from his teammates, then the parent might need to step in to protect him.

While most children will leave a bad situation on their own, a passive child might not. It is the parent's role to look at the big picture and to see where his child fits in. It is the parent's role to evaluate how an immediate experience will affect his child long-term.

The parent should evaluate the relative benefits of staying with the team to improve versus steering him to other activities where he will have success and friends.

Pulling him off the team should always be done for the good of the individual child and not to better the team's chances of making the playoffs. The purpose of kiddie league sports is child development — not trophies.

As children grow through the teen years, the selection process becomes more meaningful. While the young child needs exposure to many skills, in adulthood we pick just a few things that we do well.

By high school, an adolescent should be able to evaluate his talents and to put his limited time toward developing what he does best.

At this point, although it can hurt to be rejected, team selection is not a harmful thing, provided that the selection process is fair.

The parent of a child who does not make the team should be on hand to remind the rejected child of his strengths and to steer that child to other self-esteem enhancing experiences.

Help child to put loss into a framework

Q. We lost our home in a tornado. We were able to save a few of our belongings but also lost a lot. Our 8-year-old child is quite upset over the loss. How can we best handle this situation with her?

A. Children need help putting a loss into a framework. Children tend to live for today, and if today is upsetting, it feels as if life will be like that forever. To not have her toys right now may feel as if she will never have toys again.

Tell your daughter that while it will take time to rebuild, there will be a new house and new toys. Life will be as it once was, even if some things are new and different.

Change can be difficult, and some children will need help accepting new ways. Help your child see some similarities to her old life, and help her to see that some things might even be better. While she may miss her old home, she might enjoy a bright new one.

Help children to see the positive. Actively teach your daughter to see the glass as half full and not half empty. If no lives were lost, point this out as the most important thing. If a special toy or heirloom was saved, let your child know that you feel fortunate.

Let your daughter to talk to other victims. Sharing the experience will help her to feel less alone in her sadness. In speaking to others, she may discover something that she hasn't lost. Special friends are often formed out of shared experiences.

Replace her favorite toys as soon as you can in order to put some security back in her life. You do not need to shower her with gifts at this time, but if she can't sleep without a special teddy, do try to find a new one that will please her.

Establish a routine as

quickly as possible. Some parents think that a child should miss school after a trauma, but for most children the more quickly they return to school, ballet and Scouts, the sooner the child leaves the trauma behind and returns to her reality. When normal routine is re-established, the tornado returns to being only a day in her life, rather than seeming like all of it.

Children who were only peripherally affected by the storm should not be expected to have nightmares, but children who witnessed death or who were trapped for some time may have difficulty falling asleep or staying asleep.

If your child awakens frightened, comfort her by repeating that the danger is past and she is safe once again as she has always been before. Don't try to argue that her dream is not reality. The specific theme of her nightmares is not the issue. The dream is the expression of her fear and insecurity, and this is what you need to address.

Listen to your daughter when she tries to talk about what happened.

Repetition is part of the healing process. Don't, however, allow her to use the trauma as an excuse for school absence or for impolite behavior. The trauma is only one aspect of her life, and the other expectations upon her continue.

She still can be expected to answer parents and teachers respectfully and to do her schoolwork, even if she is upset about the storm.

Find supports for your own needs. You may need adult friends to share your experience with. Let your children know when you are too preoccupied with things you need to do to hear their stories.

Just be sure that you provide some other time for them to tell you. It is OK to say, "I can't listen right now, but I'd like to hear about your day as soon as I make this phone call."

Give your child something to do to actively take charge of her own safety. Talk about what to do in the next storm, but don't have daily tornado drills. Find a balance between expecting the normal and being prepared for the unusual.

Worried child's self-talk is scary, negative and critical

Q. My 8-year-old daughter tends to worry about everything. She thinks she will fail every test at school. She thinks her friends won't like her. She's afraid of the dark and hates to go anywhere alone. How can we get her to relax?

A. Worry exists because it serves a purpose. It allows the person to anticipate danger and avoid it.

The problem arises when the child or adult fails to see the difference between situations which pose no threat and those that do. He or she approaches every situation as if it were a dangerous one.

Worry is a conversation with yourself — a self-talk, if you will. The content of that talk shapes how you feel. Worriers' self-talk is scary, negative and critical, while non-worriers stress positive, optimistic and "can-do" ideas.

The worrying child sees the worst in every situation. If she goes to the mall, she anticipates becoming separated from mother. When she goes to sleep at night, she feels quite sure someone will break in.

Worrying children focus only on their worry and tend to blot out all else. The child who worries about being lost at the mall can't see the toys or clothes in the stores.

She keeps her eye on mother, out of a fear that mom might disappear. She fails to enjoy the scene of shoppers and decorations. She sees only the peril.

Worriers tend to be passive. They tend to see the world as jostling them about. They feel they have little control over what happens to them. Rarely do they try to influence or execute a better outcome.

They think in a cycle of worry, without a way out. The worrying child is not confident that he can study for a test and avoid failure. He feels that failure just happens and is beyond his control.

Worriers tend to exaggerate risks. They see only the downside without considering the possibility of a good outcome. They see the glass as half empty and never half full.

They tend to worry repetitively about things they cannot change, while happier children separate out what they can do something about and what is beyond their control and not worth their effort.

While worriers mentally replay a frightening situation over and over, putting themselves into increasing levels of anxiety, optimistic children think of solutions.

If they are scared of riding a bike to the store alone, they will call a friend, while the worrywart will just think of all the scary possibilities and avoid going.

To help a worrier, you must break the pattern of thought and help the child see his own power in determining the outcome.

Fix real problems for him. If your child is a weak student who fears failing, get her a tutor and teach her study skills. If she worries about drowning, teach her to swim.

Actively teach her to see the glass as half full rather than half empty. When she gets into a negative pattern, ask her how else she might view the situation in a more positive light.

Practice seeing every situation as both positive and negative. Discuss these as options she can take.

Ask her to think of how a friend, parent or grandparent might view the same situation. Ask her to talk herself through the situation as the other person might see it.

Tell her directly and openly that you are powerful and that you will protect her from harm. Tell her also that she has the skills to protect herself.

Let go and give her the freedom to be independent to the degree that is appropriate for her age. Children who never fend for themselves worry that they are incapable of being alone. They never get to practice skills and experience their own power.

Curbing unkindness is part of raising children

Q. My daughter gets picked on and teased at school. She is a good student. She has friends and she is attractive. She is not an obvious target, yet peers sling hurtful comments. Why?

A. From the situation, I would guess that your daughter is in the fifth or sixth grade at school. These are the years when the mean comments are at their peak.

Preschoolers are sometimes insensitive, but they typically do not mean to hurt. They may ask about differences quite bluntly, but they don't consciously take aim and shoot.

In the early elementary school years, children are generally accepting of a large number of children in the group. It is not until somewhere around the fourth to fifth grades that children become mean with the aim of bettering themselves at someone else's expense.

Children are mean because they are allowed to be so. Curbing unkindness is part of raising children, and children need to be raised and not just allowed to grow. The parents and teachers who come down hard on a child who says unkind things tend not to have this kind of open unkindness in their homes and classrooms.

The child who gets away with saying, "Your shirt is ugly," will say it again. The child who is told that that is rude and unacceptable might think twice before repeating that behavior.

Unkindness is modeled. While most adults have learned not to openly say rude or hurtful things to another person, many will say unkind things behind the other person's back. Often these things are said at home, where the child hears them and incorporates the parent's values. Our children behave as we do. Our words are less-powerful teachers than our behavior is.

Older elementary school children are mean in part because they are together all day long. They become a cohesive group with insiders and outsiders. By middle school, students are typically scrambled into different groups each hour as the bell rings for a new class. It is harder for the cool kid to re-establish his power with a new group of children seven or eight times per day.

As a parent, you probably will have little impact on changing the children who are mean to your child. Most are that way because they have parents who are either ineffective or who actively encourage meanness and competition with the thought that being aggressive will make their child come out on top.

Although you might want to let the parent of the offending child know about the situation, concentrate on inoculating your child from the barbs. Build your child's self-esteem by working on skills that she can be proud of. De-emphasize the importance of being popular and stress the value of having a few close and loyal friends.

Help her to see that she is special. Develop talents and skills that make her stand out. Popular children tend to be those who are very average. They don't stand out in any way, but they do represent the most typical interests of the group.

Give your daughter perspective by showing her that in the future, her skills will help her in life while being popular won't matter when she is out of school.

Do be sure that your child has basic social skills. Don't let her set herself up as a target for teasing by calling negative attention to herself. Beyond this, encourage her to have an inner sense of who she is that is not peer dependent.

The meaning of money is learned from parents

Q. My children learn about making change and converting from dollars to cents at school, but they don't seem to teach the value of money. When we go to a store, they want everything they see. What is the best way to teach children about money?

A. Children learn about money from their parents. When they see how parents budget, spend, save and make choices about purchases, children absorb parents' values and imitate their behaviors.

A good way to teach about money is to give your children control over some amount of money. By giving a regular allowance, you remove yourself from the decision of whether or not they can buy a thing they want.

If they ask you for it, you can simply say, "Do you have enough money for that? Are you sure that is what you want to spend your money on?"

Often simply having to spend their own money is enough to curb the endless string of requests. It is surprising how much more conservative a child's spending becomes when it is his own money he is spending.

For an allowance to work as a teaching tool, children should get just enough money to cover their weekly expenses, such as school lunches, plus a small amount extra for luxuries.

If the child gets so much money that he can still buy everything he sees, you have lost the lesson. Similarly, if he gets only enough for necessities, then he doesn't gain the experience of budgeting, saving and making choices.

Allowance should usually not be tied to chores. If you pay a child for doing chores, then you are saying, "If you are willing to forgo the money, you do not have to do your share of the family work." If he does not do his chores, leading him to lose his allowance, are you willing to let him go hungry? Probably not.

Better is to give allowance with no strings attached and to expect basic chores to be done as part of family membership. Extra tasks can be done for pay, to help the child earn money for more expensive or longer term goals.

Include your children in family finances to some degree. You do not need to share your exact salary, but it is helpful for a child to know, "Dad has lost his job, and we won't be able to eat out every Wednesday like we used to do until dad has a new job."

A child can better tolerate limited birthday presents knowing the family's financial limitations than when he is kept in the dark and suddenly gets less than he has come to expect from previous years.

Six-year-olds can learn about bank accounts. They can be told that the bank pays you money for your money because they can lend money out at a higher rate. By age 12, it is a good idea to expose children to other investment options, sharing with them your feelings about risk and reward. Many schools participate in the stock market game, a national, computer-based program where children choose stocks and pretend to invest. This can provide a valuable experience provided that it is carried out over enough time so that the child sees both gains and losses.

Teach your child a balance between spending and saving. Often, adults are better at one or the other. For a child to have a healthy attitude toward money, he must not only learn to save but also to spend wisely.

You might want to read consumer magazines with your child or simply talk out loud when you go to the grocery store, explaining why you choose one size or brand of a product over another.

Children are not born knowing how to use money. They are taught spending, saving and consumer choices by their parents. Share your knowledge with your child.

Age 12 to 18
The bridge to adulthood

Adolescence is often the stage that parents find the most difficult. The difficulty arises from the fact that the parent has the least control and the child has the most mobility of any stage of childhood.

This is the stage where if all has gone well, your child is delightful and independent. He can think abstractly and hold a conversation of interest to an adult.

If there have been problems all along, they will be evident now in reckless behavior, self-centeredness and lack of motivation to develop the job skills needed for adulthood.

Some parents have a hard time giving their child freedom as he reaches the late teens. Parents have spent so many years protecting and nurturing that they cannot readily change roles and let go.

The joy of parenting an adolescent is watching your child leave home, a confident individual, ready to go forth to make his mark in the world as an adult.

Teachers select students for for advanced classes

Q. My sixth-grade child is a good student and will soon start junior high school, where both regular and advanced courses are offered. How do parents decide which level class the child should take? Is a B in an advanced class better than an A in a regular class?

A. Most advanced-class placement is by recommendation from the teacher. Teachers see large groups of children of the same age and generally have a very good sense of where an individual child falls within the group. In most cases, you won't go wrong if you follow teacher recommendation.

In some cases, you may know of a strength your child has that he has not demonstrated well at school. This is particularly true of children who are late to mature in organization and focus.

Some young children are not meticulous about detail, yet master the general concept very well. These children may not have high test grades due to sloppy errors, yet do know the material being taught. Many of these children will mature as they enter junior high and can benefit from the stimulation of an advanced class. The performance of a bright but sloppy 10-year-old can easily improve as the child acquires maturity at age 13.

Parents need to look not only at each individual class choice, but also at the child's overall schedule. In some schools, each department makes a placement recommendation in its own subject, yet nobody considers the total number of advanced classes recommended. The math teacher may not know that your child has also been selected for advanced English. The child who can handle one advanced class might not be ready for the load of three advanced classes, even if he or she is capable of advanced work in each single subject.

The school guidance counselor can be a valuable resource in helping you to make schedule decisions with and for your child. Many advisors, however, have a formula — for example: "Don't take more than two advanced classes." While formulas can be helpful as a general guideline, the parent's job is to look at his child as an individual. Some gifted children may be bored in less than all advanced classes.

Testing can be of help in making a decision about advanced class placement. The child who scores well above the cutoff on tests of achievement and IQ will likely handle advanced work with ease. The child who is right at the cutoff might handle one advanced class, but not several.

Whether a B in an advanced class is better than an A in a regular class depends upon what you want to get out of the class. Generally, exposure to more information will leave your child will a larger knowledge base than mastering a larger percentage of a weaker curriculum.

This assumes that the child can understand the subject matter presented. While a B in an advanced class may be better than an A in a regular class in terms of the amount learned, an F in an advanced class is not better than a B in a regular class.

Colleges will look not only at the grades your child receives from the ninth grade on, but also at the difficulty level of his courses. The brochures of the most selective colleges specifically state that they expect the students' grades to come from the most rigorous courses.

State colleges, on the other hand, typically look only at grade point average. Yet even in this case, your school might weigh advanced and AP courses more heavily in computing class rank and GPA.

The general rule is to give your child exposure to the best classes he can take without overwhelming him. Choose with your child's interests and ability in mind. Don't place your child to compete with your friends.

Behavior and emotions are separate issues

Q. My 13-year-old son came to me and told me that the window in his room "got broken somehow." His hand was bleeding, and I know that he did it in anger but was sorry that he had done it.

During this semiconfession, he apologized for all his other minor unpleasant behaviors in the past weeks, yet he could not admit that he had broken the window. He has never done this before and is generally a good kid.

His father and I are in the middle of a divorce, and I know that he is angry and struggling. To make matters worse, he left right after the broken window incident for a weekend with his dad, so that dealing with the incident will have to be postponed for at least two days.

Should I confront him as soon as he gets home Sunday night and make him tell me that he broke the window? What should I say? Should he have to pay for it?

A. Your child is angry and struggling to deal with the changes in his family. While you do need to address his anger and his refusal to admit what he did, there is no rush to do it the minute that he walks in the door.

Instead, re-establish your relationship first. Nurture him with words and in tangible ways such as cooking a meal for him or turning down his covers at bedtime. Give him the message that you love him before you ask him to tell you why he broke the window.

To admit to something which he fears will cause the loss of his mother's love is too scary for a child. Any child can be pushed to lie if the stakes are high enough, and there is nothing higher than loss of parental love.

His security has been shattered by your divorce. This loss of security is what his anger is about. Before you can discipline, you have to make him feel secure again.

Then you do need to address the out-of-control episode or you will have taught him that his behavior is acceptable.

Many parents make the mistake of thinking that because there is a reason for a child's anger, you can't set consequences. This is not true. Without consequences the undesired behavior will happen again.

The behavior and the emotions are separate issues to deal with. You need to help him with his feelings while at the same time teaching him that explosive behavior is unacceptable.

Instead of asking him if he broke the window — which is likely to lead to a denial — tell him that you know that he did it. Ask him if his hand still hurts to show your concern about him. Let him know that you are aware of the feelings that led up to his explosion but do tell him that breaking a window is not a good way to express his anger.

Feelings and needs do not take away the fact that it will cost money to fix it. Tell him that he will have to pay half the cost of the glass repair and that you will pay the other half. By making him pay half, you reduce the cost to an amount that a 13-year-old can realistically handle.

You punish him with logical consequences because it will cost money to make the repair — it is not an arbitrary fine you are imposing. At the same time, by paying some of it for him, you give the message that you are in there with him. I would not do this for a child with repeated explosive behavior. Paying half is a one-time lenience.

To avoid repeated episodes of explosive behavior, be sensitive to issues or times of stress that lead to his explosion. This one seems to have been triggered by the transition from mother's home to father's. Give him permission to go, so that he does not struggle with guilt when he leaves you. Don't make him feel that you will cry while he is gone or that you will be out dating. These are difficult issues for the "newly divorced" child, that he will deal with over time.

Be lenient with your child's feelings but firm on his behavior.

Parent must set limits to create a likable child

Q. We recently went on vacation with another family. I watched the 12- and 15-year-old children argue with their mother over every little thing. Some of the decisions were not very important, but the children didn't seem to have any respect at all. They debated and evaluated the merits of each request from her. She is not happy with her relationship with her children. How can I help her?

A. The pleasant part of parenting is nurturing and giving. Most parents love to offer their child a gift and see the happy face in return. We enjoy saying yes. While much of parenting can be this way, not all of it can be. If parents don't set limits, they create a child they find difficult to live with and who is difficult to like.

Popular psychology has taught that it is good to run a family as a democracy. This only works in families with two parents and one child — and not very efficiently even there. Giving the child the impression that he has an equal vote makes him feel that his opinion is weighted equally with that of his parents. Without respect for parental authority, there is endless debate over small matters. Parents who run their family in this way find themselves frustrated with how much time it takes to get simple tasks done.

This doesn't mean that we return to autocratic authority or to beatings. The successful parent can say, "Do it because I say so," but he has other techniques in his repertoire as well. He also has a mutually respectful relationship with his child.

Let's look at some examples: Four-year-old Lisa had happily attended an eight-week summer school program where she had become quite attached to her teacher. On the last day of the program, she refused to get out of the car, crying and clinging to her mother.

Should mother say, "Get out of the car and go to school?" I don't think so. This is not an example of a disobedient child, but one who is emotionally distressed. Understanding her real fear on the last day of her program and addressing it solved the problem.

The explanation, "Teachers go on to new classes, but mommies never go away," was enough to quiet her and allow her to attend her program. This child was not debating with her mother about school attendance; she was expressing a fear that if her teacher could leave her, maybe her mother would too.

Contrast this to the following situation: A 12-year-old has a friend who attends a different school. The friend has the day off and is going to the lake for the day. The 12-year-old wants to go with her friend, but her school is in session. She tells her mother, "What difference can one day of school make?"

This is not an emotional problem, and parent should respond with a statement that reflects parental authority over the decision. "Today is not a vacation day for you, and you must go to school." The parent should cut off any further argument from the child. Discussion will lead nowhere. This is the time for the parent to say, "There will be no further discussion."

While it is important to listen to a child's needs and feelings, it is not necessary to discuss a nondebatable issue. In this case, the parent must take charge.

Children feel more secure when there are rules and limits. Parents who set limits create children who are likable. A balance between listening to children who are distressed but ending discussion when children seek permission for behavior outside the rules will create a family that enjoys each other and makes decisions efficiently and effectively.

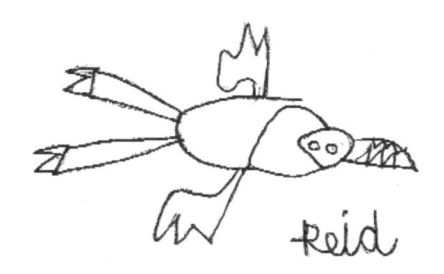

Parents should be parents — not peers

Q. I went to college in the turbulent 1960s. During that time I experimented with drugs. I don't think we were as aware at that time of the deleterious effects. Now I have a child who is about to become a teenager. I do not want him to do the things I did. How do you tell your child not to do something that you are guilty of? How much do you share with her about your own experience?

A. Parents should be parents and not peers. If you are to gain your child's respect, you need to set a good example.

"Do as I say and not as I do" doesn't work in child rearing. Your child is likely to hear your confession as evidence that you did the very behavior that you are forbidding him to do. He will not necessarily hear your confession as a way to learn from your experience, but as permission to do as you did.

There are some times in the course of instructing your child when it is helpful to share your personal experience. This usually happens when the child has already done the misdeed — not as a preventive measure. Most parents who tell their child about their own transgressions before there is reason to discuss the topic do it as a confession or as an attempt to show their child that they are or were "cool."

Children do better when they see parents as strong and infallible. The child doesn't wish to see his parent as a peer. He is confused by the parent's confession. He fares better when the role model is clear. While adolescents of adequate ability are capable of dealing with shades of gray, it is easier for them to sort out right from wrong when the values presented are black and white.

If you must share your experiences with your child, it would be better to do so when he has reached adulthood. By then his values and behaviors are formed. Until then, let your young teen see you as an unblemished example. After his personality is solidly formed, you have more options.

Examine your own need for confession and choose an adult to confess to. Like the adulterer who tells his spouse "for the sake of honesty," you seem to need to "come clean" at your child's expense. The adulterer feels better after the telling, but the betrayed spouse feels worse.

Most children attend a drug awareness education program at school. Reinforce what he is taught there without ambivalence. The fact that you may have experimented does not change the risk for your child.

Watch your child's peer group for evidence of drug abuse and remediate weak academic or social skills so that your child can feel good about himself. Drug abuse often begins as a way for vulnerable children to be included into the drug-using social group when other groups of children won't accept them.

If your child does try drugs as he gets older, you may at that time use your experience to tell him that he can stop. At this time you are not giving permission to start (as an earlier confession would have conveyed). You are telling him that one episode of abuse doesn't need to lead to a permanent habit. Reinforce the negatives of drug abuse and point out all that you have achieved that you would not have had you continued on that path.

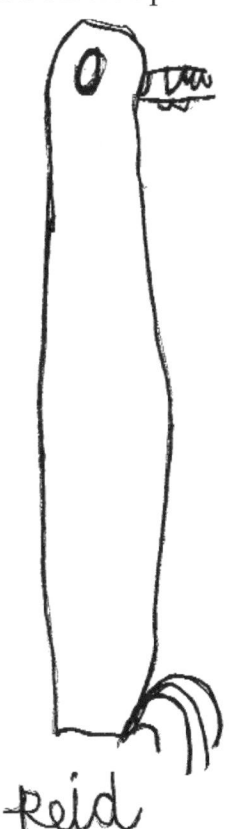

Assess child's effort at schoolwork — not grades

Q. My son, who is in the 10th grade, is a good kid. He has had excellent grades in the past, but this year he has started to have some B grades. The low grades are in advanced classes at a competitive high school. In his regular classes, his grades are A's.

I went to a selective college and I want the same for my son. I'm afraid that with B's he won't get in. When I push him to do better he gets teary and is upset with me.

He is about to turn 16 and we were planning to get him a car, but now I wonder if we should hold off buying a car for him until his grades improve.

Should he drop back from advanced classes to regular ones to get the grades he needs to get into the colleges we want for him? Should I just back off and let him be?

A. It is not the grades that parents should look at but the effort the child is putting into his schoolwork.

If a child is studying, turning in assignments and attending class, then he is doing his job. The grades follow from effort.

Beyond putting in the study time in a goal-directed manner, the child has no control over the outcome. No child should be punished for something that is not within his control. Punishment should be reserved for intentional defiance.

By the same reasoning, you should not withhold the car as punishment. You need to think what you are punishing him for.

If he is studying to his maximum, what can he do to earn the car? You cannot increase his performance with increased pressure to perform, but you can increase his anxiety.

This may backfire for you, as anxiety can decrease test performance.

Excessive parental pressure often leads to

depression or rebellion.

If your goal is admission to a selective college, he will need the advanced classes. The college admission officers are wise to the fact that an A in a regular class is not the same as an A or even a B in an advanced class.

Selective colleges look at more than just grades. Many students who are selected for admission have more than one or two B's.

It is better for your son to stay in advanced classes if his teachers think that the classes are appropriate for him.

Encourage him develop a special talent, such as music, debate, journalism or athletics, if he has the time to do so.

Do not, however, push a child to remain in advanced classes if they are too difficult for him. It is better to attend a level of class that is comfortable, where he can master the material, than to be lost in a class that whizzes by.

If you are in doubt about the suitability of the class for your son, ask his teacher. Teachers see large groups of children of the same age and have a good sense of where your child fits in with his peer group.

Children should not be expected to get straight A's. With only a few exceptions of very bright children who can get all A's in all advanced classes without excessive stress, if your child is making all A's beyond the fourth grade, the curriculum is not challenging enough for him.

The balance of A's and B's suggests that he is suitably challenged but not overwhelmed.

You refer to his B's as "low grades." B is not a low grade. B shows mastery of more than 80 percent of the curriculum, which, in an advanced class, is quite a bit of material. It is the knowledge and not the grade that is important for life.

Go ahead and get your son his car if he is a good kid who studies hard. Give the control of his future back to him if you want him to learn responsibility. It is he, and not you, who is in the 10th grade.

Even if the college you attended does not accept him, he will find a school where he can get a fine education.

Song choices reflect child's beliefs

Q. Some of the lyrics of the songs my 15-year-old son listens to are offensive to me. How much do song lyrics really affect a child's way of thinking? How can I limit what he listens to? How do I change his taste in music?

A. Music is a powerful way to teach. Just think about what you remember of what you learned at age 3 or 4. Most likely you can still sing all of the songs you learned at that age. You probably can recite little of what you learned at that time in words.

Your child learns material at school from only one or two repetitions. Imagine the impact of words set to music that he hears over and over again.

While your child may argue, "It's just a song, mom," you should not take it lightly. There are many songs out there, and your son is selecting from among his options. The songs he chooses reflect his thinking and his choice of peer group.

Teens flock together around music choices, and if your son is listening to music with violent or sexually exploitative lyrics, unless he is withdrawn and alone, he is likely to be hanging around with a peer group that does the same.

Parents always have the right to set limits on behavior they think is inappropriate. Do not be afraid to parent. If you do not like your son's choices, step in.

You will not be able to control what he hears outside the home, but you will be able to take a stance on what is played and heard in yours.

Even if he continues to listen to bad lyrics outside the home, you will have cut his exposure down considerably. You will have given a clear message that you think the lyrics and the concepts expressed to be unacceptable.

If you allow him to listen to offensive lyrics in your home, you are condoning it.

Some parents back off wearily stating, "You have to pick your battles." While it is true that you have to let some things go, you cannot let basic values slip by without comment. It is one thing to let a bed go unmade. It is another for you to let your child listen to violent or sexually exploitative words.

The issue is not only changing his taste in music. The issue is changing his values. A child who respects others does not choose exploitative lyrics.

The child who is drawn toward music with inappropriate lyrics is seeking to have his maladaptive personal belief confirmed as acceptable by a larger group.

I was recently at a Brownie meeting where each 8-year-old girl was asked to name her wish for the world. One child wished for a cure for all diseases. Another wished to be able to meet the Spice Girls.

This presented an opportunity via discussion to shape values and teach concern for the larger group over the needs of one person. By seizing these opportunities as they come up, we shape the values of our children.

You may need to get involved at the level of the underlying problem. The child without friends or the child who has not had much nurturance is an often an angry child who looks for causes on which to attach his anger.

It is difficult but not impossible to go back and nurture a teenager who has missed those basic building blocks of personality earlier in life. Much easier is to start out with a young child and meet his needs for attention, affection and guidance toward kinder, gentler thoughts.

By the time he reaches age 15, you must set firm limits. Listen to every recording that your son owns and remove those that you feel are unacceptable.

Don't make excuses or negotiate. If he lives in your house, he must go by your rules. Offer to replace some of his unacceptable music with some that you can agree on, but do so only if he is cooperative. Don't bribe cooperation but reward it.

Send a child away only from a secure home base

Q. My 14-year-old child is very immature. She does poorly in school although she has academic ability. I am a single parent who has worked outside the home her whole life. She complains that I am not home with her after school, even though she is only home alone for two hours until I get home from work. Do you think that sending her to boarding school would increase her maturity and make her more self-reliant?

A. Although there are situations in which a troubled child can benefit from separation from the family, in most cases you should not send a child away from home, unless he is leaving from a secure base. The children who do best in boarding school are mature and independent children who ask to go away to school.

Except for the child with serious behavior problems who requires therapeutic schooling or the special-needs child who might benefit from specialized training that might not be available locally — such as at a school for the deaf or blind — children should generally not be sent away against their wishes.

If the parent sends a child away when he wants to stay home, the child will experience this as a clear rejection. In most cases, he will sabotage the plans and will misbehave at school until the school calls the parent to take him home.

Some underachievement is caused by a desire to remain dependent. This underachieving dependent child doesn't want to master skills because she doesn't want to be on her own. If this is the case, sending her to boarding school will not increase her maturity and self-reliance. It may lead her to fail in order to be sent home.

If you do send a child away, there is a vast difference between sending a child 1,000 miles away as compared to letting her board at a school in the same city as her home. Being away during the week and coming home on some weekends can be a good transition for some children.

Parents need to examine their own motives when they consider boarding school. Many parents sacrifice to provide the best education they can for their child, and boarding school might offer special opportunities.

On the other hand, the parent who wants to send a child away might simply not enjoy parenting. Your child is likely to sense this and to respond emotionally to your real feelings. She may cling even harder.

If your 14-year-old is unhappy when left at home alone for less than two hours, she is likely to feel worse when asked to be without her parent for weeks on end.

On the other hand, if she is unhappy when left alone at home, she just might find living in a dormitory with other people around all the time to meet her needs.

The success or failure of her stay at boarding school will depend upon her ability to form relationships with both peers and the caretaking adults at the school.

If you want to send your child away to school, begin slowly. Take her to visit a few schools that you are considering. See if the administration will let her spend part of a day at the school, possibly attending classes or other school activities. Most schools will assign her to a buddy. See how she likes it.

Some children will feel better about boarding school once they see the actual school. Others will close themselves off to any positive aspect of the experience, insisting that they don't want to go.

If your child doesn't warm to the idea after exposure, it would be best to seek local education for her.

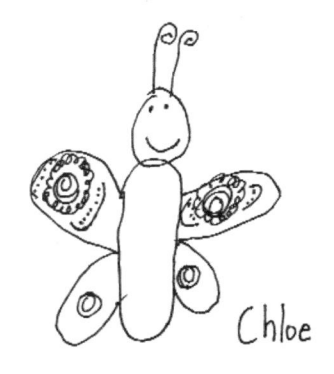

Chloe

Parents don't need to solve problem, only to listen

Q. I am the mother of a 15-year-old girl. My sister's daughter tells my sister everything that is going on in her life. She talks about classes, boyfriends and which of her classmates is smoking pot. When I ask my daughter what happened that day, she says, "Nothing." I am afraid that if she were in trouble she would not come to me. How do you raise a daughter so that she will confide in you?

A. Closeness between mother and daughter begins early in life and is forged out of nurturance. The parent who takes time with her child is more likely to have a close relationship.

The relationship is built upon a certain type of listening. It is easy for the busy parent to tune out the prattle of a young child, but the child who is not heard, soon stops talking. The child who is encouraged to talk when she is 4 and 5 is more likely to continue talking to her mother when she is 10, 14 and 16.

When children bring their problems to a parent, the parent often makes the mistake of feeling that he needs to solve the problem. Actually, a too-quick solution shuts off conversation and is rarely helpful.

Most of the time, if the problem could be solved easily, the child would have already done so. When he is stuck and unable to move on, the tangible solution a parent might offer does little to make the child feel better. His issue is not the tangible one, but the underlying feelings.

Being around at the moment that the child is ready to talk promotes conversation. The child who is distressed when she comes home from school at 3 p.m. may be ready to share her feelings right then.

By 7 p.m., when mom has time to talk, she may have moved on to homework or a telephone conversation with a friend.

On the other hand, parents can set up a regular time for family closeness. Often, children will share their feelings as they are being tucked into bed.

Honesty and trust are important aspects of close relationships. If the parent promises confidentiality and then tells the other parent or a friend, the child might not confide again.

On the other hand, a parent should not get in the bind of keeping secrets from the other parent and can avoid this by not promising confidentiality that she cannot or will not keep.

When your child approaches you and says, "I want to tell you something but I don't want you to tell dad," you might respond, "I will not share personal feminine things with your father, but I cannot promise not to tell him something that both parents should know."

This leaves open some room for using your judgment in what you share, and gives your daughter the message that you will be open and honest with her.

When a parent has an absolutely rigid position on some subject, the child is not likely to share an opposing opinion. For your child to talk to you, he or she must feel that you will at least consider her point of view.

This does not mean that you have to give her permission to do something you feel is wrong, but it does mean that you must at least be willing to hear what she has to say.

This is where the time you put in when your children are young pays off. Guide your children to your values while they are young, and you will have fewer areas of disagreement when they are teens.

Even if you nurture your children, listen actively, respond honestly and are open in your thinking, some children will talk more than others.

Temperament, insight into problems and degree of verbal skill are what the child brings to the relationship. Closeness and willingness to confide come not only from the parent's behavior, but also from the child's.

Teen won't stay in "time-out" chair

Q. There is a lot of material available about how to discipline young children. How do you discipline a teenager? They won't stay in a time-out chair!

A. Teens do not spring forth full-grown. They emerge gradually after 12 years of childhood discipline. The way you raise your child during the early years will create the kind of teenager you have. If you have parented well early on, your teen will need primarily guidance rather than punishment.

Some parents ignore fresh behavior in a 3- or 4-year-old, thinking that it is cute and that he will grow out of it. Unfortunately it doesn't happen this way.

The 4-year-old who can have his own way becomes the out-of-control teenager. Although the behavior is not cute even at age 4, the child may be. By the teen years, no one finds rude and disrespectful behavior cute, and the teen is on a downward spiral of rejection and further angry behavior because of that rejection.

Assuming that you have given lots of love, set firm limits and had high but reachable expectations for your young child, you probably have a pretty decent teen now. It is his push for more freedom that is making you wonder what to do next.

One of the hardest things about parenting is that it requires the parent to change roles as the child grows. In almost everything else we do, the job description remains consistent.

In parenting one must devote oneself intensively to the infant, then gradually let go to share the child with teachers and friends during part of the day during the elementary school years, only to have the role change again in the teen years. The parent must give even more freedom then, while remaining securely and firmly present in the child's life. The successful parent must not only bond to his child but also let go at the right time.

The teen needs a parent who is there but who remains in the background. The parent must know where the child is, and with whom he is, but not necessarily be with him.

By being involved in parent support groups for your child's activities (PTA, band parents' association) you can know his peers and their parents. Your hanging out with his peers, though, will keep him from moving on towards adulthood.

Parents must leave room for a teen to make decisions, even though some of the choices might not be as wise as the ones the parent might make. Unless the decision would cause permanent damage or limit the child's future, he should be given some real-life experience with choice.

The parent who makes all decisions for the teen sends him out into life with little experience. It is from mistakes that the child learns. Of course this only works with a child who is already on the right path. The rebellious child may not be ready yet for adolescent freedom.

If you have raised a basically good teen, you can use what I call "invisible fence" discipline. You draw an imaginary box around the behaviors that are acceptable to you, much as a pet owner invisibly fences his yard. Inside the box are all the allowed behaviors. Outside are the unacceptable ones. The teen never experiences any discipline at all as long as he stays within the limits. It is only when he steps outside your rules that he needs your input.

Because the teen is moving away from the family and out into the peer group, grounding back to home is an effective punishment. Grounding is, in effect, a developmental regression. You are saying, "If you can't handle the freedom of a teen, I will take you back to the restrictions of a child."

Make it clear to your teen that freedom is earned, but be sure that you are ready to let go when he is on the right path.

Maturity determines if 16-year-old may drive

Q. My 16-year-old son wants to get his driver's license. We don't want him to drive yet. Is it fair to refuse to allow him to get his license when he is old enough by law to get it?

A. The law sets a minimum age for driving. It does not say that every person who attains the age of 16 years belongs behind a steering wheel.

Parents should always consider their own child's maturity and readiness for responsibility. They should make a decision based on their own situation without following what "all the other parents" are doing.

If your son demonstrates responsibility in keeping school assignments up to date, keeps his room reasonably clean and avoids inappropriate peers, then he is telling you that he is ready for the adult freedom that comes with driving.

If, on the other hand, he fails at school despite adequate ability to do better, he drops his clothes on the floor when and where he takes them off and he expects you to provide for all of his needs, then you might want to put off letting him drive.

For many teens, a driver's license is a powerful motivator. You can use the privilege of driving to help shape the behaviors you want to encourage.

For the child who tends to be lazy during the summer, you can set up a logical consequence. He can drive but must provide his own insurance and gas.

If he chooses to work to earn this money, then he gets to drive. If he doesn't, then like a younger child, he must stay at home, dependent upon rides from others. The choice is his.

One key indicator of readiness for driving is how the teen handles frustration. The child who puts his fist through the wall when he doesn't get his way is not ready to be behind the wheel of a potentially lethal weapon.

If he can't handle frustration, you should not provide him with an accelerator pedal and thousands of pounds of force.

While coordination and reflexes are at their peak during the late teens, other emotional issues work against safe driving.

Many teens feel invincible. They don't imagine that life can end, and therefore they may take risks that adults would not take. If your teen is reckless in other ways, you might want to hold off allowing him to drive.

If a child is abusing drugs or alcohol, he is giving you a clear sign that he is not ready to drive. He is not ready to drive even when he is not under the influence.

If your child is smoking cigarettes, you can use the leverage of car privileges to discourage this drug. While cigarette smoking does not automatically lead to other drug use, many drug abusers do or did smoke cigarettes.

The majority of teenagers are not reckless. The teen who takes responsibility for getting his school assignments done neatly and on time, who does chores at home without undue fuss, who holds a job in his spare time or who is involved in school government, band or volunteer work is probably ready for increased freedom.

If you are reluctant to give driving privileges to a mature and responsible teen, you may need to examine your own feelings.

Obtaining a driver's license is a developmental milestone for both parent and teen. It allows the child to stray farther from home than he could do without a car.

When a teen drives himself it takes away the time that was once spent in the car in conversation with parents who drove him.

For many parents and children, driving is the last cut of the apron strings before the child leaves home for good.

If you are reluctant to let him get his license, you might want to think: Is it an accident you fear, or do you fear watching your child drive away from home?

Address the real issue, not just the wish to drop out

Q. Our 14-year-old son is a poor student who makes little effort. He plans to quit school when he turns 16, which will be in the 10th grade. We are quite upset about this. How can we make him understand what his life will be like without an education? How can we keep him in school?

A. To keep your son from dropping out of school, you will have to understand the problem he is having staying in. Dropping out of school often can be prevented if the reason for the child's unhappiness at school is understood and addressed.

Most students who drop out of school have struggled academically for years. They suffer daily humiliation from failure, and they are bored because they cannot understand the lessons.

Some dropouts suffer from specific learning disabilities such as dyslexia. These students find school to be a daily confrontation with the skills they are lacking, making them feel ever worse about themselves as each day passes.

On some level, they understand their strengths and long to be out in the adult world where they can do only what they do well, rather than being tested weekly on the broad range of skills needed for school success.

Other students drop out because their home is so troubled that they can't keep their mind on academic matters. Their thoughts are on the problems at home. It is hard to focus on history or geometry when you are wondering if your father is drinking again and if there will be money for food.

To keep your child in school until graduation, you must first understand your child's problem with school. Listen to what your child is really saying. "I want to drop out," may really mean, "I feel anxious, depressed, worthless, stupid, frustrated or disconnected from others." Treat the real problem, not just the wish to leave school.

Your child's wish to avoid school may be his way of telling you that he has no friends or that he can't deal with the feelings he has about family problems.

He may be telling you how frustrating it is for him to study and to still do poorly on a test. He may be telling you that he is involved with a group of friends he wants to leave but doesn't know how to.

Intervene early. Don't wait until age 16. Most students who eventually drop out have skipped classes for years. If he has failed to connect to the school — if he doesn't participate in extracurricular activities or has frequent absences or behavior problems, he is giving signals of his need for help.

Have a psychologist assess your child's academic problems, and do so now, not after the decision to leave school is final. While some successful students may drop out for reasons of emotional distress, most good students like school and stay in. It is school failure that is the most common cause for dropping out.

When he says he wants to drop out, broaden his choice from "in school or out" to include other options. Children lack the experience to know the alternatives.

Consider changing schools, but only if the program is significantly different from the one he is in. Special education or vocational training might make a difference. Just another school probably will not.

Vocational education, where he can demonstrate his skill at carpentry rather than his failure at creative writing, might give him a degree, an employable skill and self-esteem.

If your child is determined to leave school and will accept no alternative, offer him a leave of absence. Encourage him to see it as a year off rather than a permanent termination. Insist that he take a job and earn money if he is not in school. Don't provide free room and board with laundry service.

Consequences must follow logically

Q. My 16-year-old daughter was caught smoking with her boyfriend. She has never done anything like this before, and we feel it is his influence. She spent the night at a girlfriend's house with our permission, but she and the girlfriend snuck out of the friend's house, picked up four other teenagers, drove around and didn't return until 4:00 a.m. My daughter was the driver in a car we had just bought her six weeks ago.

We were concerned not only about the hour and the sneaking, but the fact that there were six teens in a car with four seat belts. She is otherwise a responsible and sweet child. She works part time and does her homework without prodding from us. How should we handle this? Can we forbid her from seeing her boyfriend? She loves to ride horses, and we are thinking of taking away her horse for a while as punishment. What do you think?

A. The punishment should fit the crime. If her disobedience occurred while she was driving, she should lose the privilege of having a car.

Because she left the friend's home and not yours, until you are certain that she will remain where she tells you she will be, she cannot spend the night away from your home. These consequences follow logically from the crime she committed.

To take away her horse might or might not serve as a motivator for her, but it would not have any connection to what she did. Many teens who are punished by taking away what they value most, simply lose interest in what was taken away.

She can have just as much fun with her friends as with her horse. She just might increase her time with the boyfriend you don't like to take up the time she is not spending riding her horse.

It is difficult for parents to forbid a teen to see a

particular friend and to enforce it. If you are unhappy with her choice of boyfriend, fill her time so she has little left to spend with him.

You might want to increase her riding time or her hours at work. It is much easier to encourage other activities that would not allow your daughter much time with this boy who you feel is a bad influence than to directly forbid her to see him.

Let your daughter know that you are disappointed in her behavior. Comments like, "I'm disappointed in you when you..." or, "You hurt my feelings when you ..." will not harm her but will serve to guide her to your values and standards of behavior.

Let her know how you feel about the boyfriend and his behavior and give her your reasons for your concerns. Make "I" statements ("I'm concerned about his influence on you.") rather than "you" statements, ("You make bad choices.")

Spend time with your daughter in situations that are not conflicted. Be sure to have casual conversations about boyfriends and behavior choices at times when it is not a heated issue.

It is hard to influence a child when both of you are angry. Lessons work better when you are both calm and feeling close.

Ask her what she likes about the boy she has chosen. Let her share her feelings with you without judgment before you point out that he is leading her to behaviors that will harm her. Remind her about how you and her dad feel about smoking.

Require that she save a certain percentage of her salary from work, both to teach her long-range financial responsibility and to reduce the money available for impulsive and inappropriate activities. Be especially careful that she doesn't have enough money to purchase illegal substances.

The task of the late teen years is to break away from family and establish autonomy.

Allow her to have freedom in areas that she handles well, while pulling in the reins at those times she makes poor judgments.

"Do as I say and not as I do" does not work

Q. I found cigarettes in my 14-year-old son's pocket. I am a smoker but I don't want him to smoke. I have also heard that cigarettes are a "gateway drug" leading to other, illegal drugs. Is this true? How do I get my son not to smoke when I do?

A. Cigarettes have been called a gateway drug because looking at children who use illegal drugs, most were found to have started with cigarettes.

This does not mean that all teens who smoke cigarettes will use other drugs. However, children who are smoking because their friends do are also vulnerable to participate with the group in illegal drugs.

The best way to keep your son from smoking is to show him by example. "Do as I say but not as I do" doesn't work. Join a program to stop smoking so that you will have peer support. Do this or he will follow in your smoking footsteps. Your child is likely to notice your concern for him as you try to set a good example.

Smoking is not a pleasurable experience at first. The child has to force himself past the unpleasant taste. Find out why your son wants to smoke and help him with the underlying problem.

When children begin smoking, it is almost always out of an insecurity that leads to a desire to be seen as cool by the group. Unfortunately, the students who smoke are typically troubled children. This is not the group of children you want as your son's support system.

Build your son's self-esteem by really listening to him when he talks. Don't be too quick to offer pat solutions. Do more listening than talking. Include him in those family decisions where his input is appropriate.

Children appreciate having their opinions considered even if their choice does not prevail. Just listening to him confirms for him that you think his opinion matters. Children expect their parents to make the final decision, but he will gain self-respect if you value his thoughts.

Spend time with your child and know his friends. By the teen years, the parent does not have to be present at peer activities, but your child should know that you expect him home at a certain time and that if you have doubts you will be there to check up on him.

Don't send him home to an empty house. He will get the message that no one cares for him, and he will find a group that does. This group may not be to your liking.

Set firm limits. Don't allow contact with older children or peers who are smoking. Know where your child is and with whom so that you can enforce your rules.

Keep your son busy in constructive activities. The child who is at sports, school or church activities, or in the band is not hanging out on street corners. The children who are involved in these activities are less likely to be the ones who are themselves in trouble and who will set a poor example for your child.

Teach your son to handle money wisely. Give him just enough for his needs but not so much that he has cash to spare for cigarettes. If he has to decide between spending his money on a CD he wants or cigarettes, he just might think twice about smoking.

Make him earn his money by doing chores. If the money doesn't come easily, he might be more careful how he spends it. Smoking is an expensive habit. You enable smoking when you give your child too much money.

If he works for his money, require that he save some of it. Excess money is necessary for cigarette or drug abuse.

Offer an incentive not to smoke. The incentive must be something that means more to him than smoking and being accepted by this group of children. A continuing need will work better than a one-time purchase. Know what your child values and individualize the reward for him.

Parents' influence typically is stronger than peers'

Q. I have heard that there is a book that claims that peers influence children more than their parents do. It claims that parents have no power in influencing how their children turn out. Is there any validity to this?

A. The book you are referring to is "The Nurture Assumption: Why Children Turn Out The Way They Do; Parents Matter Less Than You Think and Peers Matter More." In it, the author, Judith Rich Harris, claims that all the previous studies of causal effect between parental actions of nurturance and discipline are based on faulty reasoning. Harris claims that the studies merely show that kind parents have kind children but not that the parenting methods of kind parents cause their children to be kind.

She claims that personality is largely genetic. This part is probably true, but she goes on to say that peers can change your child, while you, the parent, have little influence.

Harris' opinions are based on her own home laboratory. She has one biological child who was easy to raise and who excelled academically, and one adopted child who gave her much trouble before settling down as an adult. From her own experience, with a sample of two (a sample size much too small for a research study), she concludes that nothing the parent does matters and that her child was influenced solely by her peer group.

While she begins her book with a scholarly review of the research, she quickly deviates to a personal and scientifically unsound analysis. She confuses what she calls personality with what is actually behavior.

Personality is a set of enduring traits, largely determined by heredity. Harris states that a child has two different personalities when he behaves one way with his parents and another way with his friends. These are simply two different sets of behavior.

Another fallacy of her argument lies in her assertion that the peer group influences personality. In fact, the child's personality is apparent and formed long before the peer group has much influence on or even contact with your child.

Before age 6, the parent is the focus of the child's world. Peers are not really salient until adolescence, although as early as second or third grade the peers may influence limited areas such as clothing choices.

By the time the child is influenced by peers, he has long ago absorbed the teachings of his home. The selection of peers is caused by the parental values, genetically endowed skills and temperamental factors. The peers don't cause the selection.

The problems Mrs. Harris had with her adopted daughter may well be a function of her not fitting into a home where high academic achievement is valued. The fact that she straightened out as an adult is a tribute to her having absorbed the values she was taught in this home.

Even in Mrs. Harris' home, her two children were raised with different parenting. Mrs. Harris became seriously ill with an autoimmune disease when her younger adopted child was only 6. The older biological child was much further along in her development and well on the road to independence before she lost a functioning mother.

No, parents, you are not off the hook if your child is badly behaved. Certainly there are children who are more difficult to raise than others, and some will turn out badly no matter what the parent does, but most parents can work with their children's shortcomings and soften the sharp edges to make them turn out better than if they were just left to grow.

So keep on setting limits, reading bedtime stories and giving hugs and kisses. Your child is not a blank slate on which to draw, yet nor is he born unyielding and unattached either. Parenting matters.

Child doesn't need to know mom's mistakes

Q. My friend had a turbulent adolescence with drug abuse and promiscuity that produced two children before she was married. She gave the first child up for adoption but is raising the second child in a stable marriage that came when she turned her life around, two years after this child was born.

This child is now 12 years old. The adoption contract for the first child stated that at age 16, she would be told who her birth mother is and would be given help to find her. Now that this child is nearing her 16th birthday, my friend wants to tell her 12-year-old about her past, including telling her about the two illegitimate births. I think that the 12-year-old is too young to understand all this. What do you think?

A. Young children think concretely. Things are either right or wrong without shades of gray. They don't take into account the motivation of the person doing the wrong. To the young child, breaking four cups by accident is worse than breaking one cup on purpose because more cups are destroyed.

Somewhere around age 12, the child begins to be able to think abstractly. He gradually acquires the ability to consider many aspects of a situation at once. He gradually comes to be able to consider the motivation of the offender.

He rethinks right and wrong for himself, rather than just accepting and parroting what parents have told him. This process happens gradually and over time. It is not fully developed at age 12.

Even when abstract thinking is in place, children still fare best when they can see their parents as all-powerful and infallible. The child who has the ability to objectively see the flaws in a friend or teacher still cannot see his or her parent with the same objectivity. The child needs the parent to be a role model who doesn't stray.

It is unlikely that the adopted child will appear unannounced on the doorstep. More likely is that she will make some contact with the mother, and the mother will then have time to prepare her other daughter. The conversation should include an explanation of adoption as a loving act: that the mother who couldn't care for her child but wanted the best for her allowed another couple who wanted a child to give her their best.

It is not wise to discuss promiscuity and illegitimacy with a 12-year-old who has had no personal involvement with these herself. In the current vogue of total openness and honesty, we fail to give our children a childhood where things are as they should be.

Children need to feel that the world is just and that parents do what is right. Adults who do not screen what their children hear make it easy for themselves at the expense of their children.

The parent of these two girls should share the positive parts of the story with her 12-year-old daughter. She can know that she has a sister. She should certainly be told about her sister when the older child makes contact with the birth family and comes into the younger child's life.

Spare the 12-year-old the mistakes of the mother's early adulthood. Telling her too much, in graphic detail, will only teach a 12-year-old that there are alternatives to marriage and family for producing children. While she will certainly know this by age 16, she can still be sheltered at age 12.

Ages and stages of development are not equal and the same. What is honest communication at age 20 is overwhelming at age 10. Share with children only what they are developmentally ready to hear.

Give them a childhood free from adult worries and concerns. Let them see parents as better than they may really be. They will see their parents' shortcomings when they are old enough to handle the news.

Teach child to make wise decisions on his own

Q. My son wants to take Latin next year when he starts foreign language. I would rather that he take French or Spanish, as they are spoken languages. At what point should a parent impose his will? Should the child have the right to choose his own schedule?

A. The parent's job is to guide his child and to teach him how to make wise decisions on his own. If the parent makes all decisions for the child, he will not learn how to consider all his options and how to gather information upon which to base a wise decision.

If the child makes all his decisions on his own, he will make more mistakes than if he has the benefit of the wisdom and knowledge that his parents have acquired over their many years of experience.

One can learn by trial and error — but it takes much longer, and the path is rougher.

Rather than making a decision for your son, sit down and talk with him about his interest in Latin. Explore his passion with him and hear him out. Parents should only set limits after hearing their child's logic.

Share your excitement about a living language. Positive reasons for taking French will have more impact than a parental decree that he can't take Latin. If possible, take a trip to a place where a foreign language is spoken. A trip may awaken his desire to learn a spoken language.

Air your views on the practical aspects of a living language, but don't squelch his purely academic interest. Enjoy the fact that you have a child with a desire to learn. It is less important what he learns than that he is interested in learning.

Taking Latin now will only increase his ability to learn French later. Don't get stuck thinking that he can only learn one thing. Your child sounds like a lifelong learner.

Be careful to guide your child only on the right path but not necessarily your path. Because you would prefer French to Latin doesn't mean your child will only make a good decision if he makes the same one as you would make.

Parents should set limits when the child strays off the path, not when he takes a different but reasonable one.

In some cases the child may even have a better sense of the options. While a parent may focus on one language or the other, or one level of math versus the other, the student may know that one subject is taught by a talented teacher while the other is taught by a weaker one.

A good teacher can make any subject worthwhile and sometimes the ability of the teacher to excite students is more important than which subject he or she teaches. Any knowledge is enriching.

When a choice is between two equal options such as French or Latin, it is best to let the child choose.

Parents can justly intervene when a child is choosing between two unequal choices.

If a student is avoiding subjects that require effort or filling his day with nonacademic classes, then the parent should step in. Here you are not dealing just with a difference of interest but also with how much your child will learn.

A parent should also have a say, but not always the final one, when choosing between different levels of a course. The gifted child who avoids advanced classes should be encouraged to work to his potential.

The average student who chooses to get in over his head by taking numerous hard courses should be steered to trying one challenging course but not so many that he will fail.

Choosing a schedule can be a dialogue in which both parent and child contribute their knowledge and opinions.

Where the choices are between equal options, the child might have the final say. In the end, he is the one who has to take the course.

Restrictions need to be fair and rational

Q. My 16-year-old son got his driver's license three months ago. We have not seen him since. I did not anticipate the degree of freedom he would have when he was allowed to drive. Is it fair to limit the amount and kind of driving a teen living at home can do?

A. Parents always have the right to set limits on their child's behavior and freedom. Teens don't yet have a grasp of all the dangers in life, and they certainly have less experience than adults. The parent's role is to teach and to guide.

There are some ways of establishing rules that work better than others. Force and coercion are likely to lead to power struggles rather than cooperation.

To win the respect and compliance of your teenager, make the rules fair, and be sure that your motivation for establishing the rules is for the benefit of your child and not just to meet your own needs.

The parent who uses rules to force the child into compliance with the parent's interests will create a rebellious child.

The father who was an athlete and who ties the use of the car to his son's choosing sports over participation in the school drama production will not win the child's respect.

The child will quickly see the rule as one meant to control, rather than protect and guide. He will get around the rule when he can.

Parents need to watch their own need to hold on to a maturing child who is moving away from parents and home.

Limiting the child's freedom because the parent has trouble letting go or because he is reluctant to lose the company of the child will not be seen by the child as a fair and rational restriction.

Limiting car privileges just to keep a child at home

may not be fair. Teenagers often want to spend time with friends rather than parents.

While some family obligations teach the child social responsibility and awareness of the needs of others, keeping the child with the family most of his free time holds him back from normal development.

It is age-appropriate for a teen to move away from the family and to form bonds with peers, teachers, coaches and youth group leaders.

In setting limits on driving, consider your child's level of maturity and responsibility in other areas of his life. The student who is doing his best in school, who turns in assignments on time and gets to class punctually, is showing you that he is ready to make some decisions on his own.

The student who skips homework and classes and who chooses inappropriate company is telling you that he needs supervision rather than freedom. It is appropriate to provide external limits on his freedom while he works on developing internal controls.

Even for responsible children it is wise to create a framework for driving privileges. Some parents set boundaries of how far teens can drive away from home. Others limit nighttime driving or driving on highways.

The specifics should be determined by the tolerance of the parents, the driving skills of the child and the reality of where he needs to go. The child with a job across town may need more freedom to travel than the child who goes to school just down the street.

While a child can get a license to drive on his 16th birthday, parents are not obligated to allow every child to have one at this age or to allow unrestricted driving just because the law allows this.

Driving privileges are a powerful motivator for improved behavior for many teens. Driving privileges can be tied to compliance with rules and execution of chores. Just be sure that the behavior expected is within the child's ability and that the rules and chores are for the good of the child not just for parental convenience

The child who does not feel heard stops talking

Q. How do I keep lines of communication open with my 13-year-old?

She seems to be getting increasingly private. I hear her on the phone with her friends telling them all the details of her life, but she doesn't talk to her parents. What can we do?

A. The best way to keep the line of communication open is to listen. The child who doesn't feel heard eventually stops talking.

The most common mistake that parents make is to give a solution too quickly. When the child comes to tell a parent about a bully who is bothering him in class, many parents are quick to say, "Just ignore him."

Most children need to talk about the situation at greater length. The parent has cut off conversation, and the child feels dismissed.

If he were able to perform the simple "fix it," he probably would not have come to you in the first place. We all get entangled in our feelings and can't always take the most obvious step toward fixing the problem.

By talking it out, we often come to our own solution. You can't make the solution happen faster by cutting off talking it out.

Better is to listen to the whole story, drawing your child out with open-ended questions.

"What happened next?" "How did you feel about that?" and "What do you think he was thinking?" will not only encourage conversation between you and your child, but it will also help your child to sort out her own feelings and formulate a plan of action.

Children differ in their ability to communicate. Some children are very talkative while others keep much to themselves. By asking open-ended questions, you can help a child who has difficulty expressing feelings put his thoughts into words.

Some children don't talk because they fear that they will be punished if they reveal something that won't please the parent.

It is important that when your child comes to you with something that he has done wrong, you hear him out before responding.

Consider the fact that he knows that he did wrong. He may need no further punishment. While you don't want to actively reward him for wrongdoing, you can tell him that you are proud that he could tell you about it.

Some children don't talk because they are ashamed of themselves. This child doesn't talk because he feels he has nothing to say about himself that is good.

The child who doesn't talk about his day may be unhappy about grades or about having few friends.

He may not talk because he feels he has nothing to say that will make you proud. He may fear rejection if he shares his real self with you or with others.

Some children withhold communication out of defiance. They realize that not talking hurts the parent. This child may even flaunt the fact that he shares with others but not with his parents. If this is the case, you will see defiance in other areas a well.

Your daughter's choice of friends over parents as confidants may be due to nothing more than her age.

If she shared with you as a young child but now hangs on the phone with her friends, you may be seeing nothing more than normal development.

Teens shift from parents to peers for support as they prepare to leave home and become independent adults.

When your child does come to you to talk, don't feel that you must generate a solution. Most problems don't have a simple solution, and offering one makes you less helpful to your child.

What children want most is someone to listen and someone to allow them to talk so they can think through the problem out loud. Just the experience of talking it out is helpful. A specific action may not be necessary.

First girlfriend is unlikely to be the final choice

Q. My 15-year-old son has a girlfriend — his first. While we do not dislike the girl, she is not as talented or bright as our son. She dresses in a sloppy manner, often wearing torn jeans, and has little sense of style. How can we tell him that we think he should aim higher? Why do you think a gifted and talented boy is choosing a girl who is neither ambitious, talented nor well groomed?

A. Teenage boys are typically insecure in romantic relationships. Because they fear rejection, they are often attracted to girls who give them a clear message of acceptance. The appeal of this girl may not be that she is the most talented of all the girls he has met, but simply that she likes him and has let him know this. The relationship is secure and comfortable. He doesn't feel threatened.

First loves are not the final life decision. Your college-bound son is not likely to marry at age 15. Parents often put too much weight on decisions which for the teen are just what the Brownie Scouts call "Try its." The weight, significance and permanence the parent attaches to a teen's decision are far greater than how the teen values it himself.

At this point in his life, your son is gathering experiences. Over the next few years he will sort out what he has learned and use his acquired experience to make good choices. He may date for 10 or more years before he makes the final choice. Parents need to be careful not to overreact to an experience that is just an experiment for their child.

Even if the relationship should persist into adulthood and become his final choice, it might not be a negative thing. It is hard to predict what traits make a relationship work. Many an attractive and vocationally successful couple find that they are not happy together over the years, while other, less-endowed couples thrive.

Emotional support is probably the most important part of a romantic relationship, and that aspect may be hard for a parent to judge. Compatibility is not based on the girl's report card or her clothes.

Choosing a girl who is not a challenge to him does not carry much significance for a first romance, but choosing a girlfriend with bad habits that he might imitate should arouse your concern.

The insecure boy might be flattered by the attention of any girl who accepts him, even one who is abusing drugs or cutting school. If your son is changing his good habits to be more like a peer group that is less desirable, then it is time to intervene.

Relationships in the high school years tend to last about one school year. The choice of a first girlfriend who is not his intellectual match is not significant, but if your son shows a pattern of repeated relationships with women who you feel do not match his achievement and potential, you might want to share your feelings with him.

On the other hand, parents sometimes have such an admiring eye for their own children that no one seems good enough. This unconditional love is good for an infant, but when it is applied to a teenager, it stifles the teen's ability to realistically evaluate his own behavior, and it kills relationships.

This kind of admiration from a parent is self-serving. It reserves the child for the parent at the expense of letting the teen move on in his own life.

Annie

Son struggles with move to new town

Q. We moved to Birmingham just before the start of this school year. My ninth-grade son continues to mope and has not made any real friends. He compares everything to home and finds everything not quite as good as it was there. Even though he is in an excellent school system, he thinks all his classes in his old school were better. I may be guilty of furthering his attitude because I too miss our old city. How do I help him to make his way here?

A. You and your son seem to be suffering from what I have come to call "newcomer syndrome." While there are many different ways to do things, when people move to a new place, they tend to define the correct way to do a task or view an issue as the way it was done in their old town.

No matter how good the new way or place may be, if it is not exactly as it was at home, it is wrong. Until time passes and the new ways and places become familiar and accepted, the new place seems awkward, wrong and unfamiliar.

People vary in their openness to change. Some people cling to old ways longer than others. The longer one holds onto the old way of doing things, the longer it takes to feel comfortable with the new one, but even under the best of adaptability, it often takes one to two years to feel completely at home.

The age of the child determines, in part, the length of the period of adjustment. Preschoolers make friends easily and quickly forget their old home. In grades K through three, children are open to new friends, and most children with adequate social skills are quickly accepted.

The very fact that they attend school and are introduced to peers often makes the adjustment easier for the children than for the adults. As long as the family structure is in place, children will soon adjust to their new room, new teacher and new class.

Teens, on the other hand, are much slower to adjust to change. Because they are so sensitive to doing things exactly as their peers do, it takes time to figure out the new style and to blend in to new ways.

To fit in, they feel they must be just like the others. Since the new town is likely to be different, and different is bad at this age, it can take time to adjust.

Young children are also more open to different kinds of peers, while by the teen years children are more selective in friendships. Until your son finds his niche, he may feel like an outsider.

You can help him by keeping an open attitude yourself about the new ways of doing things. If you make fun of, for example, the lack of a beach here, then your son will also view his new home as lacking. If, on the other hand, you take the attitude that, "Well, we lost the beach but gained the beautiful hills and trees," your son may also begin to find something he likes in his new home.

Most adjustment problems are within the person, but the environment may aggravate some. Birmingham is not just one uniform city but also an area of many different neighborhoods.

It is hard to have a sense of the different neighborhoods when you first come to find a place to live from out of town, but after a few months here, if you still don't adapt, you may find that a different neighborhood may suit your needs better.

Teens adjust best to school when they find a small subset of the larger group. Capitalize on a talent or interest and help him to find others who share this with him. If he plays an instrument, encourage him to join the band. If he is talented in theater, encourage him to try out for the spring play.

These are activities that create close bonds among its participants and will help him to develop common memories with other schoolmates.

Competitive child shuns correction

Q. Our daughter is an eighth-grader who puts intense athletic and academic pressure on herself. Whenever we talk to her about school or sports in what we think is a supportive, non-threatening manner, she accuses us of expecting her to be perfect.

Actually, she imposes standards of perfection on herself and gets angry when anyone offers suggestions on how she might do something differently. How do we get her to tolerate correction and to give up her perfectionism?

A. Your daughter's perfectionism seems to be part of her need to compete. Rather than comfortably working to improve her own skills, she seems to find it essential to be the best.

This leads her to resent any suggestions from others, particularly her parents. Corrections or suggestions mean rejection to her.

I would guess that she has one or more siblings at home. She doesn't take the limelight for granted but seems to be on the alert to assure her share.

While some aspects of competitiveness come from inborn temperament, parents can foster competition by giving the impression that there is not enough love, attention and approval to go around.

The parent who is too busy with the baby to attend to the preschooler leads that child to intensify his behavior in order to be noticed. The less-noticed child may feel he has to be perfect or win awards to get his share of the parents' love.

Some parents control and motivate their children by setting them up to compete. A casual, "Let's see who can finish their vegetables first," might not be harmful but when this is used as a constant mode of controlling behavior, the siblings learn to compete.

It increases sibling

fighting, and it leads to a child who measures himself in terms of the performance of others instead of working to achieve his personal best.

Being good is not enough anymore; you have to be the first or the best, because there can be only one winner.

In families with more than one child, each child tends to find his own niche. Your daughter seems to have found her place in the family as the academically and athletically successful child.

She defends her turf by not allowing anyone to better her. To accept criticism, or even suggestions from you, threatens her role. "Perfect" is who she is and how she gets love — at least in her eyes.

Changes in behavior come slowly and over time. Even if you alter your patterns of parenting, she won't wake up suddenly one day and say, "Tell me about that suggestion you made last night. I'm ready to hear it now." It will take a steady repetition and lots of praise and attention to cause a gradual change in your daughter.

Add noncompetitive activities to her athletics, and limit the competitive sports to one at a time. She might find that she enjoys art lessons or ballet class, where there isn't a winner and a loser at the end of each day. It may take her time to get used to this.

Use other children to make your point about not having to be perfect. She can hear it better when it is not about her. When her teammate makes a less than perfect play, point out how she is such a nice kid or such a good team player.

When she gloats about winning, point out the good plays of the other team. Shift her focus from winning to the effort and steps it took to get there. Point out how her view of people is fairly stable and not dependent upon one action. Remind her that she doesn't change her friends, or her feelings about them, based on how they performed that day.

Watch your own need for perfection. If she is doing so well already, it may not be necessary to show her a better way to do something. Let the small things slide and accept her as she is.

Don't pressure child to get grades — motivate him

Q. How much pressure should a parent put on a child to achieve good grades? Should a parent allow a child ever to fail? What about choices between enriching extracurricular experiences (such as piano lessons or participation in the school play) versus studying?

A. Parents shouldn't pressure a child to get good grades, but they can motivate a child to want to achieve by creating a love of learning.

The parent who takes his child to concerts and plays teaches a love of culture. He encourages his child to think and to analyze at more than one level.

The parent who forces a child to achieve may push a child to cheat. This child does not learn to value learning. He values only a number on a test or a report card.

Pressure to get good grades is not likely to improve a report card, but encouragement just may do so.

Reward effort, not achievement. Notice your child when he is studying. Praise him when he goes to bed early the night before a test.

The child who studies every night but still gets low grades should be commended for his work. You can enjoy the interesting paper he wrote for English class whether or not he gets a high grade.

Reward frequently, and use praise, not gifts, to reward. Nine-week grading periods are too long to wait for encouragement.

The most powerful reward is parental approval. You don't need to buy a Nintendo game to encourage your child. Your words are sufficient and won't lead to the secondary problems of spoiling.

Keep your praise short and positive. Many parents use praise as a time for a lecture. Your child won't hear the compliment if it is buried in a long speech, and "You got a good grade this time" is a reprimand, not a compliment.

Experiences outside school are important too. These can provide learning experiences that are not always available at school.

Most children can handle both school and some outside activities. If your child is struggling academically, you will need to consider his overall load, but just because he is failing math doesn't automatically mean that he shouldn't play baseball. Success outside school may be just what he needs to maintain self-esteem.

Sometimes psychiatric problems can get in the way of a child's successful performance at school. Treat depression, anxiety and attention deficit disorder so that the illness does not get in the way of your child's academic success.

While some parents are fearful of using medication to get rid of troubling symptoms, not treating is not benign either. The untreated child can slip into a downward spiral where low grades and lack of friends lead to low self-esteem and increased depression or bad behavior.

Should a child ever be allowed to fail? It is not the parent who is in the fifth, seventh or twelfth grade. The child is the student. He should be responsible for doing his own work.

Parents should not bail him out. Sometimes failing makes the child realize he has hit bottom and it gets the child's attention. Sometimes it shows both parent and child that another path, vocational training for example, might be a better fit.

"I don't care" may be cover for "I can't"

Q. My 14-year-old son is a very poor reader. The children tease him at school about this, even though some of his subject grades are OK. He gets in trouble for misbehaving, but it is not really big stuff — just being the class clown. He is great at sports. How should we handle his behavior problems? Could it be that he has attention deficit disorder that is preventing him from reading?

A. Reading problems often run in families. Chances are, if you explore your family history, you will uncover close relatives who are also dyslexic — the technical word for inability to read fluently.

Your son's behavior problems are likely tied to his poor reading. When children struggle with mastering a subject at school, they often find it embarrassing to admit that they are trying as hard as they can to learn the material but still can't master it.

It is less humiliating to act the clown and portray an "I don't care" attitude than to show your desire to learn when you can't.

Both in families and in classrooms, children find their own niche. A niche is a way to be noticed and admired. When children can't find a way to be recognized for things that please adults, they find another way.

It sounds as if your son can get positive attention on the football field so he is no trouble there. In the classroom, he settles for the laughs of his classmates that he gets as class clown because he cannot win their admiration for academic achievement.

To solve the learning problem that underlies his behavior problem, you need a better understanding of the specifics of what he can't seem to learn.

Your first step should be to have him tested. You want to see his pattern of strengths and weaknesses. The child who is slow at everything is a very different student than the child with a specific deficit.

Testing can help you to find areas of strength to use to build self-esteem. It is easier for a child to accept a reading problem if he is a strong math student.

Testing can be used to find strategies that can teach around the brain pathways that are weak. When skills are taught in a different way, they use different parts of the brain.

In one hospital in Boston, stroke patients who lost the function of the part of the brain that controls speech were taught to sing to communicate. This worked because singing comes from a different part of the brain than speech.

Although attention deficit disordered children often have learning disabilities, just having an area of learning deficit does not mean he has attention deficit disorder.

Children who are dyslexic do not necessarily have any other problem other than the secondary problems with self-esteem and behavior that arise from being unable to read.

Medication for attention problems won't fix a reading disorder. It is only helpful if he isn't learning because he isn't paying attention. This might be the case in first or second grade. It is not likely the case in ninth grade.

Accept his reading problem for what it is and define it for your son. Point out his strengths in other areas. Make it clear that you will not tolerate misbehavior at school and set up consequences. Talk with him about realistic career plans for the future that will maximize his strengths and minimize his reading deficit.

Disrespectful son treats parent as peer

Q. When I tell my 14-year-old son to clean his room, he tells me to clean mine. When I complain that he is late for dinner, he lists all the times that I have been late. How do I get him to stop this back talk and listen to me?

A. Your son is disrespectful. You probably arrived at this state by failing to discipline when he was young.

Parents who want to be the child's friend rather than the parent, and who think their children will love and respect them because they set no limits, end up with the exact opposite of their goal. The child, who has not had an authoritative parent, typically has little respect for adults.

Parents who are uncomfortable being in charge defer many decisions to the child. The child, who has had his way when he was young, is not likely to change and respect the opinion of the adult as a teenager.

Some parents are absent during the formative years of a child's life due to depression or dating after a divorce. Then when life stabilizes for them, they want to resume the role of the parent. Typically, the adolescent who was on his own as a child will not accept a parent's return to authority.

Children need and want structure. They need rules and boundaries. They want consequences for transgressions. When seventh- to twelfth-grade students were questioned about the traits of their favorite teachers, students named "control over the classroom" as the most desirable trait.

This was followed by "fair" and then by "able to clearly impart information." These adolescents are saying that structure and discipline in the classroom need to be present before learning can take place. They are also saying they appreciate discipline.

The most common

error that parents make in disciplining a child who talks back is to get bogged down in the content of the child's argument rather than disciplining the child's lack of respect.

When you tell him to clean his room and he tells you to clean yours, the issue is not about clean rooms. It is about back talk.

The parental answer should be: "You may not talk to me this way. I am the parent and you are the child." You must say this from a position of authority and not as a begging, whining parent.

Parental respect both is earned through parental behavior and comes automatically from the role as the older and wiser person. It is hard for a teenager to respect a parent who makes foolish decisions or who is lazy and slovenly in his or her own life.

On a first offense you may assume that your child didn't know that he was doing wrong. Instruct him that you will no longer tolerate his talking back and that you will provide a specific consequence if he does.

Cultivate a tone of voice that lets him know when he is in dangerous territory. This will serve as a warning for him when he begins to transgress, giving him an opportunity to retreat and correct his misbehavior.

If he continues to disobey, then he receives a consequence. While some would suggest that an appropriate consequence for disrespect is being sent to his room, a more powerful punishment is one that is related to the crime.

If your child cannot accept your authority as a parent, then he must lose one of the benefits of your parenting. Doing his own laundry might be such a punishment. It serves to remind him of your role and to deprive him of the benefits of your role if he doesn't value it.

Savannah

Teach child to make lemonade out of lemons

Q. My 13-year-old daughter tends to see things at their worst most of the time. If she has a test the next day, she thinks she will fail. If she hears that a friend is having a party, she expects that she won't be invited. My friend's daughter has real problems in her life but always seems to find the positive in every situation. How do you raise an optimistic child, and what can I do to turn my child's attitude around?

A. Some children seem to come into the world with a positive attitude while others tend to expect the worst. You may recognize yourself or your spouse in your child's personality. Personality is not destiny, however, and children can be taught to make lemonade out of lemons.

The most powerful influence on a child is the role model she sees daily. If you view the glass half full, your child most likely will too.

If your child tends to see the half-filled glass as half empty, you will have to show her the other side. Point out specifically the good parts of any situation. Confront her doubts and pessimism rather than just letting her negative statements go by.

When she says, "Janie is having a party but I bet she won't invite me," you can respond, "Sounds like you are worried that you won't be included." This rephrases her pessimism and opens conversation.

Often when a child makes a negative comment, it is more a worry than a firm belief in the less desirable outcome. By rephrasing her statement into a worry or concern, you have already given her the message that the negative alternative is not the only possible outcome.

When a child firmly believes that something bad will happen, instead of saying, "No, it won't," open other alternatives.

Lead her to think of other possibilities. When she says, "I'll fail this test," ask her what would happen if she studied for it.

Sibling conflicts present a wonderful opportunity to help the child see a situation in a different light. When a child complains that her sister has taken her favorite blouse, you can say, "Your sister really admires your taste in clothes."

Children who have a positive outlook tend to be children who feel that they are in control of what happens to them. By overcontrolling your children and by trying to make everything perfect for them, you place them at greater risk for pessimism.

The child whose parents have intervened in every conflict with a teacher or friend have taken away the child's sense of power. They have taken away the opportunity for her to learn that she can turn bad situations into better ones by taking action.

She has learned from their constant intervention that only others can make the outcome she desires happen. Helplessness is closely tied to hopelessness.

Setting up your children to compete with each other is an easy way to motivate children to compliance but creates a troubled world for the child. Competing for limited goods is stressful.

By telling all of your children that there is enough love, attention and material stuff to go around, you make the world a more benign place.

Watch your own behavior. When you fret and worry, you convey to your child that life is difficult. When you look at the bright side, your child learns to expect mostly good outcomes.

But don't smile when things are going badly, either, or your child will not learn to think positively but instead will learn to deny reality. To have a positive outlook, your child needs to learn to turn lemons into lemonade, not to smile as he sucks lemons.

By meeting your child's emotional needs, by being realistically optimistic and by guiding your child to see the positive, you can help her to see the good in life.

Needs of individual and group are not always same

Q. My daughter is in a public middle school in a good neighborhood where most of the children are reasonably well behaved. We have a new principal who comes from an area where he had to impose very rigid codes of dress and behavior to maintain order and prevent chaos. He is now applying these rigid rules to our school, and the children are upset. While they used to enjoy going to school, many now don't want to go. My daughter even says that she will drop out of school when she is 16. This principal requires that every child tuck his or her shirt in. This is upsetting to some of the girls who, with the hypersensitivity of preadolescence, feel that their stomachs stick out. Is it really necessary to have such rigid rules? What would it do to school discipline if the girls were allowed to wear their shirts out at an age when they are so self-conscious about their bodies?

A. The needs of the group as a whole and the needs of an individual are not always the same. What may be good for the general maintenance of order in the school might be difficult for an individual child.

Well-behaved children can be given greater freedom than children who have demonstrated that they cannot monitor their own behavior. A small group of disobedient children can make it necessary for more rigid discipline of the whole group.

Your principal comes from a situation where harsher and more rigid discipline was likely necessary to maintain an environment conducive to learning. He did what it took to keep his students safe during their day at school.

Ideally the control should come from each child internally, but when this fails, the structure has to be imposed from outside in the form of rules.

Children learn to control themselves by being controlled first by others. They take the rules and values of their caretakers and gradually make these standards their own.

This is a developmental process. As the child matures, others can set fewer rules as the child takes over control on his own.

Your new principal may be out of step with the developmental level of his new students. Just as the parent who is used to a toddler that he must watch constantly may overprotect a 4-year-old he is caring for only once, so your new principal may be overprotective and out of step with the developmental level of his new students.

Because he is new to the school, he may feel he has to establish his authority. Possibly after he adjusts, both to the good behavior of his new students and to his position, he can be persuaded to lighten up on the rules. You may need to give him some time in his new position before you expect change.

Most students will accept rules that are for their own benefit although they might not see the benefit right away.

The problem comes when the rules seem arbitrary to the children. Tucking in shirts may seem this way to them. The principal probably reasons that neat dress will create an orderly school environment.

If your daughter is talking about dropping out of school, there is a larger problem than just rules. You may need to teach her the reason that she is in school and help her to establish long-term goals rather than choosing to attend or not based on how happy she feels each day.

After giving the new principal a time for adjustment, a concerned group of parents, or parents and teachers, might approach the principal for an evaluation of the rules.

This group should be selected carefully to be a rational and respectful one. The principal has the right to make the rules in his school. Discussion and support will go further toward change than angry and adversarial criticism.

Teens should have only the freedom they earn

Q. My 16-year-old son is basically a good kid, but since he got his driver's license and the freedom to go with it, he has made some bad choices. Each time he does something wrong, we rein in the rope and keep him closer to home. After his punishment is over, we give him some slack, but each time he has the rope he hangs himself with it, and we rein in again. Am I wrong to watch him so closely? Am I not giving him the freedom a teenager should have?

A. Teenagers should have only the freedom they earn through appropriate behavior and rational decisions. They do not earn independence simply by being 16.

Some teens are quite adult. Others are impulsive and reckless. Teens who can't make wise decisions still need close supervision and tight limits imposed by parents, school authorities and the law.

It sounds as if you have a good balance between freedom and rules. You provide the opportunity for your son to earn his freedom. When he shows good judgment, he gets a longer rope.

When he makes bad choices, you read his message correctly — that he needs an outside force, his parents, to set limits. Freedom is earned, and he is not earning it.

Your method sounds quite fair. You punish him with a logical consequence. If he cannot handle his freedom, then he loses it. You don't punish him forever. When his punishment is over, he gets another chance to prove himself.

The most common mistake in discipline — other than not disciplining at all — is making the punishment too long so that the punishment is not enforceable and/or the child is always on punishment.

You are not wrong when you set limits for your son. It is the parents of teens who do not watch their children closely who are making the mistake.

While the task of the teen years is to move away from parents into autonomy, it is the job of parents to teach their children how to behave when they are on their own.

If a teen is moving away in a reckless or thoughtless manner, the parent must make the child take a step back into the home to learn the basics he missed when he was younger.

Parents overprotect a teenager only when they keep a child close to home to meet the parent's own needs. They do not overprotect when the child behaves recklessly and the parent reduces freedom.

As long as the parent is willing to give the child the freedom that is appropriate for the child's maturity level, no harm is done.

Maturity and chronological age are not the same thing. One 16-year-old may do his homework diligently, be respectful to teachers and other adults and maintain good grades, while another child of the same age may drive too fast, drink alcohol and not perform up to his potential in school. These two children should not have the same freedom just because they are the same age.

On the other hand, teens should not be reined in for things that are beyond their control. The child with limited ability who is doing his best in school but still making mediocre grades should not be held back from age-appropriate freedom if he is otherwise making good choices. Expectations should be individualized for each child.

If you maintain consistent expectations and consistent consequences for misbehavior, your son will eventually grow through this stage. Not only are you teaching him how to behave responsibly, but you are also teaching him how to parent.

Even while you are distressed by his seeming failure to learn the rules, you might be surprised to hear him apply them to a younger brother or to a friend.

Keep on doing what you are doing. You are on the right track. He will eventually get it.

Rudeness is not a developmental stage

Q. Our only child is a 14-year-old daughter who has always been a delightful person and has brought us much joy. She has always been outgoing and independent. When she turned 13, she began to spend a lot of time in her room with her door closed, watching TV, talking on the phone or doing homework. I respect her privacy even though she occasionally overdoes it and I find myself having conversations with her through the closed door.

She is becoming increasingly private and distant, which I think is probably normal. However, when her aunt and uncle visited us recently, she wouldn't spend time with them, and their feelings were hurt. At dinnertime, I called her, and she refused to come downstairs for dinner.

Her aunt and uncle are childless and have always doted on her and treated her as a special person. They are hurt and I am upset. I am praying that this is only a teenage phase. Do you have any advice?

A. While it is normal for a teen to begin to pull away from intense closeness to family and to move into the peer group, it is not normal to be rude. Rudeness is not a stage. If you ignore it, it will become her permanent way of acting.

When she ignores her guests, she is acting in a self-centered way. She is accommodating only her feelings and not those of her aunt and uncle. If you don't want to raise a selfish person, you must set some rules and consequences for her behavior.

You should not be talking to her through a closed door. Open her door after knocking and face your child when you speak to her. To continue to speak to her through the closed door is to teach her that this is an acceptable way to behave. If you allow her to be rude to you, how can you expect her

Raising Children

not to be rude to her aunt and uncle — or to her teachers at school?

By speaking to her through the closed door, you think that you are teaching her respect by the example you set. It doesn't work this way. What you are really showing her is that she is quite powerful. You are failing to teach her that the world runs in hierarchies of power and that parents, and not children, are in charge. Why should she strive to achieve at school in order to get a good entry position in the work force when she is already at the top of the power hierarchy?

Take the bull by the horns and insist that she eat with the family. At first she may be sullen and may ruin your dinner, but do not give in. After about one week expect her to be not only present, but also pleasant. If she is not, reduce her privileges. You must set consequences for rude behavior or it will continue. Praise her when she is well behaved.

Children only have power if their parents give it to them. The do not have transportation or financial resources without their parents. Make all that you do for her contingent upon respect within the family.

Remove the TV from her room and give her chores to do. She needs to hear not only about her rights in the family, which you have stressed by respecting her closed door, but her obligations to the family as well. While for most teens chores can be responsibility for their own things, your child may need to have chores that benefit the whole family.

She is not too young to take out the trash, to do a load of laundry or to cook dinner one night a week from among a few recipes that you have taught her to prepare. She will appreciate the skills when she leaves home, and may learn that she must give to others and not only take.

Cooking and sewing are still important skills

Q. My son's 14-year-old girlfriend came for dinner. She offered to help me make the salad, but when she tried to cut a bell pepper she didn't know how to cut it so the seeds didn't end up in the salad. She said her mother didn't ever cook and they lived on frozen dinners and restaurant food. Further conversation revealed that she didn't know how to sew on a button either. Shouldn't parents teach their children the basics of housekeeping? Has this gone out of style?

A. I don't know of any research study that has investigated how many children are being taught to cook or to sew on a button, but you do make a valid point. These skills are important, and children today, unlike previous generations, are not automatically exposed to housekeeping skills.

Some may argue that in today's society, where you can take your clothes to the tailor for alterations and buy ready-cooked food at the grocery, it isn't important to have domestic skills. However, without someone doing these things, the house is not a home and the children don't have a sense of being nurtured.

It is not important to be a gourmet cook. That comes under hobbies and special talents. It is important to be able to provide a family with basic home cooking so that not every meal comes prefab.

If you do not teach the basic life skills to your children, they may not learn them later either. A motivated young adult can pick up a few tips from roommates and mentors, but their exposure is not guaranteed and the lessons may be haphazard. There is little substitute for daily exposure to doing basic tasks at home.

If you lack these skills yourself, you can at least convey to your child that these skills are important. Typically, the mother who cannot cook devalues cooking as important, and so the teen is discouraged from learning from others.

Skills can be learned from sources outside the home, but the parent has to value the skill in the first place. One way to get this message across is to take a class together with your teen.

There are cooking classes for children, and there are classes for adults that accept teen participants. For the initial lessons, find basic courses — not specialized menus.

Sewing skills can be learned in sewing classes, but the basics — threading a needle and hemming a skirt — can be learned in organizations such as Scouts and 4-H. If your child's Scout troop does not do basic skills, you can suggest that they do, and find a volunteer willing to do a few sessions.

No child of either sex should leave home without knowing how to sew on a button and do a basic sewing stitch to mend a seam in a pinch.

Children should know how to boil pasta, brown meat and fry and boil an egg. This is not gourmet cooking, but survival skills.

Take your college bound teen to the grocery store with you and teach him how the grocery is arranged. You may be surprised to find that he looks haphazardly for items. Teach him how you shop for value and which brands or products you like. If you never shop or cook, ask a friend to do this with you and your child.

If you are the mother of the boy who comes home with the girlfriend with few domestic skills, take her on as a daughter. If she is willing, offer to let her cook with you. She just may be thrilled at the opportunity.

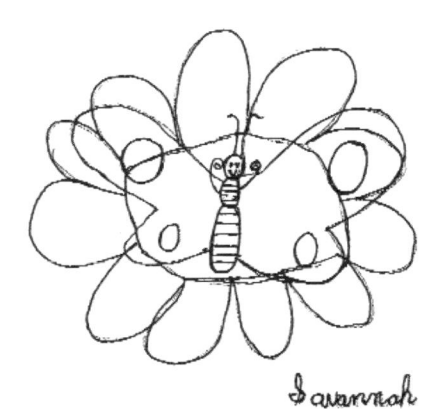

Savannah

Smiling child is easier to like than moody sister

Q. We have two daughters, ages 11 and 13. The older child tells us that we yell at her for parts of chores not completed that we let go by in the younger child. We don't feel that this is true, but the younger child does everything to the best of her ability and with a smile on her face, while our older child resents anything she does and does a sloppy job with minimum effort. How can you get a child to do a better job and change her attitude so she doesn't feel like only she gets scolded?

A. Tell your 13-year-old how you feel. Tell her that when she resents doing a task, she does a minimal job. Tell her that her attitude affects how you feel about her work. Tell her that a task done with a smile on her face and with her best effort gets rewarded even if the job is not perfect.

Catch her when she does well and reward even the smallest step with praise. When children get into a pattern of negative behavior and endless scolding, they have trouble breaking the pattern. A word of praise can sometimes stop the downward spiral of sloppy work that leads to criticism that leads to resentment. Praise can turn things around.

Do keep in mind that she is at a more difficult age than her sister. At 11, her young sister is in the relatively uncomplicated elementary school years, while your older child is dealing with hormonal changes and the social and academic pressures that accompany the teen years. She may need more guidance in handling her emotions than your younger child.

Some children are temperamentally more difficult than others. A smiling, positive child is easier to like than a moody, demanding, what-have-you-done-for-me-lately child. Find an activity that your 13-year-old enjoys and does well, and spend time doing this with her. If she hates to clean her room but would love to make dinner with you, be sure to do the activity that will give you positive time together.

When you give your older child a task to do, write out the steps you expect her to take. Rather than saying, "Clean your room," write out, "Pick up your clothes and put them in the hamper, empty your trash and put your books on the shelf."

This leaves her no room to guess what will please you and gives you a firm list to review. If she still doesn't comply, then you can show her that it is her behavior and not your attitude that causes the conflict.

Sometimes parents inadvertently teach their children to compare and compete. When parents try overly hard to be fair, they actually tell their children that things should always be equal. Sameness is not what parents should aim for. What you want is to meet each child's needs. Doing the same for each won't do this.

They may need to see this for themselves. If one child complains, tell her that you will do exactly the same for both children for three days. When one child wants a peanut butter sandwich, make two. When one child wants her hair cut, make both do the same. When you buy one child a size 12 dress, buy the same size for the other. They will soon get the message that they want things to be fair, but not exactly the same.

Don't set your children up to compete with each other. Parents sometimes use comparison to motivate children, but that has its problems. A simple "let's see who can eat their vegetables first" may seem harmless at the time, but over the years, with repetitive use of competition, the children get the message that there can be only one winner.

Watch your real feelings. Parents don't always like their children equally. Often there is one child who is easier to like than the other, but do be careful not to criticize only one. Nothing breeds resentment between siblings faster than when parents favor one child.

13-year-old has the right to be told the truth

Q. My sister committed suicide four years ago, leaving a now 13-year-old son. He lives with his grandparents, my mother and father, because his own father didn't want him. He is a very angry child with lots of behavior problems despite having been in therapy for years. He has not been told that his mother's death was a suicide. Don't you think that we should tell him? If so, who should tell him and how? Is it too late to tell him now that we have kept it from him for all these years? Will he be angry that we didn't tell him right away?

A. A 13-year-old child has the right to know the truth. He is old enough to understand parts of the situation and old enough to ask about the parts he doesn't understand. He doesn't need to grasp it all at once. His comprehension will continue to grow as he does.

Family secrets rarely work to keep information from the person they try to protect. Instead they create a situation in which everyone has the knowledge, but each feels he or she must keep silent to protect someone else. This results in family members isolated from one another, unable to turn to each other for support.

Instead of a shared tragedy, each is alone in his pain. The 13-year-old is likely to be protecting his grandparents by not telling them what he knows, just as they are protecting him with their silence.

It is almost impossible to hide family events from children. The community and extended family know the truth, and he is bound to have heard it. When you try not to let him know, you are probably not sparing him knowledge of the truth, but simply are denying him permission to talk about it.

When you don't talk about the suicide openly, you

leave him to create his own distortions of the facts. He most likely knows some of the facts already, but instead of knowing for sure, he has pieced together bits of information and has used his fantasy and feelings to fill in the missing pieces. He is unlikely to have done this completely accurately, and his fantasy is probably worse than the truth.

Nearly all children who have lost a parent feel guilty. They worry that the parent left because the child was bad. When the secret is out in the open, the child's self-blame can be corrected.

Without honesty his therapy has little value. He can be in therapy for years with little progress, as he has been, if his therapist participates in hiding the truth from him.

As he probably knows or suspects the truth anyway, in hiding the suicide from him, his therapist has effectively said, "You can't really talk about your feelings here either." Therapy has become for him no different from any other place in his life. The task of therapy is to work though feelings, which can't be done if the therapist is participating in the deception.

While he might initially be angry that he hasn't been told sooner, that doesn't mean that you shouldn't tell him now. His main caretakers, his grandparents, should be the ones to tell him but they might want to break the news to him during his therapy session so that both they and the child can have the support of the professional.

While the caretakers seem to fear an emotional outburst from their grandson, they might be surprised to find that his reaction, rather than shock at the disclosure, is one of relief that the secret is now out in the open.

If the therapist is uncomfortable with breaking the family secret, you will need to find another therapist who is not afraid to deal with strong emotions and tragic events.

Recovered child simply needs to catch up

Q. My eighth-grade son has missed a week of school due to illness. He has several tests to make up and a lot of reading to do. How do you get a child caught up after illness? Should the parents intervene with the teachers? I know they make modifications for children with learning disabilities. Is there such a thing as temporary academic modification for children who miss school?

A. For most good parents, nurturing comes easier than letting go, but at some point, the competent parent must back off and turn over responsibility to the child. A good time to do this is as the child makes the transition from elementary school to junior high. It is not your responsibility to get your eighth grader caught up. It is his job to make up what he has missed.

While most teachers are reluctant to make the special effort it takes to bring a child up to speed after missing a week of school for a family vacation, most teachers are quite helpful when a child has been out ill. When your child returns to school with a note to readmit him to class, he can ask his teacher for a list of his assignments and for help if he needs it.

The solid student will usually be able to make up most of the work on his own if given a few days to do so. The more marginal student may need extra help learning the material he has missed.

This is not entirely the responsibility of the school. Parents should be prepared to share the effort. Teachers teach many children. Parents, only a few. No one is as concerned about your child's education as you are. If he needs help, help him.

Your eighth-grader is old enough to work things out with his teachers without parental intervention. At the eighth-grade level, parents should only step in after the child has tried. To step in pre-emptively robs your child of an important life experience. He cannot learn to fend for himself without the chance to do so. If you do it for him before he has had a chance to try, you give him the message that you think he is incompetent.

As he makes up missed work, parents need to focus on the child's mastery of the content, not on the grade the child receives on the first test after his illness. While grades do provide feedback for parents, they do not measure your child's identity.

If you know that your child's test grade dropped because he missed the lesson, you should not be alarmed. Instead of seeking a modification to raise his test grade, simply go over the work with him.

Academic adaptations, those which lower the standards for performance by the child, are needed only to prevent a child from experiencing constant failure. The child who is out for a week doesn't need a formal modification with a written individualized education plan. He simply needs a few extra days to turn in assignments and to make up tests.

This can be done by agreement between teacher and child. Academic modifications enable a learning-disabled child to have some degree of success at school, but they do not change the underlying deficit.

The child who is out for a few days does not have an underlying deficit, nor is he lacking experience with success. The recovered child is simply behind in his work and needs to catch up.

Give him some extra time. Help him with academics if he asks. Don't stress grades but do expect effort. Most children will catch up without a problem.

Artsy son feels he can't please athletic father

Q. My 15-year-old son does poorly in school. He is bright enough to be at least an average student in his school but he has no self-confidence. He seems to give up before he even tries. My husband is a very successful businessman, and he has a hard time understanding my son's lack of drive. They also share few interests, as my husband was a football player and my son shies away from anything aggressive, preferring art, reading and music. What can I do to help my son?

A. A child who has a successful and aggressive father and who is himself athletically talented and assertive will tend to model his father and become like him. Because their temperaments and skills are alike, the son has open to him the option of defining his success in the same way as his father did.

He might choose to play football like dad, thereby gaining father's approval. This approval, in turn, makes him feel even more confident, and so the child is on his way to emulate dad's lifestyle and dad's success.

The gentler and temperamentally more passive child might see a powerful and successful father as an overwhelming obstacle. Instead of following in his footsteps, he learns early on that he can never measure up. This happens so early in life that he may not be able to put these feelings into words.

Boys are not equally vulnerable to the effects of a powerful father at every age. Between the ages of 3 and 6 they are especially sensitive. At this time, boys try to win their mother's attention by being like a man. This is the stage when little boys might say that they want to marry mom.

When the dad accepts his son as a little man without either ridiculing his attempts to copy him or abandoning the boy to be the man of the house, then the boy gives up his intense attachment to mom and moves on to learning the skills he will need in adulthood.

When dads take the young child's interest in mom as a threat and come down too hard on them, the child can learn to fear competition. Any assertiveness on the child's part may lead to anxiety, and the child learns not to compete, not only with dad, but also with anyone, in order to avoid the bad feelings.

It is sometimes hard for a parent to accept a child who is different from the way he is, but it is important that the parent work on this. Your child is not likely to suddenly become an aggressive athlete, even if he wanted to do so to please you.

Yet, with your acceptance, he can develop the drive to become successful within his interests, personality style and talents. You can have a son who is successful in the arts if you allow him to be so. Drawing or painting is just as valid a way to fill leisure time as is playing sports.

To help your son you will need to accept your son as he is. Value his gentler skills and work with dad to accept his son's talents.

Back off on pushing him to success but do steer him to experiences which will build his self-esteem. Bolster his self-concept by making it clear to him that you love him for what he is.

Dad will need to search inside himself to understand his need to devalue his son. Would dad be threatened if his son were successful?

Because your son's fears have been with him for many years, changes will not come quickly. Over time, however, you should be able to help him accept himself as he is and to shed both his fear of failure and his fear of success.

Parent's job is to help child evaluate risks

Q. My son has started back to high school, and on his first day has already started talking about liking a certain girl as a steady girlfriend. This girl is a very popular girl, who by reputation has broken the hearts of several boys whom she has dated and left. I think my son should stay away from her. How can I help him avoid what I think will lead him to be hurt?

A. Children encounter many risks as they move from total dependence on parents to being able to live on their own.

Without taking risks, no child would learn to swim, ride a bike or skate. Children would not perform on stage in the school play or try out for the debate team. Part of growing up and gaining new skills and new experiences involves taking risk.

The parent's role is not to hold the child back to absolute safety, but to help the child evaluate what risks are worth taking.

When you think that he is taking on too much, ask your child to identify the risk, identify the potential reward, and estimate his chance of succeeding. Think with him about whether the potential for reward is enough to overcome the risk.

Impulsive children need to be helped to slow down. When the impulsive child wants permission to climb a tree, the parent might want to go to the tree with him and talk about just which branches he will step on to get up. The child just might discover that he won't be able to get up because the branches are too far apart.

It is the parent's job to teach him to think before he acts, but not necessarily to make the decision for him. Some lessons are best learned from experience.

Children who are careful by nature may not need to go through this process out loud. These children already do this in their own mind and would only be discouraged from risks worth taking if they have to stop and analyze every step.

For the overly cautious child who never ventures into the risk zone, you might want to encourage him to try by asking, "What do you think might happen if you do this?" "How would you feel if you were successful?" "How would you feel if you failed?" "What would you lose by not trying at all?"

Sometimes it is wise to let the child make his or her own decision about participating in something that the child perceives as risky. There are other times when the parent can help a child over a hump of fear.

If you know that your child wants to try out for the school play but backs down as the time for auditions approaches, you would do more for him if you asked questions about his change of heart than if you simply accepted his decision to back down.

Your son seems to have no trouble taking risk in romantic relationships, and this might mean that his feelings are not as fragile as you believe. He goes to school with this girl and probably hears the same rumors about her that you have heard, yet he is still eager to take the chance.

You might ask him how he would feel if she dates him for a while and then they break up. Keep in mind that short-term is the normal pattern for most adolescent relationships. At age 17, most relationships are not for life.

Instead of preventing him from approaching the girl he likes, it would be better to help him learn to be a good judge of people. Be careful that you don't view your son with such affection that no one is good enough for him.

Focus on teaching what character traits you think he should look for rather than trying to prevent this specific relationship out of fear that he will be hurt.

Teach him the skills to make a good judgment rather than making the decisions for him. You won't be at his side forever.

Crazy and angry are not the same

Q. We heard about the boy who shot his mother, his girlfriend and other students at his high school in Mississippi. What would make a child go to those extremes? Is he crazy?

A. There is a difference between crazy and angry. When we are angry, it is possible to act impulsively to do something that we might not do if we were calm. That does not make us crazy (psychotic) in the technical sense.

Yet in popular use, there is a connection. The word "mad" can mean either crazy or angry, but there is a big difference. In anger, but not always in psychosis, the person still remains aware of his behavior.

Shame, not craziness, is the motivator for most impulsive aggressive acts. One psychologist, Michael Nichols, in his book "No Place to Hide," says, "Rage is very close to shame... Whenever someone responds with an aggressive reaction — a hot retort or sharp retaliation — it's a safe bet that they felt attacked in a way that made them feel diminished and ashamed...As long as we can hang on to our anger, we can focus outward — 'I'll get them!' — instead of accepting the hurt and shame."

Sad and mad feelings are closely connected. The child who shifts quickly from sad to mad doesn't even have time to recognize how bad he feels. It is easier to be mad than sad. Mad doesn't hurt as much. Revenge can, unfortunately, even feel good to the insulted child.

This reaction is helped along by a tendency to externalize blame. "It's not my fault. You caused this." The child who never looks at his own contribution to a problem is more likely to feel insulted by others. He feels like a passive victim. Things happen to him, rather than his controlling and determining the path of his life.

Although there are some children who seem born to blame others, parents teach children to externalize blame when they take the child's side in disputes.

While parents should not just assume their child is wrong when they get a note home from school, the parent who immediately attacks the teacher or the other child who was involved in a conflict with his child gives the clear message that the fault is all external and not within the child's control.

Feelings build up over time. Most people can handle some insults, but over time anger builds. The child involved in the Mississippi school incident was picked on for years before he took revenge.

Unfortunately he hurt the people who gave him a chance — not the ones who never liked him. These were the people whose rejection hurt him most, and he was unable to tolerate it.

Rage can also come from a lack of nurturance. Children who are ignored and emotionally neglected grow up to be angry. The child who is left daily after school to wander the stores until 6 p.m. grows up with little concern for others. He is angry and empty.

Parents who manipulate and overcontrol their children may have angry children as well. This is particularly true for children of parents who withhold love to manipulate the child's compliance.

The mother who tells her child that he can do no wrong — as long as he does exactly as she says — but rejects him if he has his own opinion sets him up for rage.

When we read about adolescent murders in the media, the first reports always show surprise at the sudden aggression from a quiet child.

As more information becomes available, what typically emerges is a profile of the murderer as a rejected and neglected, often academically unsuccessful child — a child full of shame.

Under these circumstances, it takes only one trigger event of perceived humiliation to set off the powder keg.

Many older siblings can be capable family babysitter

Q. I have three children ages 13, 9 and 6. Until now, when we went out for the evening, I hired teenage babysitters. Now that my oldest daughter is the same age as the sitters we hire I wonder if I can leave my other two children with her. Do older sisters make adequate babysitters?

A. Children vary in their maturity and readiness to assume responsibility, but generally a 13-year-old is old enough to take care of younger siblings, especially if these sibling are not infants.

Readiness can be seen from her behavior elsewhere. If she is fighting at school and is generally a behavior problem, then you know she is not ready to assume the responsibility of taking care of others.

Having a sitter who is a sister has many advantages. She will know where everything is kept. She will know the family routines and just how the family does things. When the sibling relationship is a good one, the younger children might feel more secure with a sister than with a stranger.

Some brother/sister relationships can lead to trouble when the parents are not around. If your children generally have no more than an occasional squabble when you are home, they are likely to do well when you are not at home. If, on the other hand, they fight constantly and despise each other when you are there, they will do the same in your absence. Without a parent home to keep the older sibling's anger in check, the younger child can feel quite insecure.

If you leave children home alone, be sure to listen to any feelings they express about the experience. While you might brush aside the typical protest that a young child makes at his parent's leaving, you need to keep an ear open for serious concerns. If the younger child feels frightened or threatened or if the older child feels burdened or resentful, you might want to consider other arrangements.

The amount of time the children are alone is an important factor to consider. Going out for three hours in the evening is different from leaving the children home alone all day every day for the whole summer. For the working parent, a day camp or full-time day care might be a better alternative when school is out.

In your family there is a large age difference between the children, and the oldest can be left in charge. In families where the difference in age is small, it might be better to say, "You are both in charge. You are each responsible for yourselves."

Impress upon them that being allowed to stay home alone is a privilege. Most children will rise to the occasion and surprise you with their maturity. This, of course, assumes that you have judged their readiness for responsibility accurately.

When you do leave an older child in charge, leave a clear set of rules. What you allow and expect should be known not only by the sitter but by the younger children as well. Leaving structured activities and steering them toward an activity before you leave can help them pass the time without conflict.

Should siblings be paid for babysitting? It depends. Children are part of a family and should not be led to expect payment for participating in what needs to be done to make the family system work. No amount of payment can equal the pride at being trusted to be in charge.

However, you might want to offer your child compensation for giving up her time. You are teaching her not that she must be paid every time that she helps at home, but that she can work to earn the things she wants.

Do be sure to leave your teenager enough time to be with her peers too. Too much responsibility for younger children can keep her from taking the step away from the family out into the peer group that is the normal developmental task of adolescence.

Child with plenty is still stealing

Q. My 13-year-old daughter has been caught stealing small items from stores. I don't really understand why she is doing this because we give her what she needs. Why does she steal when she could buy what she is taking?

A. Stealing is a behavior that parents should not ignore. You are wise to take a serious look at why your daughter is doing this.

Very young children do not know that items have an owner. The 2-year-old simply takes what he sees that catches his fancy. When he takes what is yours, he is not stealing. He is simply meeting his own needs without regard for yours.

By age 6, a child should know the difference between right and wrong and should have knowledge of basic social rules. Stealing by children can happen for several reasons.

The child whose parent is absent, either emotionally or physically, may steal an object from the absent parent. He does not do this to sell the object for profit, but to have a piece of the parent to hold with him.

The object represents the parent. At the same time, by stealing, he may make the parents mad, causing his parents to notice him. Negative attention is better than no attention at all.

Insecure children may steal to buy friends. By having money or trinkets to share with others, the child thinks he can win acceptance.

This child has low self-worth and feels that others will not be interested in him unless he has something tangible to give them. The teen may steal clothing to have what peers value and to fit in.

When a parent favors one child over the other, a child may steal to make things equal. By possessing things, the rejected child tries to balance what the sibling gets in affection.

Tangible objects come to take the place of love, but things never fill the child up, and so he steals more and more.

Because stealing also hurts most parents, the child is also getting revenge by taking what is not his.

Children can steal to get attention. In families preoccupied with divorce or illness or in affluent families where social and business concerns hold the parents' attention, a child can steal to be assured that he will not go unnoticed.

Children may steal because they model what they see. Parents need to be sensitive to the subtle messages they give to their children.

When they tell the child not to steal but they engage in questionable business practices, the child gets a mixed message.

Children under age 14 who take what is not theirs once or twice are not necessarily hardened criminals. They may just be testing the limits. Parents need to define the limits emphatically or they will be giving permission for the undesirable behavior.

Because stealing has its own reward (the object stolen) stealing may not represent a deep underlying problem, but it does represent a break in moral development.

A parent will need to put a quick stop to the behavior by expressing clear disapproval and by making the child return the stolen object with a public apology.

The child's embarrassment is an essential part of the cure. Sparing the child the embarrassment is missing out on an important deterrent to future theft.

Stealing can be a difficult habit to break because it is self-rewarding. Like most bad behaviors it is easier to stop it before it starts.

By setting a good example for your child, by giving nurturing and caring attention and by rewarding your child for taking small steps toward long-term goals and building frustration tolerance, parents are preventing the problem of stealing before it starts.

Strong will works better for adult than for child

Q. I have a very strong-willed daughter who is in the 11th grade. She is a very good student and does not do anything major that we don't approve of. The problem is that she talks back to everything I say to her. We bicker over going out with her friends at night or staying up too late studying. She seems to always need to have the last word in any discussion, even over trivial things such as what she eats. How do you handle a strong willed 16-year-old?

A. The personality traits that are useful later in life are not always easy ones for a parent to deal with. The child is in a role where a submissive personality works better than an assertive one, but submissiveness is not always the trait that is best after the transition from childhood to the working world.

Your daughter sounds as if she has the makings of a very successful attorney, particularly for a situation where she would head her own firm. She would not do as well in a job where she would regularly have to take instruction from others.

Not all "having the last word" is disrespectful. While it may be difficult for you to tolerate her back talk, if she is arguing her point as a debater might do, she is not necessarily being rude or out of control. This requires a different parental reaction than the child who, in anger and disrespect, calls a parent names or simply ignores the rules.

If the argumentativeness is in the form of a substantive argument, you might want to take her on in a debate for a short while but cut it off if it goes on for too long. Parents do have the right to the last word and can establish rules without the agreement of the child. After listening to her for a while, it is OK to say, "Just because I said so."

Some arguments are related to the age of your child. The teenager has far less fear of harm than does his parent. Many parents and teens argue about curfews, driving in bad weather or being at the mall at night. Using humor sometimes gets you past the fact that you will never see eye to eye on some things.

At these times it is sometimes better to say, "It is your job to push for new freedom but it is my job to set limits so you can be safe," and to end the conversation with a statement that you are not of the same age and you may never agree on that particular issue, but that you are the parent and will set the rules. You may need to agree to disagree.

Build your relationship with your child during times where there are few conflicts. Go out to lunch together to converse when she is not straining for freedom. Bake a cake together to take as a gift for one of her friends. Create a relationship outside the sphere of conflict. While you don't want to put yourself in the position of trying to win her approval as a peer, you do not have to have a relationship that only emphasizes the power structure.

Guide your strong-willed child into areas where her will will be her strength. Steer her away from careers where her temperament will work against her. While children need to be guided and taught, they are not blank slates for the parent to write on either. Work with, rather than against, her temperament.

Know that she is fighting for her independence now because it is the developmental task of the teen years to do so.

She is developmentally right on target. As she matures and is secure in her independence, she will be better able to take your advice.

Of general interest
The diverse issues

Some issues are universal and don't apply to a specific age group. Some issues of child rearing don't end when the child turns 18. Not all children leave home when they reach the end of adolescence.

For some, the job of parenting largely ends when the adolescent leaves home. Adult children still call for advice from time to time, but they are independent and on their own. They are adult.

For a few parents the job of parenting continues. Their children don't fully grow up. They reach physical maturity without attaining maturity in their societal role. They return home after college graduation or job failure, and the parent must set limits for an adult who no longer wants to be ruled as a child.

Some children live on their own but want the continued financial support of parents. Both parent and adult-child need to define how much autonomy is lost when the child fails to assume a key role of adulthood — financial independence.

Tenth year anniversary column

This is the 10th-year anniversary of this column which debuted in March 1988. During this time I have watched the 2-year-olds that I wrote about then turn into 12-year-olds and the 7s into 17s. Toddlers then are now in junior high. Elementary-school children then are graduating from high school now.

I don't remember aging during those years, but I can see the passage of time in the maturing of your children and mine. The 18-month-old who used to crawl under my desk while I was writing now won't let me kiss him in public.

I find myself writing more about teenagers than I did 10 years ago, now that I have not only professional experience with that age group, but personal experience as well. Driving and girlfriends, curfews and college are not just issues I deal with from afar.

While our children have grown and changed a lot, the parenting issues have changed very little. Parents 10 years ago were worried about their 11-year-olds being rejected by friends and, although there is a new group of parents of 11s, they are having the same concerns.

Parents of nonpotty-trained toddlers are still concerned today, as they were 10 years ago, that their children would go to kindergarten in diapers. They won't, but it's hard to feel that when you are in the midst of a struggle.

It has been my pleasure to meet many of my readers in person at the numerous PTA and church group talks I have given around the city. I am always struck by how much parents have in common — how universal the concerns are. We share the same joys at our children's successes — not only in ways that bring academic or sports awards, but also in watching them turn into the kind, caring, generous, polite people we want them to be.

I am struck by the commonality of fears among

parents — fears that a child will be rejected by friends, will fail in school or not exert his best effort, fears that a child will turn to drugs or alcohol or make bad choices in friends.

I have enjoyed meeting your children, some at my office and some at school meetings. As my children grow, I enjoy your little ones even more than I had time to do when my own four were small.

I am meeting readers who are new parents now, parents who were not old enough to have children 10 years ago. I am hearing from grandparents who read the column and send it to their children in other cities. Some readers tell me they are learning new things about child development. Others tell me that what they like most about the column is that it confirms that they are on the right track.

Some readers who were dealing with parenting issues when this column began are now trying to reorganize their lives around a home without children, as their success as parents has made their children into independent young adults. As children leave home for jobs or college, there is a lot of time, once so packed with child care, that is available for new interests in this next phase of life.

Many of my readers worried about children leaving home, but as their children are in their last year or two at home, these parents have shared with me that they are comfortable with their child's leaving, that the person leaving is not the 12-year-old child they worried about, but a young adult approaching age 18 with good judgment and a kind heart.

Parenting is the best thing I have ever done. I hope you share that view. I hope that this column has helped some of my readers to come closer to being able to mold their children into people they can really like. Just about all of us love our children, but not every parent really likes them.

Thanks for joining me in this 10-year odyssey. I have loved traveling with you.

Healthy conflict resolution can be model for children

Q. My friend and I got into a discussion about arguing in front of children. She thinks it is never OK to disagree with your spouse when children are present. I think that gives the children a real view of life. Are there ever times when it is OK to let children see their parents disagree?

A. Children don't learn how to resolve their own conflicts with their peers now or with marital partners later in life if they never have any exposure to conflict and conflict resolution.

While children should not be exposed to a no-holds-barred war between their parents, healthy disagreement will teach the child that adults can have different opinions and still remain friends.

When children have never seen any conflict at all between their parents and the parents then suddenly divorce, the child is bewildered. He feels insecure in all subsequent relationships, because he learns that there are no cues prior to separation. In his experience, relationships can break up at any time with no warning.

By contrast, the child who has been exposed to civil and open disagreement can trust good relationships, because he can distinguish them from relationships that are in trouble.

He knows that he will see signs of disagreement before the relationship splits apart.

Seeing parents argue in a controlled and civil manner teaches the child about his own emotions. It gives him a model of how to handle anger and frustration.

It confirms that emotions exist. It allows him to accept his own feelings rather than to repress and deny them.

Children learn how to argue effectively by watching their parents work out their differences in a civil manner.

The key is to model compromise and persuasion rather than shouting insults and committing physical abuse.

By observing parents in a rational and controlled argument, the child learns how to limit and control his own anger.

By watching his parents resolve their differences through seeing each other's point of view, he too learns to see the other side of an argument.

Girls, in particular, benefit from seeing their mom stand up for herself. Girls traditionally tend to take a more passive role in conflict, deferring to the male.

By viewing her mother standing up for what she believes, a girl can model appropriate assertive behavior. Of course, if the parents are out of control, she will model this maladaptive behavior too.

By seeing appropriate conflict resolution, children learn to express their concerns rather than letting anger smolder until it tears the relationship apart. They learn to express rather than repress tension and to let their feelings be known rather than pretending that everything is OK when it isn't. They learn to accept people in all their complexity, rather than looking at them as simply friend or foe, right or wrong.

Some parents don't have open conflict but still give opposing messages to their children. When one parent tells the child that it is bedtime and the other one lets the child stay up, the child loses.

While this child is not exposed to open conflict, he sees a much more confusing variety of parental disagreement. Because it is not open, he cannot understand it or discuss it. It would be far better for the parents to discuss their issues openly, although probably not in front of the children.

Out-of-control conflict is very frightening to children and should be avoided. If parents cannot disagree civilly, then they should have their arguments away from the children. Generally, disagreement that is accompanied by rage or insults is best discussed in private.

Nurture the young child, wean him as he grows

Q. My sister expects her children to make their own breakfast, both on school days and during vacation. I have always prepared my children's breakfast and done many other things for them. As a result, her children are more advanced in things like dressing themselves and tying their shoes, but my children seem happier and more relaxed. How much should you do for your children and how much should you expect them to do for themselves?

A. Children need nurturance. When you nurture children, you create happy, sweet children who can give back to their own children and to others what they have received. The key is to nurture and not to spoil or to hold a child back from normal development.

You spoil a child when you give him everything he wants and expect nothing in return. You do not spoil a child when you make his breakfast at age 6 or 8 or 12 but at the same time expect him to save part of his allowance for a birthday gift for his grandmother.

You teach him to think of others and do kind things for others through your kindness to him. Go ahead and make his breakfast, but expect him to consider the needs of others at a level appropriate for his age.

Some parents think that they are fostering independence when they expect a 3- or 4-year-old to dress himself and make his bed. While it is true that these children will have earlier dressing skills, by age 7, both nurtured and neglected children will be able to dress.

Your child can always acquire the ability to put on shoes or pour a glass of milk later, but he can't go back and make up for a lack of nurturance that is the cornerstone of a sweet and kind disposition.

Think of your child's needs when determining how

Raising Children

much to do for him. The parent who expects a 3-year-old to dress himself and clean his room without help is not making this decision in the interest of the child. He or she is simply delegating a task that needs to be done.

Similarly, the parent who goes to the movies every Friday night with his 16-year-old is not entertaining the child. He is meeting his own need for company that should be met by other adults — not by children.

Parents who nurture their young children should expect increasing independence and skills as the child grows and matures. Most children who are loved will gradually take on more tasks on their own, without much push from the parent. Independence and competence feels good to the emotionally stable child.

The exact age that a child is ready for independence may vary. Some children are born saying, "I can do it myself," while others seem to live by the motto: "Never do for yourself what mother will do for you." The very independent child will be easy to wean from the parent. The dependent child will have to be actively weaned at some point. If at age 10 he still wants you to tie his shoes, you will have to express your expectation for independence.

It is OK to nurture the nurturance-seeking child for a bit longer than the independent child, but by high school, the parent is creating a handicap if he does everything for the child.

Your goal is for your child to be independent with cooking, cleaning, laundry and basic sewing skills by the time he or she leaves home. The more independent and skilled your child is, the better the job you have done at parenting.

Nurture your child when he is young; gradually wean him as he grows. Expect independence from a teen who is close to leaving home.

Nurturing sick grown child is probably OK

Q. My college-age child has left school but doesn't want to work. She takes on various menial jobs, which last only a few weeks, and then she finds a reason to quit. She chooses jobs we are skeptical about, so we are not upset when she leaves the inappropriate jobs she has chosen. We want her to work toward a goal — not to endanger herself at work. Because she upsets us when she is home, we have paid for the apartment she wanted but drew the line at paying for her food, entertainment and gas. Recently she got sick, and I found myself taking a plate of food over to her apartment. Did I back down on the agreement?

A. There is a difference between enabling and nurturing. Providing everything for a child over 18 who is neither in school nor working is enabling. If you do this you are making it possible for the young adult to live without providing for herself — something that is not likely to happen to her in real life.

When you take a plate of food to a sick adult child, you are nurturing her. It is this nurturance and love that builds self-esteem and security and quells anger. Without nurturance, children become hostile and vengeful. The unnurtured, angry child tends to engage in behaviors that are intended to hurt the significant others in his life, but that in fact hurt the child himself the most.

Past about age 18, in most circumstances, a child should be mostly self-supporting unless he or she is in school. The parent who allows a child to sleep all day and play all night or to otherwise loaf about is hurting the child they mean to help.

Some young adults are subtle about this, and the pattern can continue for some time before the parent catches on. This child, instead of being at home doing nothing, has a series of unsuccessful attempts at work.

The jobs are often dangerous and serve to evoke the parent's ambivalence. The jobs are typically underemployment — employment below the child's level of ability. These jobs are jobs for the moment. They are not steps to a future career.

To move a reluctant child out on his own, a parent will want to provide the basics but leave the child to fend for all luxuries above a meager existence.

If you expect this child to be totally self-supporting, you will have to be prepared to let him go hungry or even to be out on the street. As most parents would not follow through under these extreme circumstances, it is better to take a more moderate road.

Close loopholes such as parent-paid credit cards, but do help your child with business contacts that might lead to a job. A family dinner out or at home once or twice a week will assure you that he is OK, and will offer the child a sense that you have not abandoned him. Cancel these if the adult child uses these to manipulate you.

At these reunions be careful not to fall victim to the child's attempts to arouse your guilt. Separate your problems from those that belong to your child. Her inability to pay for a new dress for a friend's wedding is not your problem. Don't let your child blame you for his shortcomings.

Be sure to notice and praise small steps of success. If the apartment is clean or pleasantly decorated, note this in a positive way, but do be aware that even what you intend as praise can be heard as criticism. Some children are prepared to hear the worst, and a comment such as, "Your home is neat and clean," can be heard as your expectation that his home would be dirty.

Enjoy those small moments when you can nurture without risk of causing your child to backslide in autonomy. Go ahead and bring your sick child chicken soup. These moments of non-regressive nurturance are those that both you and your daughter will remember.

Too high self-esteem can lead to rage at reprimand

Q. I read with interest your column about children with high self-esteem who become aggressive when criticized. I found you describing my 18-year-old son, who for the most part is easy to get along with except when you disagree with him. He becomes verbally aggressive and tunes out anything that is said to him. He can tolerate no instruction or criticism. He is absolutely never wrong. It is always someone else's fault.

Both my husband and I grew up in homes where there was little praise or encouragement, so I guess we were overly attentive to our son. He was a wonderful youngster, always eager to please and easy to be around. Although I did discipline, my husband thought his son could do no wrong, even when he said or did bad things to me. He had poor grades in high school so we thought he might be ADD. We saw a psychologist, who thought he was just spoiled. Not until I picked up your article did I even remotely think that our son's high self-esteem could be the culprit. We were a big part of the problem. I guess the question is, what do we do now? We have a big problem.

A. It is always easier to discipline when a child is young than to try to correct a grown child, but it is never too late. Your son is an older child, but a very young adult.

At this point, you don't want to continue to support or enable his behavior. You can send him out to sink or swim on his own. This is not easy for most parents, who would much rather give than withhold. This is your chance to teach responsibility via natural consequences rather than through words, which he neither hears nor heeds.

If he can't hear you

when you try to correct him, try writing to him. He just might read your words when he doesn't have to face you. He can keep your letters to read when he is ready to absorb them. You can put your expectations and rules in writing.

When children are little, it is very easy to be only the loving, giving parent, but when you don't also guide, constructively criticize and correct a child, you create a person who thinks he is the center of the world. That is, he becomes a narcissist.

When a child gets in trouble at school and the parent bails him out, the teacher has a problem for a few months, but the parent has a problem for life.

Children must be taught that they are not the center of the universe. They aren't born knowing this. They must be taught to give as well as to receive, to think of others as well as of themselves.

An 18-year-old should either be in college, trade school or at work. Unless he maintains adequate grades at school, you should insist that he work to support himself. To let him live at home without working or to support him through school with barely passing grades is to enable him to continue his grandiose expectations.

You must have the support of your spouse for this plan to succeed. If one parent undermines the other's rules, it cannot work. The child will destroy the marriage if you don't work together. He will continue to mooch off the parent who lets him.

Help him to find something he enjoys and for which he has some aptitude. Don't value school over all else if he is just going through the motions of being a student but not really trying. He may need to work for a few years to mature.

You don't need his college education or his job. He does. Give responsibility and consequences back to him.

Stability and happiness are not forged out of money

Q. We don't have a lot of money to spend on Christmas this year. How do we tell this to the children? Will it spoil their childhood memories of Christmas?

A. A child's stability and happiness are never forged out of money or gifts. Indeed there are many children who are showered with material things who are quite deprived emotionally. Sometimes it is easier to show your love when you cannot just go out and buy the latest fad toy.

Children are overwhelmed by excess. Having less can give the child an opportunity to recognize what he or she has. I have never known the child with fifty Barbie dolls to be any happier than the child with three.

The most meaningful childhood memories are built on emotionally satisfying moments together. Baking cookies, decorating the tree and visiting family are what children remember. Ask anyone the name of the fad toy he asked for in 1988, and I'll bet he can't tell you.

The desire for many gifts is taught; therefore it can be untaught. Instead of asking your child to give you a list of things he would like to get, listen to him throughout the year and notice the general types of thing he enjoys.

Tie the few gifts you do get him to his interests and talents rather than to the latest fad. He will use these gifts much longer than the ones that he has asked for just because they were "cool."

Instead of asking your child for a list of wants, select some gifts for him. We give our children too many choices. We ask them what they would like to do, where they would like to go out to eat or what gifts they would like to get.

While giving choices is not always unreasonable, we tend to ask for the child's opinion as if he has the same range of experience that an adult has. It teaches the chld that he is more important than he actually will be outside his family.

When an adult makes a choice for the child, he is lending him the adult's greater experience. Based on your knowledge of who your child is, you might conclude that he would like to try, for example, chess.

He might not ask for this gift on his own, but if your understanding of your child is accurate, he might just love a chess set as a gift. An inexpensive gift that is matched to your child is often more successful than a very expensive one that your child just chose because his friends are getting one.

Children learn money management from watching their parents. If you overspend at Christmas, don't be surprised if your child cannot live within his means as an adult. Your financial constraint can teach your child budgeting and value shopping — skills more important to success in life than getting what he wants for the moment. This lesson in delaying current wants for longer-term goals carries over to school performance and to general control of feelings, including anger.

Model values and attitude for your child. If you feel terribly deprived, he will feel that way too. If you are cheery and grateful for what you have, he will absorb that. You can teach your child to see the glass as half full or as half empty. The younger you start this lesson, the more effective your teaching will be. Teenagers are more difficult to influence than young children.

Use creativity to replace cash. Children have more fun making holiday decorations than buying expensive ones. Few children recall going out to buy ornaments, but many will remember making paper chains or stringing popcorn. It is your time and attention that makes the holiday for him.

Help your child to focus not only on what he gets but also on what he gives to others. Expect him to give of himself — not only of his money.

Too high self-esteem is as bad as too low

Q. I have heard that self-esteem determines how well a child does in life. That is, that the child who thinks that he can do something will be able to do it while the child who thinks he can't, won't be able to do it. How do you build self-esteem in a child?

A. To a certain extent, high self-esteem can be a good thing, but after years of advocating building self-esteem, researchers are discovering the downside of self-love.

Psychologists Bushman and Baumeister, working independently in two different universities, found that college students with too much self-esteem became aggressive when insulted or criticized. It seems that self-esteem crossed the boundary and became self-love or self-interest. Piercing the illusion that this person was perfect led him to rage.

Yet there is a difference between narcissism and self-esteem. Self-esteem causes a child to value himself and to realistically assess his own behavior and skills. Narcissism leads a child to self-love and an inflated sense of self-importance with a lessened concern for the feelings and needs of others.

The narcissistic child, at least superficially, thinks himself to be quite competent and wonderful. He becomes enraged when others don't mirror his opinion of himself. This child is handicapped by his high selfregard, because he often doesn't feel that he has to correct any shortcomings.

Typically he cannot view how he looks to others, and so he behaves in a way that meets his immediate needs but causes him to lose the friends that would fulfill his long-term needs.

The mother of the narcissistic child does him no favor when she tells him that he is never wrong. This is the parent who goes to school to blame the teacher when her child is in trouble. She tells him that the blame lies outside himself.

While this fosters closeness to the mother, it doesn't prepare the child for life. It is a very self-centered form of parenting, in which the mother's need for companionship with her child takes precedence over the child's need for appropriate limits and realistic evaluation of his behavior.

The good parent tells his child when he is wrong. The self-interested parent uses the child's need for approval for the parent's own benefit and tells the child that he is right even when he is not. This parent's aim is to make the child love the parent, not to mold the child into a person who will be liked by others.

The narcissistic child is sensitive to criticism because the mother who builds the child up to think of himself highly holds her child in high regard only when he sacrifices his separateness and individuality to do exactly as she says. When he deviates from her exact wishes, she rejects him. The result is that the child is angry at any criticism because it is not just a criticism of his minor behavior, but also a threat of loss of love.

Artificial praise, praise when he is wrong or lowered expectations so that he can get artificially high grades won't create the self-esteem that will carry him though life. Instead, build healthy self-esteem by encouraging good study habits so that your child can have real achievement. Identify your child's talents and strengths, and give him the opportunity to develop these skills. Offer love that your child can count on so that he feels secure.

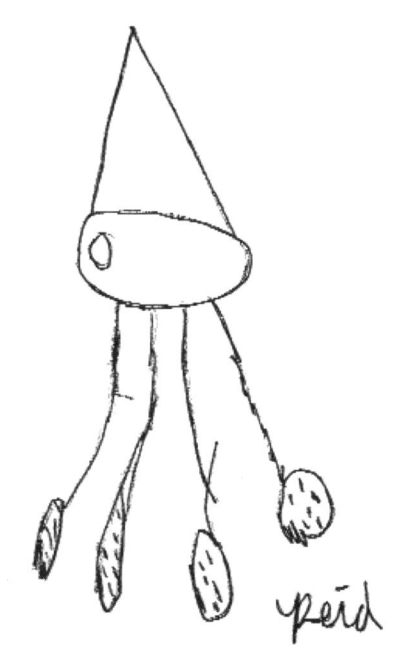

The value of neatness must be parent-taught

Q. My 4-, 8- and 12-year-old children do not pick up their clothes or toys unless I sit over them. How do you teach neatness? How important is it that their rooms are picked up and their beds made? Is it worth the constant nagging that it takes to keep it up?

A. Neatness means different things to different people. For one person, neat may mean the beds are made and the room is dusted but the desk is piled high with papers. For another person, the house must look like the Decorators' Show House to be acceptable.

Perfection is hard to achieve with children, especially with more than one child, but total chaos in the home gives the child a message that details and order are not important.

The child who has no respect for his own property may not learn to respect the property of others. The child from a messy or dirty home is more likely to abuse his textbooks or to turn in sloppy schoolwork.

Cleaning the house is not on the agenda of most children. For all except a few children born to be orderly, the value and standards of neatness must be parent-taught and often parent-imposed.

Like most things, if this is taught early in life, it is easier than if you try to suddenly impose order on a sloppy teenager.

The training goes better if you do it with positive comments and requests for cooperation than if you impose your demands arbitrarily.

If you ask for cleanup when the child is tired, he is less likely to comply than if you do it when he is rested. If you interrupt another activity and demand cleanup without time for transition, you will encounter more resistance than if you give an older child a time when you expect the job done and a younger child a 5- or 10-minute warning.

Cleanup should be expected at the beginning and end of the day but not necessarily all day long. Learning, exploring and creative fantasy play may not always look tidy. Some of the most creative children pull out blankets to make tents and build bridges out of items found in the room.

The child who vegetates in front of the TV may have the neater room but a mind cluttered with junk. Don't expect neatness at the expense of play.

The message to your child should not be that neatness is expected at all times. Rather it should be that, "We can make a mess and we can clean it up." The idea to convey is that at the end of the day or at the end of a project, cleanup is expected.

Tasks that are too big for them overwhelm children. Set a rule that a second game cannot come out before the first one is picked up. By allowing only one thing out at a time, you keep the mess kid-size and manageable.

Instead of constant nagging, set a time for cleanup before bedtime. Stay in the room with your child until the task is done. Nagging only takes place when you have to give the same command over and over. If you remain in the room while the task is in progress, you can give different suggestions to direct your child toward the goal.

For your older child this can be quality time as you discuss other topics while he or she cleans up. Your goal is to make cleanup a habit so that you don't have to nag or police. All parenting involves repetition, so don't expect one-trial learning.

Yes, it is worth the effort it takes to maintain a reasonable state of order. Children who are orderly are better students and are more likely to be able to hold a job. On the other hand, you will need to be flexible, maybe bending the rules during finals or helping a child who is not feeling well.

A middle ground, with sensitivity to other demands upon the child, will lead you to a comfortable sense of order.

Young children cannot be left alone

Q. I am going through a difficult time and have periods when I am teary and depressed. I am shorter-tempered with my children than I was before. What is the best way to deal with my children when I really want time out from parenting?

A. If you want time out, you may need to get some help. Although you did not mention the ages of your children, I will assume that they are not infants. Teens can cope with a short period of parental time out, but young children need at least one parent nearly all the time.

If you are depressed, you need to seek professional psychiatric help. There are many medications that can help you to feel better. With the edge taken off your depression, you will gain the energy and lose the hopelessness that is preventing you from taking steps forward to improve your situation.

Set schedules and goals for yourself, and try to meet them. Your ability to do this will serve as a good measure of your level of depression. If you can still cope and meet goals, you can still parent. If you cannot get even the most mundane things done, you may need psychiatric hospitalization and the help of others to care for your children.

If the situation is one that will resolve in a short time, you can share your feelings with your children honestly. Don't burden them with details that are of an adult nature — such as the infidelity of a spouse — but do let them know that you are sad and don't right now have the energy to do some of the things you used to do with them.

Suggest alternatives to make up for their loss. If you used to play a game with your 6-year-old every night before bed, suggest that she play with her 9-year-old sister instead. Try to maintain as much of their routine as possible. Even when you are not parenting at full speed, you must still be there to create the structure.

Get as much help as you can from friends and family. Let your parents take your children for a few days when they are not in school. Let your friends take you out to lunch to cheer you up. If you are not socially connected in this way, you may need to work on this issue with your therapist as well.

When you are short-tempered and scold your children for something that you might have handled better before, apologize to them and let them know that you are just out of sorts.

Make it clear, if it is true, that their behavior did not merit the intensity of your response. Tell them that what they did was really a small error and that you did not mean to make them think that you were very angry. Go back over the scene and handle it better.

Let your children know when you need small amounts of time out. You can't take a day or a week, but you can soak in the tub and ask them to hold your phone calls. Don't do this during their homework time when they need your help, but do settle them down in an activity and then take your needed time.

Use your moments when you feel better to reconnect with them. Give them a hug and find something to laugh about together.

Offer the children professional counseling if you cannot meet their emotional needs or if they are confused about the changes in their mother.

Children can handle short periods of parental depression after they are 6 years old. They do not fare well with a chronically depressed parent unless there are others to care for them.

Some children are easier to love than others

Q. It is very hard to love my two daughters evenly. They are very different children. The younger one is athletic and sweet. The older is academically gifted but nasty. How can a parent be fair when the children aren't the same?

A. Most parenting advice focuses on the parent-to-child effect — how the parent's behavior effects the development of the child. There are, however, child-to-parent effects too. The temperament and behavior of the child causes the parent's reaction.

Some children come into the world sweeter than others. They seem immune to jealousy and are inclined to see the glass half full. They are delighted with the smallest things in life. These children are easy to love.

But sometimes the parent's favoritism is not the fault or credit of the child. Often a parent will favor a child with a skill the parent values. One parent may value academic achievement. Another may admire athletic skill or beauty.

While it is OK to love your children differently, it is not OK to show consistent partiality. If you do, you will bring out the traits in the less-desirable child that you most dislike.

The child who tends toward jealousy will be consumed with envy. She will take it out on the younger sister, causing you to like her even less. As she senses your feelings, she is hurt and feels even more justified in her anger. You have set up a downward spiral, which typically ends with the bitter child leaving home as soon as she can.

The favored child will fight to preserve the favorite-child status, which he comes to take as his rightful role, while the other child spends much energy in trying to knock the favored sibling off the throne.

The partial parent undermines the sibling bond and sets the children up to be rivals instead of partners. This rivalry may affect not only the sibling relationship but also how the child-turned-adult relates to his marital partner.

The favored child fares only slightly better. She may harbor guilt at her role in ousting the sister. If she can succeed at making the parent like her better, then she too is vulnerable because parental love is not guaranteed.

Both children lose when the less-loved child bonds with the other parent and the parents are split by the children. Both children lose when there is turmoil and fighting in the home. Both children lose when they don't have the closeness and security of that special sister bond.

Better would be to hold both children in your lap and tell them that there is enough love, candy, toys or whatever to go around. Tell them that the most precious gift you have given them is each other. Tell them that they are a team and they must work together, as you work on the traits of the child that irk you and prevent your complete love.

Work on your own feelings as well. You do not have to like your children evenly, but you do have to treat them fairly. Instead of disliking the less-favored child's traits, look at them as a problem that you must solve. Work on improving the negative behaviors just as you would correct a deficit in academic or physical skills.

Don't take sides in the arguments between your girls. Do prevent them from hurting each other, both physically and emotionally. Do it from a neutral role.

Your efforts may be rewarded with kinder behavior from your child. Remember — you are the adult.

Ashley

Teach child to see the other person's point of view

Q. I have watched a friend's marriage fall apart because each of them focuses on his own needs and cannot see the other person's needs in order to meet them. I also encounter parents who expect the school to cater to their own child's needs without being able to see that what is good for their child might not be good for every child or for the group as a whole.

I don't want my own children to be handicapped by an inability to view the world from another person's perspective. I fear this personal limitation would hurt them later in life. How do you teach children to be able to see things from another person's point of view?

A. You are a wise and farsighted mother to have this concern. Intelligence alone is a poor predictor of success in life. The kind of "people skills" you describe go a long way toward bringing happiness and success in life. Indeed, research studies have linked social popularity in elementary school to the ability to meet the needs of others.

Intuitively this makes sense. Most of us don't choose as friends people who only think of themselves. By teaching your child to reach out to others, you are giving him the opportunity for friendship and social support.

While some children seem to come by the ability to walk in another person's shoes as soon as they are mature enough to relate to others, some children must be taught this skill.

Babies are egocentric. They think only in terms of their own needs. When they are hungry, they cry loudly, with little regard for the fact that mother may be tired or busy with something else.

By the preschool years, however, the child can begin to accept that others have needs too. At this age the child can be taught the concept of fairness — a concept, which is based on recognizing that another person has needs too. Children of ages 3 and up should be taught not only to take turns and share toys, but also to understand why they need to take turns and share toys.

Moments of conflict in day care are opportunities for lessons. The young child must be told, "When you hit Tommy, it hurts him." Adults take this for granted, but not all children realize this spontaneously. The child who is lacking an awareness of others needs explicit instruction about other children's feelings.

You can help the child who seems to have missed this ability by doing a simple exercise with him. Sit at the opposite end of a table from your child. Take out three objects and put them on a table in a line so that one is closest to you, one is in the middle and one is near your child.

Ask him to tell you, in order, what he sees. He may say, "I see a toy truck, a key and a spoon." Then ask him to tell you what you see. Now he must take your point of view and say, "You see a spoon, then a key, then a toy truck."

After he has become proficient in looking at a situation from the other person's point of view with tangible objects, you can ask him to do this with social situations. You can ask him to look at situations from both sides. Hear him out as he tells you how he sees it, and then ask him to tell you the same story from the other child's vantage point.

As with all child rearing, repeat concepts without nagging. Set a good example with your own behavior, and your child will develop this important life skill.

When behavior is out of line, the parent must act

Q. Recently there was a story in the news about the 13-year-old girl who died in bed weighing 680 pounds. Her mother is now on trial for fault in her death. What could this mother have done to prevent it? Do you think she should go to jail for the death of her daughter?

A. Children are not a completely blank slate for parents to write upon. They come into the world with a personality or temperament, which leads them to react to situations in a certain way.

While one child might approach a crowd of people with shyness and hide behind mother's skirt, another child will approach the same situation with curiosity and interest.

While one child might have a normal appetite, another might not be sated with an average diet. The child's behavior influences the parent's response, just as the parent's behavior influences how the child behaves.

Yet while the parent can't completely determine the child's behavior, he or she can work with his child's temperament to shape acceptable rather than unacceptable behavior.

When the behavior is far out of line, the parent needs to step in and put an absolute stop to behaviors which are hurting the child or others around him.

Intervention is most effective while the child is young. This particular child weighed 237 pounds at the age of 8 when about 50 pounds is typical. She was already seriously overweight by kindergarten.

These are the years when parents have considerable influence. Around the issue of extreme obesity, parents have control prior to the teen years. It is the parent who goes to the grocery store to stock the pantry and who prepares the meals.

However, parenting,

and particularly parenting a difficult child, takes both time and energy. This mother was working full time while caring for elderly, demented parents in addition to the child who died.

She may have been doing more than any one person could handle — certainly more than she could handle. The fault, if any is to be assigned, seemed to lie with the extended family, which offered her little help.

Yet one does not get to be 680 pounds through only neglect. Without active help in maintaining that exceptional weight, she would have lost weight or not gained it in the first place.

This child was unable to get out of bed or to attend school. Someone in the home was providing the calories to not only keep her at that weight, but also to continue to gain.

While there may be some blame for missing doctor's appointments or stocking the pantry excessively, I don't think we need to focus on punishing this mother. She is unlikely to harm others in the future. She is a danger to no one.

We do need to work at being sure that this could not happen again. We need to track children who are not attending school and to accept that exceptional obesity is as potent a psychiatric symptom as hallucinations or suicidal thoughts, which would quickly gain professional attention.

Arrival of child can change your life

Q. I am about to have a baby — my first. I have heard from friends that adding children puts stress on the marriage. Is this true? If so, what can I do to prevent marital problems when our baby arrives?

A. Most of us are creatures of habit, and any change causes some degree of stress. What causes significant problems in a marriage is not the arrival of children, but the arrival of children to parental personalities who cannot bend and adapt. Children do change your life, and both you and your husband will need to adjust to new and changing demands and schedules.

A newborn is totally dependent and can't be left alone for even a brief time. The wife who was used to running a tight ship is shocked at how little she gets done in a day with a baby. The infant's sleep/wake schedule saps parental energy, and so the first few months can be ones in which the parents, and especially the mother, have little energy for anything other than the care of the baby.

It is not uncommon for the husband to feel some jealousy of the new baby who commands so much of his wife's time and love. Most men are adult enough to join in the love of the baby rather than continuing to feel left out.

It is only a few troubled adults who cannot let go of their role as the nurtured one to make room for children. If a spouse cannot be an adult partner in the care of the infant, but instead wants to be cared for too, marital problems can surface.

As children grow, the issues change. By the school years, children no longer require minute-to-minute care, but families become busier. At times the wife/mother must make a choice. When her husband's business dinner falls on the same night as the child's school play, where does mom go?

In most families there is a pattern of choice, with the wife/mother typically giving preference to either the marriage or the child. Here is where the stress of children on the marriage can be seen most clearly.

Religion and money are common issues of marital conflict. Both of these are emphasized when children enter the family.

Husband and wife can have different ideas about religion and still live in harmony. When children come along, it often becomes important to both to pass on the traditions of the family in which each adult was raised.

When the children are small, the issue can be pushed aside, but at school age the family must decide what religious practices to teach, and conflict can surface.

Choices about how to spend money can also add stress to a relationship. Children add to expenses and can increase stress in relationships where money was already tight.

Parents can have very strong feelings about discipline, especially about spanking. Differences of opinion can drive one partner to leave with the child to protect him from a parent who believes he is doing the right thing. When one parent wants structure and rules and the other lets things slide by, parents can find areas of difference they did not know existed before they had children.

For most families having children is a happy event and one which serves to bond couples rather than to separate them. Differences can be resolved through compromise and through letting each parent have a domain of power.

When the dad has the final say over where the family spends the vacation and the mom has the last word on what color to paint the living room, each can come away content.

Couples who try to please each other, and who bend and adapt to the new arrival, will not be harmed by widening their circle of family. They will be enriched and bonded by the experience.

Index

abused 30, 40, 41
academic 57, 60, 82, 93, 97, 117, 141, 147, 148, 149, 170, 178, 179, 199, 204, 212, 213, 219, 222, 223, 232, 235, 236, 250, 254, 255, 270, 288, 289
achievement 99, 117, 118, 132, 156, 157, 158, 164, 173, 179, 193, 204, 219, 229, 234, 236, 283, 288
ADHD 96, 97, 156, 160
adopted 160, 218, 219, 221
aggression 93, 115, 125, 136, 137, 261
aggressive 38, 88, 89, 106, 107, 125, 136, 152, 153, 170, 173, 187, 256, 257, 260, 278, 282
allowance 134, 143, 188, 189, 274
altruistic 143
ambivalent 88, 119
anger 60, 89, 92, 93, 94, 101, 123, 125, 136, 176, 194, 195, 203, 260, 261, 262, 272, 273, 276, 281, 288
angry 60, 61, 89, 92, 93, 95, 123, 124, 136, 137, 158, 171, 194, 203, 208, 215, 232, 243, 252, 253, 260, 261, 276, 283, 287
anxiety 30, 129, 157, 185, 200, 235, 257
anxious 34, 137, 157, 212
appearance 127, 176
aptitude 118, 158, 173, 279
athletic 55, 60, 109, 143, 149, 152, 164, 180, 181, 232, 256, 288
attached 189, 196
attention 33, 36, 37, 41, 46, 47, 56, 57, 61, 82, 83, 89, 95, 96, 97, 101, 105, 109, 112, 113, 117, 118, 119, 127, 129, 132, 134, 142, 144, 146, 156, 157, 158, 160, 161, 169, 175, 187, 203, 229, 232, 233, 235, 236, 237, 241, 256, 264, 265, 281, 293
attitude 63, 94, 101, 143, 158, 179, 189, 230, 231, 236, 240, 250, 251, 281
autonomy 3, 35, 54, 132, 215, 245, 269, 277
bedtime 39, 56, 125, 194, 219, 273, 285
behavior modification 100, 101
blame 31, 35, 57, 153, 159, 166, 253, 260, 261, 277, 282, 283, 293
bond 61, 63, 208, 288, 289, 295
bored 63, 140, 158, 193, 212
boundaries 174, 225, 238
buffering 129
bully 106, 152, 173, 226
calming 52
career 158, 173, 237, 277
chaos 120, 242, 284
chores 90, 91, 134, 135, 188, 189, 211, 217, 247, 250
classroom 30, 31, 44, 89, 101, 148, 158, 161, 165, 170, 171, 172, 173, 180, 236, 238
cleanup 42, 43, 161, 284, 285
cliques 131
clothes 45, 90, 91, 113, 126, 127, 145, 174, 175, 176, 177,

184, 210, 229, 241, 248, 251, 284
communicate 29, 226, 237
compare 35, 112, 113, 251
comparing 56
competition 35, 51, 92, 167, 187, 232, 251, 257
competitive 89, 161, 167, 200, 232, 233
computer 45, 109, 154, 155, 189
confidence 145, 256
consequences 30, 41, 89, 91, 111, 195, 214, 237, 238, 245, 246, 247, 278, 279
controlled 93, 118, 123, 170, 243, 272, 273
cool 107, 174, 176, 187, 198, 216, 280
curriculum 44, 82, 148, 161, 170, 172, 178, 193, 201
daddy 60, 62, 123
deaf 204
defiant 40, 41, 42, 88
demands 37, 47, 56, 57, 80, 82, 122, 142, 143, 172, 284, 285, 294
dependency 119, 125
depressed 47, 59, 96, 158, 213, 286, 287
depression 129, 169, 235, 286, 287
destroy 123, 279
deterrent 265
development 32, 55, 115, 116, 123, 125, 127, 160, 173, 174, 181, 219, 221, 225, 227, 265, 271, 274, 288
developmental delays 57
developmental stage 60, 61, 174, 246
disability 96, 118, 161, 168
discipline 36, 40, 41, 56, 57, 83, 88, 89, 116, 117, 123, 139, 159, 194, 208, 209, 218, 238, 242, 244, 278, 295
disruptive 88, 100, 120
distractibility 157
driving 128, 210, 211, 214, 224, 225, 270
drugs 82, 97, 116, 117, 128, 129, 198, 199, 211, 216, 229, 271
dyslexia 169, 212
education 104, 128, 141, 168, 180, 199, 201, 205, 212, 213, 254, 255, 279
elementary school 79, 111, 148, 164, 171, 178, 186, 187, 208, 250, 254, 270, 290
embarrassed 125
employment 135, 277
enforce 117, 215, 217
excuses 203
explanation 56, 59, 123, 197, 221, 239
externalize 260, 261
fall asleep 34
fight 90, 262, 288
fighting 47, 122, 233, 262, 289
flirt 29
focused 33, 45, 83
food 84, 85, 212, 248, 276
friends 45, 47, 50, 62, 63, 81, 84, 86, 87, 94, 95, 103, 104, 108, 109, 116, 121, 124, 126, 129, 136, 137, 144, 145, 150, 151, 152, 153, 155, 160, 163, 166, 171, 173, 174, 176, 181, 182, 183, 184, 186, 187, 203, 208, 213, 214, 216, 217, 219, 225, 226, 227, 230, 233, 235, 264, 270, 271, 272, 281, 282, 287, 290, 294
friendship 87, 102, 290
gender differences

38
goal 32, 100, 104, 118, 119, 120, 141, 159, 200, 238, 275, 276, 285
grandparents 47, 62, 63, 120, 121, 252, 253, 271
habit 34, 43, 84, 104, 134, 199, 217, 265, 285, 294
handicap 45, 131, 132, 133, 139, 275
handicapped 46, 47, 97, 130, 131, 132, 133, 282, 290
helplessness 241
homework 81, 83, 97, 118, 119, 122, 146, 147, 159, 165, 206, 214, 225, 245, 246, 287
honor roll 141, 179
illness 44, 45, 138, 139, 235, 254, 255, 265
immature 82, 172, 173, 204
independence 34, 61, 109, 119, 145, 159, 176, 219, 244, 269, 274, 275
independent 54, 61, 87, 118, 119, 124, 185, 191, 204, 227, 246, 269, 271, 275
inexpensive 149, 281
invitation 162, 163

irritable 94
jealous 46, 89, 112, 113
kindergarten 30, 31, 44, 82, 99, 128, 270, 292
laundry 91, 147, 213, 239, 247, 275
limits 36, 37, 41, 88, 117, 123, 126, 127, 143, 196, 197, 202, 203, 208, 209, 217, 219, 222, 223, 224, 225, 238, 244, 265, 269, 283
marriage 35, 39, 60, 61, 94, 120, 122, 123, 131, 220, 221, 279, 290, 294, 295
material things 51, 112, 134, 280
math 99, 118, 148, 154, 156, 159, 165, 192, 223, 235, 237
maturity 45, 55, 137, 192, 204, 210, 225, 244, 245, 262, 263, 269
medicine 83, 131
memory 51, 79, 105
messy 284
money 51, 52, 85, 91, 104, 120, 134, 135, 142, 143, 153, 177, 188, 189, 195, 210, 212, 213, 215, 217, 264, 280, 281, 295
motivate 90, 91, 104,

150, 154, 158, 165, 178, 232, 234, 241, 251
motivating 90, 101
motor skills 160, 161, 171
nap 46, 113
narcissist 41, 279
narcissistic 282, 283
neuromuscular disease 133
obligated 50, 162, 225
organized 83, 93, 180
out of control 41, 57, 105, 208, 273
passive 92, 118, 119, 181, 184, 256, 260, 273
patience 154
performance 156, 157, 192, 200, 233, 235, 255, 281
personality 33, 54, 90, 94, 102, 172, 199, 203, 218, 219, 240, 292
popular 107, 152, 187, 196, 258, 260
popularity 79, 290
praise 89, 233, 234, 247, 250, 277, 278, 283
pride 127, 129, 135, 263
punish 40, 89, 90, 195, 244

punishment 43, 88, 89, 90, 100, 134, 167, 200, 208, 209, 214, 227, 239, 244
read 33, 84, 92, 93, 98, 99, 127, 147, 153, 158, 162, 164, 165, 168, 169, 172, 189, 236, 237, 244, 261, 271, 278, 279
reading 34, 92, 93, 98, 99, 118, 153, 155, 164, 168, 169, 219, 236, 237, 254, 256
reinforce 101, 128, 171, 199
reject 117
religious 59, 139, 295
remarry 35
resentful 263
respect 56, 100, 128, 129, 196, 198, 217, 224, 238, 239, 246, 247, 284
responsibility 35, 36, 37, 90, 126, 150, 154, 166, 201, 210, 211, 215, 225, 247, 254, 262, 263, 278, 279
reward 89, 90, 91, 100, 101, 104, 105, 119, 159, 172, 189, 203, 227, 234, 250, 258, 265
risks 185, 211, 258, 259
routine 43, 63, 108, 120, 121, 122, 146, 182, 183, 287

seductive 126, 127
self-esteem 187, 216, 257, 278, 282
sensitivity 163, 285
shouting 272
sibling 46, 47, 58, 59, 89, 92, 112, 148, 150, 167, 232, 241, 262, 264, 288, 289
size 106, 175, 176, 177, 189, 218, 251, 285
sleep 34, 35, 108, 132, 138, 139, 144, 182, 184, 276, 294
social cues 153
social skills 81, 85, 95, 107, 122, 148, 153, 172, 187, 199, 230
social status 162
spanking 105, 295
special needs 154, 204
specific learning disabilities 212
spelling 97, 118, 141, 147, 154, 161, 165, 178, 179
spoil 52, 124, 274, 280
stealing 264, 265
strengths 45, 85, 151, 173, 181, 212, 236, 237, 283
struggling 118, 140, 173, 194, 235
subjective 96

supervision 107, 133, 144, 225, 244
teddy bear 139
temperament 55, 61, 88, 113, 145, 154, 167, 207, 232, 288, 292
test scores 156, 157
tests 92, 118, 156, 157, 164, 173, 179, 193, 254, 255
toy 33, 42, 43, 50, 51, 84, 85, 105, 129, 143, 182, 280, 291
transition 62, 86, 87, 106, 165, 176, 195, 205, 254, 284
trauma 94, 183
TV 50, 80, 84, 88, 110, 117, 137, 139, 147, 158, 246, 247, 285
twins 168
unhappy 63, 95, 145, 205, 215, 227
vacation 31, 34, 62, 135, 196, 197, 254, 274, 295
weight 83, 179, 228, 293
wheelchair 46, 130, 131
winning 233

About the Author

Vivian Katzenstein Friedman, Ph.D., holds a Bachelor's degree in developmental psychology from Cornell University, a Master's degree in clinical psychology from Harvard University and a Doctorate in clinical psychology from Case Western Reserve University. She completed an internship at Boston Children's Hospital/Harvard Medical School.

Photography by John Acton

She is currently a Professor in the Department of Psychiatry at the University of Alabama at Birmingham School of Medicine, where she has been a child, adolescent, couples and family therapist since 1983.

She was the parenting columnist to <u>The Birmingham News</u> from 1988 to 2005 and is the Parenting Publications of America award-winning parenting columnist to <u>Birmingham Parent</u> magazine. She is the mother of four terrific children, ages 18 to 27.